D11193859

ANTIQUE FIREARMS

ANTIQUE FIREARMS

Their Care, Repair and Restoration

By

RONALD LISTER

BONANZA BOOKS · NEW YORK

First published in the U.S.A. by Crown Publishers, Inc.
MCMLXIV

This edition published by Bonanza Books, a division of Crown Publishers, Inc.
C D E F G H

LIBRARY OF CONGRESS CATALOG CARD NUMBER: 64-23797

Printed in the U.S.A.

DEDICATION

To Jane, who assisted in the preparation of this book by arranging, revising and typing the script and who took many of the photographs for the illustrations.

CONTENTS

Chapter

LIST OF LLUSTRATIONS

CHAPTER ONE

TIME WELL SPENT

IN the early years of my interest in antique firearms circumstances permitted acquiring specimens only at infrequent intervals and the possession of fine or rare pieces was quite out of the question; I had to be content with items which were often in neglected or damaged condition. In retrospect I believe that this was ultimately an advantage, since I soon found that with care and patience it was often possible to clean, adjust and repair, and even make new parts for, these old weapons and restore them to acceptable condition. When I was able to buy more freely, my early experience enabled me to acquire some rarer specimens, damaged or incomplete, which were capable of being restored to really fine condition.

Guns apparently in good order can usually be improved in appearance, and almost certainly internally, by stripping and careful cleaning. I have had some old guns which obviously had been cared for and appeared immaculate externally, but which, when stripped down, showed rust on the interior lock parts, between barrel and stock and in other hidden places. Every new acquisition should be dismantled, partially, if not completely, to enable the internal parts to be examined and cleaned and oiled. It does no harm to an old gun to be stripped and reassembled occasionally and the skill required is well within the capacity of anyone with average mechanical aptitude. Given patience and the will to learn, almost any gun collector can become a reasonably competent restorer. There are some jobs, however, which demand long practice and technical training and which are beyond the capacity of most amateurs; for example, rifling a barrel, checkering a stock or making a revolver cylinder. On the other hand, there are jobs in which the amateur can excel by devoting to them much more time than can be afforded commercially. If there is any doubt whatsoever about satisfactorily completing any proposed piece of work, it should be postponed until confidence has been gained by experience on simpler jobs or by practice on scrap material.

The capacity to maintain and improve his specimens offers a fascinating subsidiary interest to the gun collector. The collector who develops his skill in this way, in addition to deriving pleasure from the actual work and in pride of achievement, soon develops an almost infallible eye for quality of workmanship. He can detect at once even slight indications of alterations or repairs which are not up to the highest standard. I do not refer to such obvious and inexcusable blemishes as traces of vice marks or ill-fitting parts, but to less apparent signs as, for example, a replacement screw with a head of the wrong pattern, or perhaps a new flint-lock top jaw and cock-screw, well made, perfectly finished, but not exactly in correct proportion.

This raises an interesting point regarding the ethics of gun restoration, and one on which collectors hold a variety of opinions. It would no doubt be generally accepted that it is permissible to fit a modern flint or nipple to an old gun, or to replace a missing screw with a new one of correct pattern. At the other extreme, however, to build up a hybrid weapon from miscellaneous parts of different origins, with the deliberate object of deceiving the inexperienced collector, would be universally condemned. Where, then, is the line to be drawn? The decision must largely depend upon individual circumstances, but I have always felt that the following is a good general rule.

The character of the gun should be preserved. Lock, stock, barrel and furniture and, in the case of revolvers, cylinder and frame, should all be original, and any repairs or replacements should be such as might well have been carried out by an old-time gunsmith. In former times, when these old guns and pistols were in actual use, and particularly in the case of military weapons, accidental damage frequently occurred. In the case of machine-produced arms such as Colt revolvers, the damaged parts were seldom repaired, but were replaced with interchangeable components from stock with the result that many of these guns have genuine old parts but non-matching serial numbers, which to a certain extent reduces their value to the collector.

Bench-made, hand-fitted guns, however, were generally repaired, according to the resources of the armourer or gunsmith. It was taken as a matter of course that, during its working life, a firearm might require repairs or replacements to keep it in sound order, and the local gunsmith, called upon to "service" a client's pistols, would be unlikely to send to the distant original maker for some simple replacement such as a new ramrod, hammer or trigger, but would make as near a match as possible from material in stock. To put an imperfect weapon into good shape, it seems reasonable that the modern restorer should be allowed to work on a gun in the same manner as the old gunsmith.

The original character of many old guns has, of course, been modified quite legitimately without destroying their interest. It was common practice to convert flint-locks to percussion type, and also percussion cap revolvers to take metallic cartridges so as to bring serviceable old weapons up to date, and such conversions have their place in the collection.

Some collectors assert that replacements should be left polished or be finished in such a way that they are recognisable as new additions, but if the work has been honestly and expertly done, I see no reason why it should not match the general finish of the weapon. To take an analogy, a restorer working on a piece of antique furniture would be expected to leave his finished work as inconspicuous as possible. Why, therefore, should not the same principle apply to the restoration of a weapon? Fakes and forgeries, however, must be strongly condemned.

In my own early years of collecting I was offered a quite attractive percussion pistol with a famous London maker's name engraved on the barrel. The engraving, just a shade too sharp, aroused my suspicion. Furthermore, I would have expected this maker to have had his products proved in London rather than in Birmingham, as indicated by the proof marks, and anyway, the quality was not quite up to the standard one would expect from this particular maker. I did not buy this gun, but some time later traded a good-quality but unnamed pistol in an exchange deal at the same place, and after a week or two saw the pistol offered for sale, engraved with a well-known maker's name. Remonstrance merely elicited the assertion that it was not the same weapon. Forgery of this kind is not only commercially fraudulent but it also ruins an otherwise genuine specimen.

Whilst the collector-restorer will quickly develop a discerning eye for fakes, there are few of us who have been collecting for any length of time who can honestly say that we have never been imposed upon. I know I have.

I once had a cased pair of pocket percussion pistols knocked down to me at an auction for a fairly modest bid after a necessarily cursory examination. They were a quite ordinary attractive-looking pair of box-locks with bright barrels and what appeared to be polished ebony handles, in a nice velvet-lined oak case with a single diagonal division, which also housed a genuine old labelled tin containing a few percussion caps and another tin half full of lead balls. The pistols carried the German proof marks but no maker's name and they seemed to be in good order apart from one stiff-acting trigger spring.

A cased pair is always a welcome addition to a collection and I was quite pleased with my purchase until I investigated the lock with the defective trigger spring. The removal of the butt revealed the original brown stain of the wood. The handles had not even been removed when they had been re-stained black. The trigger spring was missing and the vacancy filled by a roughly cut triangle of soft rubber. However, that was not the end. The velvet in the lid of the case was coming loose and, on pulling it away to re-glue it, I revealed a label bearing a cutler's name. This fake, I imagine, was the work of some amateur, as the time and trouble involved would not have been worth while commercially. I still have the pistols and use the case for storing small parts. *Plate 1* shows this identical pair in the case just as they were bought.

Sometimes a good lock from a damaged gun will be exchanged for a broken lock on a good gun to enhance its selling value. Many flint-lock plates are almost identical in shape and size and can be made to fit by slight trimming of the recess in the stock. A flint-lock gun which I bought appeared to be complete as originally made, but on removing the lock it was apparent that this was a replacement. The internal trigger extension had been filed to suit the lower position of the sear arm, and the original vent, or touch-hole as it is commonly but erroneously called, had been plugged and a new vent drilled to match the more forward position of the flash-pan. The work was expertly done, but it destroyed the authenticity of the piece, and I would describe this as a fake.

It is rather different if, as occasionally happens, a good gun is acquired without any lock. In such a case I would not hesitate to fit a spare lock if one of suitable period, pattern and fit could be obtained, rather than leave the gun with an ugly gap in the side of the stock. A future buyer, however, should be informed of the circumstances and the price adjusted accordingly. I would never buy an antique firearm of any appreciable value without insisting on the removal of the lock at least, either by myself or the owner, so that a close inspection could be made.

Professional experts have other ways of treating old guns in order to increase their market value, which are quite beyond the capabilities of the amateur, but which should be known to every collector. Plain old pistols and revolvers can be skilfully engraved in traditional style, or old engraving is sometimes re-cut. In either case the specimen is ruined from the point of view of the discriminating collector. It is even possible to have an old percussion revolver, in fair condition, renovated by weld-filling all nicks and pits and re-polishing, fitting new grips and altering *serial numbers of all parts* so that they all match, finely engraved and gold damascened in the exact style of the beautiful old work found on "presentation" guns. The treatment is costly and, while these transformed weapons are marked to differentiate them from original presentation models, there is the risk that in time they will be passed off as genuine antique rarities at highly inflated prices. The work is, no doubt, of the highest quality and presumably there are collectors who find satisfaction in possessing such specimens and are prepared to pay lavishly for the privilege of owning an imitation presentation piece.

An important question for the amateur gun restorer is whether he intends to shoot with any of his old guns. There are many clubs and societies whose members shoot with muzzle-loaders and black powder, and most devotees of this fascinating sport get much of their satisfaction from using genuine old guns which have been preserved in, or put into, safe shooting condition; but the amateur who restores an old weapon with the intention of using it for shooting is very seriously urged to have it proved before he fires it. The gun may already bear an old proof stamp and appear sound, but a century or more of internal rust or corrosion near the breech may well have weakened the barrel to the point of danger. It has been stated in a gun magazine that "unless there is a defective part of the barrel, any muzzle-loading shot gun, rifle or pistol will stand a tremendous charge.... Do not be afraid that they will blow up. They are safe and very practical to shoot.... Shot guns can be loaded till they kick like a mule." The difficulty is to determine whether "there is a defective part of the barrel" and the only sure test would seem to be by proof with double normal load and charge.

British muzzle-loader shooters can have this done at either of the official proof houses at London or Birmingham at a modest charge, by sending the barrel only, in clean condition with vent clear and all internal rust and fouling cleaned out. This can be done through any gunsmith. I sent a muzzle-loading pistol barrel to the Birmingham Proof House and received it back stamped with the new proof mark and safe black powder charge and weight of shot. A gun or pistol so tested can be shot without the slightest risk of bursting and, when it is realised that according to the proof-house authorities, a substantial proportion of old black-powder guns submitted for re-proof are rejected, the danger to both shooter and spectators from old untested guns will be appreciated. There are methods of safely carrying out overload tests oneself, and experienced club members can best advise prospective muzzle-loader shooters about the procedure.

Modern-made replicas of old percussion rifles and revolvers for muzzle-loader shooters are advertised in gun magazines. These are fine weapons, but again I wonder how many of them, after some years of use, will be offered to new collectors as genuine antiques in unusually well preserved condition.

Personally, I could never get the satisfaction out of shooting with a commercial replica that I would from using a genuine vintage weapon and, in general, I do not like replicas, in spite of the fact that I have made two. They were for lecture purposes, to illustrate the sequence of the various methods of powder-ignition. It seemed extremely unlikely that I should ever acquire a genuine touch-hole hand gun or a match-lock pistol, so I made one of each type to complete the demonstration series. Both of these, though not very difficult to construct, would be valuable if they were genuinely antique specimens. I therefore had each barrel deeply engraved with the word "REPRODUCTION" and the date (see *Plate* 2). Of course, some day an unscrupulous faker might fill the engraving with welding, polish up the barrels, leave them out exposed to the weather for a period, and otherwise treat them to turn them into "genuine rare antiques", but I hope not, as I cannot do more than I have done to brand them as modern reproductions. The match-lock also bears the Birmingham proof marks and so is quite suitable for shooting, if one fancied experience and practice with this very early type of firearm.

Before dealing with the practical aspect of gun restoration it might be well to consider our responsibilities as collectors. The collector who, for his personal pleasure, accumulates beautiful or historic relics of bygone times assumes a duty to cherish and preserve these treasures, of which morally he is merely the temporary custodian. Ultimately he should pass them on in as good condition as when he acquired them; if they can, with care and treatment, be improved or restored, so much the better.

A piece of glass or china can be stored away for generations without detriment; in the same circumstances a fine firearm can deteriorate so as to become almost or entirely valueless. Firearms are somewhat unusual among antiques in having a working mechanism in the lock which can be easily taken off, damaged or lost. From such causes and other forms of ill-usage the total number of collectable antique firearms is steadily being reduced, and their loss can never be replaced.

The following chapters describe and illustrate methods of completely stripping down, cleaning and reassembling the early firearms most commonly met with today. In the early chapters it is assumed that the specimens are complete and in fair condition and need no repair. Later, when practice has made this work familiar, the various problems arising from rust, stubborn screws, damaged or missing parts involving repairs or replacements and general restoration are dealt with. This seems to be the logical sequence, since the method of dismantling will vary for different types of firearms, while repair problems are largely common to all. It is not possible to cover in a single book every pattern and variation of old firearm and the scope of this work has been deliberately restricted to muzzle-loading flint-lock and percussion guns, the term gun being used in its wider application to embrace shoulder and hand guns, whether with smooth or rifled barrels. This group probably forms the major part of most private collections, and by the time the amateur has mastered the art of working on these weapons he will be competent to deal with other types with confidence.

It will be seen that the majority of firearms illustrated are pistols, the reason being that their smaller size permits the use of photographs showing much closer detail than would be possible with shoulder guns, and the instructions given apply equally well to both types.

A book of this nature can never be complete, but at least it can definitely be stated that, unless otherwise indicated, every operation, procedure and expedient described has been successfully practised by myself during a long period of gun-collecting.

CHAPTER TWO

WORKSHOP AND TOOLS

ONE of my pistols, a fine holster flintlock, will always carry a scar caused by the use, at some time past, of an unsuitable tool. Starting at the head of one of the lock-fixing screws and running right across the polished stock, there is a deep scratch inflicted by an imperfectly fitting screw-driver that slipped from its seating in the screw-head. This accident, which permanently disfigured a fine weapon, would never have happened had a correctly ground screw-driver of exactly the right width been used.

To anyone intending to develop the hobby of gun repair and restoration, the importance must be stressed of having at hand the right tool of the best quality and in good condition for any job undertaken. The amateur, like the professional craftsman, must be prepared to invest in suitable tools, and to give time to keeping them in first-class order.

Admittedly it is quite possible to effect many repairs with a few ordinary household tools, but, as a long-term policy, this is undesirable and could result in causing permanent damage.

If the correct tool is not to hand, postpone the job until it has been obtained. By accumulating only the equipment for which increasing experience will show the necessity, a useful stock of tools will gradually be built up.

Even in the larger cities, some of the tools specifically designed for the gunsmith, such as mainspring vices, nipple keys and pin punches, are not readily on sale, even from a gunsmith. Sometimes a dealer will order such items from his trade supplier for a customer, but in general he is not interested in supplying the tools of his trade to the amateur. However, there are mail-order firms specialising in the sale of antique gun parts and tools whose advertisements may be found in collectors' magazines. Failing this, most tools and parts can easily be made, and the procedure will be described as each becomes necessary.

THE WORKSHOP

Ideally this should be a large, well-ventilated room, cool in summer and warm in winter, well lit by day and with convenient shaded light-points for evening work. It should be reserved solely for the use of the gun worker, so that jobs in progress may be left undisturbed. It should house a strong wooden bench of ample size (the advantage of wood being that it minimises vibration and sound), a power-driven lathe, drill and grinding and buffing wheels. There should also be drawers, cupboards and racks for tools and materials, and a table with a small drawing-board, T-square, etc., where work can be set out.

How close this ideal can be approached in practice depends on individual circumstances. Of necessity, however, the average amateur's workshop falls short of this; but, with some contriving and ingenuity, any drawbacks arising from limited accommodation can be overcome, so that it is only convenience and not efficiency that suffers. Indeed, I have seen work carried out on a portable bench temporarily set up in a garden shed that was equal to any coming from the best-appointed workshop.

I am fortunate in having a spare room entirely at my disposal and a description of how this is laid out may be helpful. *Fig. 1* shows a floor plan of the room which is 9 ft. square with a window facing due north.

Bench (*A*) is 5′ long by 2′ 6″ wide by 2′ 10″ high. The top outside longitudinal members and the legs are of 8″ by 3″ timber, and the middle two pieces are 1″ thick boards, giving a 2″ deep recess or well along the middle of the bench top, which allows small tools and materials to lie out of the way below the level of the front member. Filings, etc., can be brushed into it while working and then swept off the end.

The side and end pieces which frame up the tops of the legs are of 7″ by 1″ boards. A wide shelf 10″ above the floor braces the legs and is useful for storage purposes; it also allows sufficient space for sweeping out. The cross-pieces under the top and under the shelf are 2½″ square, and the whole job is assembled with 3″ long heavy wood screws.

This bench was home-made from material supplied cut to length and ready-planed and is of ample size and weight for any job of gun work. Considerations of space may dictate some variation of these dimensions, and any local joiner will build a suitable bench to given measurements.

My bench top is covered with a 6′ by 3′ sheet of No. 22s gauge galvanised iron which is easy to cut with tinsmith's shears. It is bent to fit the central well and turned down 1″ over all edges; only a few inches had to be taken off the length of the standard sheet.

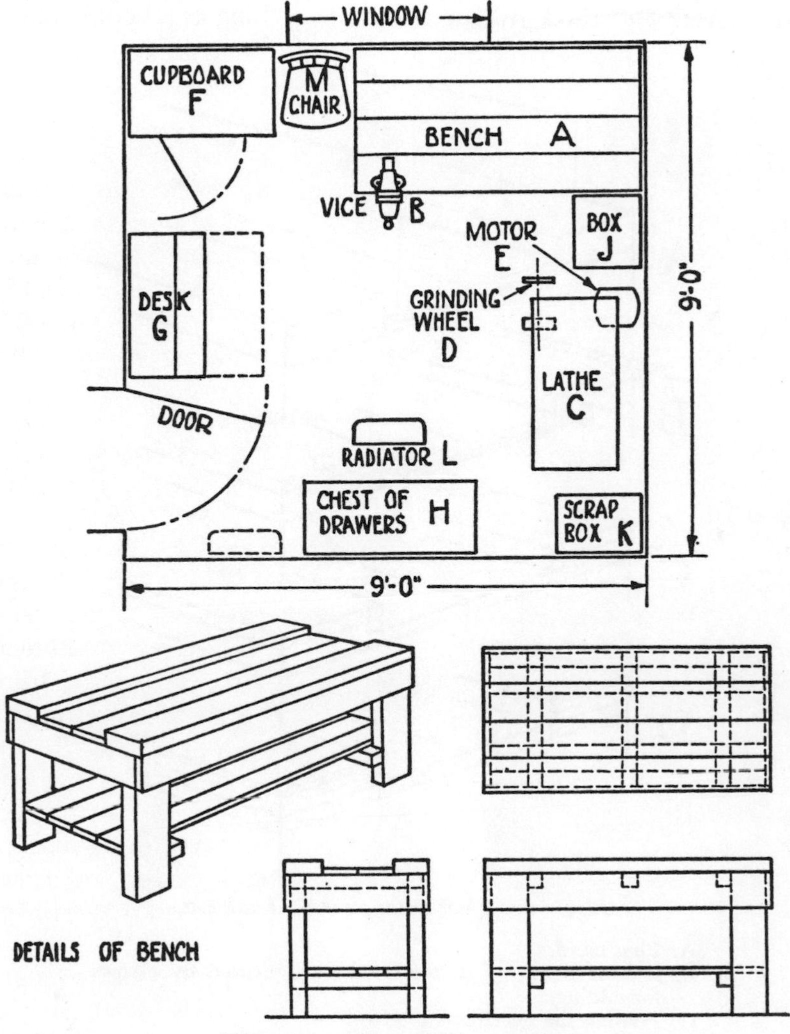

Figure 1. The author's workshop.

In calculating what would be required for a larger or smaller area, the metal should be 6″ wider and about 2″ to 3″ longer than the bench. *Fig.* 2 shows the method of progressively bending the sheet. Such a metal cover is not a necessity, but it has the advantage that there are no crevices into which small screws or parts can fall; oil can be wiped off; and the smooth continuous surface is easy to clean. When necessary to avoid marking delicate work, I use a sheet of $\frac{1}{8}$″ thick rubber 1′ wide by 3′ long as a bench mat.

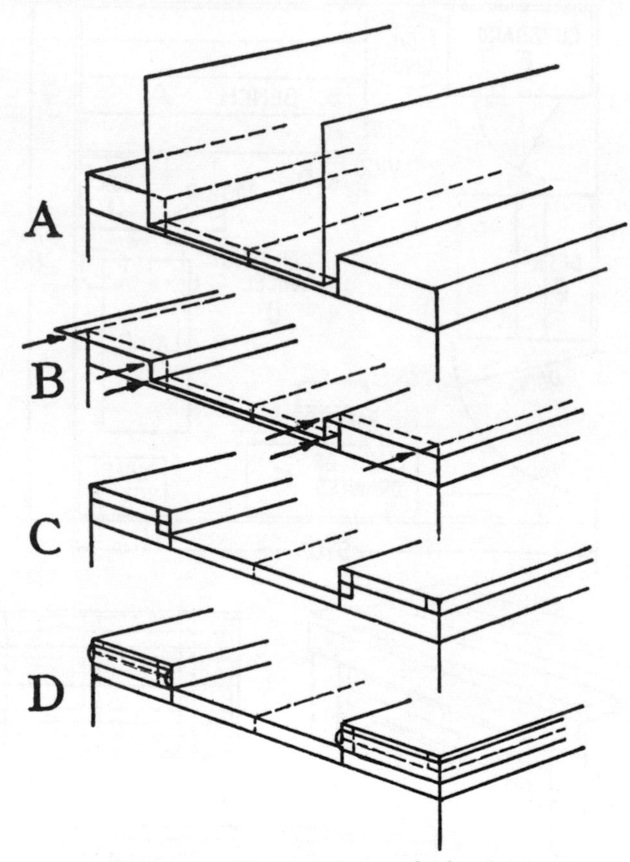

Figure 2. Sheet metal cover for bench top.

A. First bend.
B. Second bend. Cuts made where indicated by arrows for folding.
C. Folding the overlapping edges.
D. Half-round aluminium beading over edges.

In contrast to this, I worked for a long time on the portable three-legged bench shown in *Plate 3*. Its working top is only 36″ by 10″ and, like the other bench, it is 2′ 10″ to the face of the top. The legs are of 1½″ and the stays of 1″ and ¾″ external diameter electric conduit. The rectangular top is of 1″ by 1″ by ⅛″ section angle-iron, forming a recess to take a piece of 1″ thick board for the working top. The legs at the vice end are well splayed for stability, and the three legs accommodate themselves to any unevenness of the floor. The metal dealer who supplied the material cut the pieces to size and welded them up to a sketch supplied. Lugs were welded to the frame to take the fixing bolts for the vice, which is easily detachable. I have done quite a lot of gun work on this bench and its small size and portability are a great advantage.

The dimensions given are, of course, arbitrary, and these and the design can be modified. For example, the whole job could be carried out in light angle-iron and the joints riveted.

In both cases the height of the bench has been given as 2′ 10″, which I find suitable. Obviously this will vary for a taller or shorter man. There is a sound old engineering rule that the most comfortable height for the top of the vice jaws is level with the worker's elbow when he is standing upright. This is important, as a long session of filing, sawing or drilling with the work too high or too low can be unnecessarily tiring.

Vice (*B*) (*Fig. 1*). A fairly heavy engineer's-type vice is necessary. The one on the portable bench is 3½″ wide and is fixed to the frame by three ⅜″ bolts. This is adequate for any normal work but, when equipping the wooden bench, I chose the next larger (4″) size. It is mounted at the left-hand end over one leg, with the vertical face of the fixed jaw overhanging the front of the bench by about ½″, and it is fixed to the 8″ x 3″ front member of the bench by three 7/16″ bolts (*Fig. 3*). With the bench in the corner of the room as shown, the vice comes conveniently opposite the window, midway between the walls, so that a long barrel can be held by the breech with the muzzle projecting in either direction or, with the overhang of the vice jaw, vertically downwards. This vice, with the added stability of the bench, will deal comfortably with such exceptionally heavy jobs as taking out a stubborn breech plug.

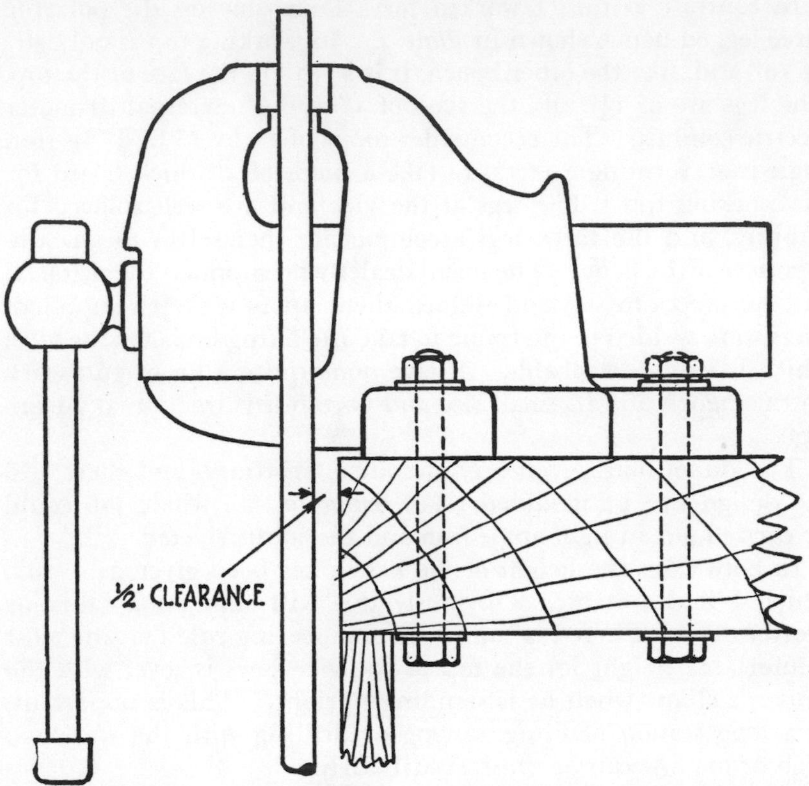

Figure 3. Mounting of 4" engineer's vice. Note position of face of fixed jaw about ½" in front of the edge of the bench, allowing long work to be clamped vertically, to reach the floor if necessary.

A 4" engineer's vice is a powerful tool. It could squeeze the breech of an iron barrel out of shape, or crush a brass fitting. One has to cultivate a sensitive control when gripping small parts and, of course, the heavier the vice, the more necessary this is. Furthermore, the file-like pattern of the fine teeth on the hardened inside faces of the jaws will be impressed on the surface of any object held unprotected between them. To avoid this, two pairs of covers should be made to fit over the vice jaws. *Fig. 4* shows the shape of these. The actual measurements must be taken from the vice itself, which can be used as a template for bending to shape.

One pair should be of 1/16" (No. 16s gauge) sheet copper or

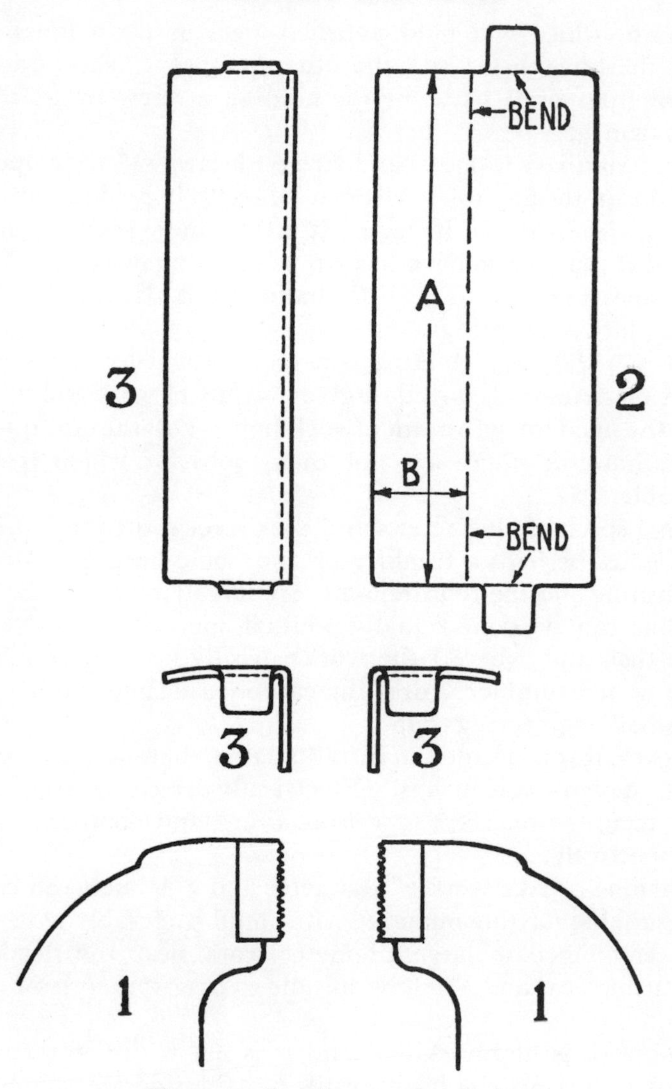

Figure 4. Smooth covers for vice jaws

1. Vice jaws.
2. Shape of sheets before bending.
3. Finished covers.

Dimensions

A. Equal to width of vice jaws.
B. Equal to depth of vice jaws.

aluminium, which will hold polished steel or plain brass parts without marking them; and the other pair of $\frac{1}{8}''$ sheet lead for small irregular brass parts, or for holding a screw by its thread without damage.

A small auxiliary hinged hand-vice with jaws $1\frac{1}{4}''$ wide opening to $\frac{1}{2}''$ is useful for fine work. It can be securely held at any angle in the big vice by one of its legs. It gives a more sensitive adjustment and it should also have its own miniature jaw covers. *Plate 4* shows such a set-up. This little hand-vice is also invaluable for removing lock mainsprings.

Lathe (*C*) (*Fig. 1*). A lathe is a tool coveted by almost every amateur mechanic. It will do a great variety of work and is essential in the modern gunsmith's workshop. For the antique-gun restorer, however, there are not many jobs for which it is indispensable.

Making special fixing screws and cock screws, turning up metal ramrod ends, perhaps a tumbler or two, some horizontal drilling and polishing and the requirements are largely covered. Some of these jobs can be done equally well, if more laboriously, with simpler tools and, where lathe work is really necessary for, say, a cock screw or a tumbler, a drawing can be made and the job given to any small engineering shop.

However, if it is decided to install a lathe, there is a wide choice of sizes, designs and prices. Electrically-driven lathes can be bought mounted on trays or cabinets, to stand on the bench or floor respectively.

A machine to take work 7″ diameter and 2′ 6″ between centres is very suitable for the amateur. It should preferably have a gap bed to accommodate larger-diameter work near the headstock, screw-cutting gear and a hollow spindle to pass work at least 9/16″ diameter.

Lathe work is highly skilled and it is not within the scope of this book to instruct the beginner in it. Considerable knowledge and practice are needed to set up even a comparatively simple job —to centre the work correctly, to adjust the right tool to the exact height and angle, to select suitable speeds of rotation and feed of cut, and to maintain tools in good order for different materials and types of work. There are excellent books written by specialists, devoted entirely to the use of the lathe, but a short course of practical instruction is by far the most satisfactory introduction to lathe work. There are some people with a natural gift for mechanics who may become fairly proficient by the trial-and-error method, but most beginners need some expert advice and demonstration.

My somewhat old-fashioned lathe is not screw-cutting, but it will turn out accurate work within its limitations. Centre height is 6″, i.e. it will take work up to 12″ diameter and up to about 20″ in length. The cross-slide is adjustable for any angle and the hollow head-stock spindle will pass 9/16″ diameter. It has a 6″ self-centring chuck with two sets of jaws for outside and inside holding, and a 3-jaw drill chuck which will take drills up to $\frac{3}{8}$″ diameter, which largely compensates for my lack of a power-drilling machine.

I have a set of parallel twist-drills from 1/16″ to $\frac{3}{8}$″ increasing by 1/32″s, and from $\frac{3}{8}$″ to 1″ increasing by $\frac{1}{8}$″s with morse taper shanks, together with some intermediate sizes which were bought as required. Drills above $\frac{3}{8}$″, however, are seldom necessary for gun-restoration work.

The lathe is mounted on two heavy cast-iron standards to which is bolted a small platform near the floor to carry the electric motor (E), which drives an overhead shaft through a two-speed motor-cycle gear-box and thence to the lathe by a pair of three-step pulleys, giving six speeds in all.

Grinder (*D*). The grinder is mounted near the end of the lathe, driven by a "V" belt from a second pulley on the motor. It has interchangeable 6″ wheels of fine and medium grit and is used for sharpening tools, and for rough shaping prior to file finishing. Its main use is for tool sharpening, and a smaller, hand-operated geared wheel to fit on the bench or clamp in the vice is a practical substitute, provided there is someone willing to turn the handle.

There is a buffing and polishing mop at the other end of the spindle which is occasionally useful, but usually I prefer to finish and polish work by hand.

Motor (*E*) is $\frac{1}{4}$ hp and drives the lathe, counter-shaft and grinder through "V" belts. It runs off the domestic power circuit.

Store Cupboard (*F*) is 5′ 6″ high, 2′ 6″ wide x 1′ 6″ deep to which shelves 10″ deep and 9″ apart have been added, leaving a 6″ space at the front from top to bottom to accommodate lengths of tube, rod, strip, etc., or a long gun-stock or barrel. The shelves take tools and work in hand, and smaller items of material.

Desk (*G*) is equipped with drawers, a hinged cover which swings down to make a writing-table and an enclosed bookcase above for technical books and magazines, drawing instruments and paper. One can sit here in comfort to make a sketch or read up a subject.

Chest of Drawers (*H*) is 3′ wide and provides additional storage for tools. This, the cupboard and the desk are all pieces of discarded domestic furniture, but eminently suitable for the workshop.

Box (*J*) contains miscellaneous items, including pieces of seasoned walnut such as the curved arm from an ancient chair, the other having been used for a pistol stock; an old ivory billiard ball, its fellow already turned to shape to replace an ivory ball butt missing from a Cossack pistol, and part of a broken tusk which has provided material for a revolver grip.

There are some pieces of ebony and other fancy woods, several round horn handles from old table-ware, ideal for ramrod ends, and a heavy horn walking-stick handle which could be invaluable for tipping the fore-end of a stock. One small box contains odd scraps of sheet silver, silver wire, german silver, mother-of-pearl and some thin discs of ivory useful for inlay repair. Another holds genuine old gun parts which I have accumulated over the years—springs and lock parts, old screws, nipples, flints, a trigger guard and trigger, a butt plate, some broken hammers and cock screws, etc. To the uninitiated this may seem a scrap box, but it is a treasure chest to the gun-restorer.

Box (*K*) is a scrap box into which are swept filings, etc. The workshop should have its own equipment for sweeping up. If that of the household is relied upon, one is inclined to leave this until "next time".

(*L*) and (*M*) are a portable electric radiator and a chair respectively.

While the obvious place for the bench is in front of the window, artificial lighting also is important, and there are adjustable light points over the vice, the lathe and the desk.

This then, is a description of my own workshop with just comfortable room for one person to work. The lay-out was evolved rather than planned, but for its size I don't think it could be much improved. It is not offered as a model to be copied, but rather as providing a review of practical and useful basic equipment.

HAND TOOLS

Screw-drivers. These are among the most important tools for gun work and there should be one to fit every size of screw which may be encountered. There is a great variety of patterns and lengths to suit different purposes and my preference is for those with round shanks of medium length ranging, say, from 4″ for a 1/16″ to 12″ for a $\frac{3}{8}$″ size.

I have nine, in widths of 1/16″, 3/32″, $\frac{1}{8}$″, 5/32″, 3/16″, 7/32″, $\frac{1}{4}$″, 5/16″ and $\frac{3}{8}$″ as shown on *Plate 5*. These have all been used on different jobs. The odd one with a taper square for square-socket screw heads was used for a quite different purpose and will be referred to later. *Plate 6* illustrates the advantage of the round shank, where a screw-driver with a shaped, flat shank would foul the trigger guard at every half-turn, and with one too short the trigger guard would be in the way of the handle or fingers. Not all my screw-drivers are of the pattern I have recommended, but any replacements would be of this type.

If all screws had projecting cheese heads, one might manage quite efficiently with two or three sizes of screw-driver, but a high proportion of gun screws are of the flush, countersunk type, and for these it is essential that the screw-driver must be a correct fit; that is, the width of blade should be fractionally less than the length of the bottom of the saw-cut. This will give the maximum grip of the blade on the screw. If too narrow a screw-driver is used, the saw-cut might be marred; if, on the other hand, it is even a shade too wide, it will not reach the bottom of the saw-cut, and the face of the counter-sunk hole in the surrounding metal or wood will be badly scraped.

The foregoing points and the obvious risk of damage by using a worn screw-driver in a worn slot are illustrated in *Fig. 5*. Even in a worn slot, a perfectly ground blade of the right width will usually grip.

Hammers. Always use the lightest hammer that will do the job. It may take a little more time, but it will incur far less risk of damage. A 4-oz hammer is sufficient, and allows very sensitive control, for removing pins, etc., when dismantling a gun. For flattening or bending material and for tool-making, ½-lb and 1-lb hammers are suitable, and I once had to buy a 4-lb hammer to deal with the distorted fork of a heavy swivel boat gun.

I have found that the most generally useful type of hammer head

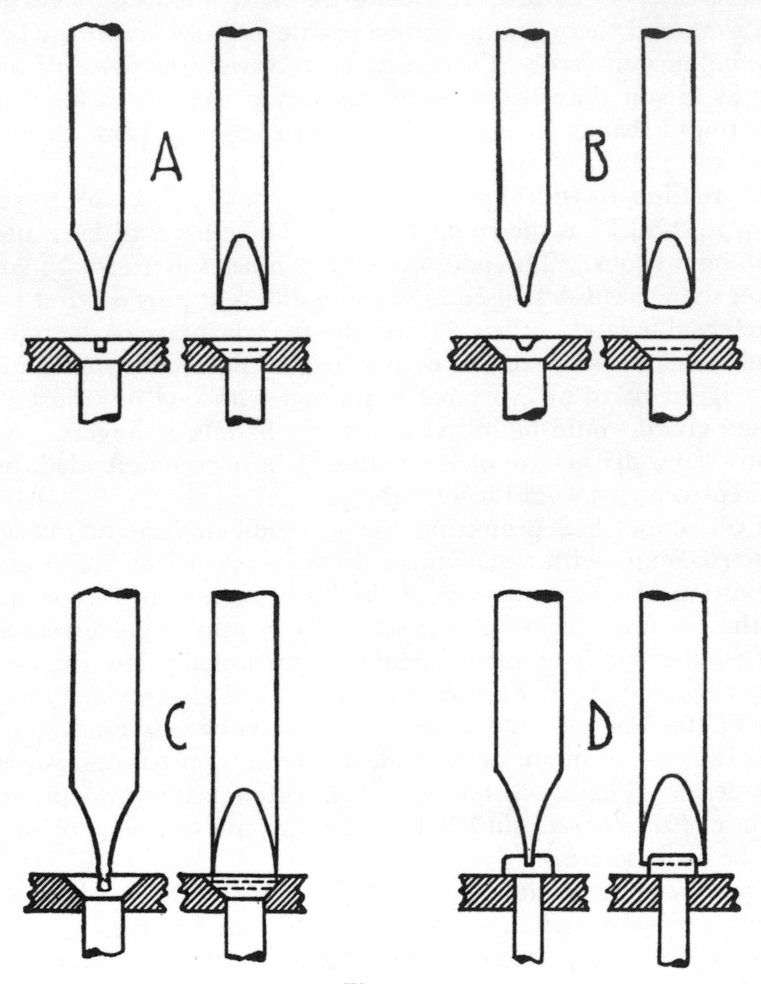

Figure 5.

A. Screw-driver of correct fit for countersunk screw.
B. A worn screw-driver and worn slot in screw.
C. Screw-driver too wide for countersunk screw.
D. A screw-driver wider than the screw-head may be used for projecting cheese-head screws.

is the engineer's pattern with a ball peen, but one of them—say, the half-pound size—could, with advantage, be of the joiner's type with a narrow cross peen.

A joiner's medium-weight wooden mallet or one of hard rubber is a useful adjunct and *Plate 7* shows the various hammers I have used for gun work.

Pliers and Wrenches. There are many sizes and patterns of these and *Plate 8* shows a number of gripping tools.

(1) is a 12″ heavy adjustable wrench and it has been used only once on gun work.

(2) A long pair of thin-nosed pliers with two sizes of recesses for gripping barrels or small round parts.

(3) A rather more powerful grip with jaws adjustable to four widths.

(4) Ordinary 6″ pliers with jaws adjustable to two widths.

(5) A miniature adjustable spanner opening to $\frac{5}{8}$″, useful for holding lock springs while these are being removed.

(6) The small hinged hand-vice. Not only can this be clamped in the bench vice for holding fine work, but it deals comfortably with the strongest lock mainspring.

(7) Taper round-nose pliers for bending.

(8) These small long-nosed offset pliers are useful for handling pins or screws in awkward positions, their particular virtue being that the hand is out of the way and the worker can see what he is doing.

Files. These are made in many shapes, sizes and grades of cut. *Fig. 6* shows a number of sections which I have used from time to time.

(1) Flat. All four faces may be cut, or one edge left uncut. The uncut, often called the safe, edge is used to avoid undercutting when filing into a corner.

(2) Flat file with rounded edges.

(3) Half-round.

(4) Round. The small ones are often called "rat-tail" and the miniature needle files "mouse-tail".

(5) Square, for finishing square holes, such as the tumbler hole in the hammer.

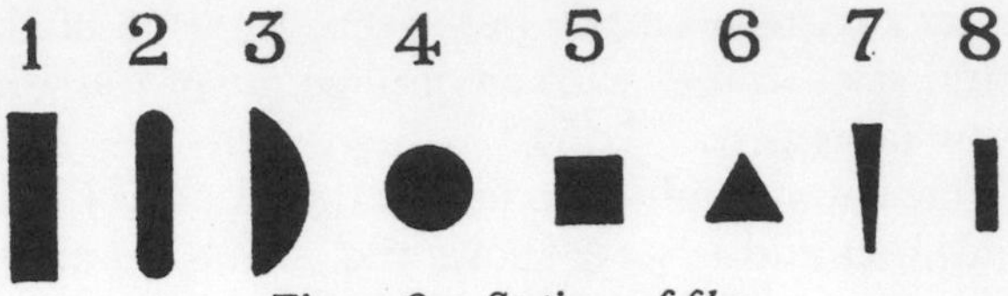

1 2 3 4 5 6 7 8

Figure 6. Sections of files.

1. Flat; 2. Flat with round edges; 3. Half-round; 4. Round; 5. Square; 6. Triangular; 7. Knife; 8. Warding.

(6) Triangular (sometimes, for some reason, called "three square"), for notches in sights and tumblers. (Also for sharpening wood saws.)

(7) Knife file, useful for half-cock notches in tumbler.

(8) Usually known as a warding file. Slender and thin and tapering in its length almost to a point.

The round, half-round, square and triangular files almost always taper in their length. This is a particular advantage with the round and half-round sections, as they offer a varying radius of curve at different positions along the file.

As regards grades of cut, there are rough, bastard, second, etc., representing the number of teeth per inch from 22 to 120.

To begin with, it is suggested that Nos. 1, 3, 4, 5 and 6 be bought in the 10″ size of medium-grade cut. Larger, smaller, rougher or smoother types and other sections can be added as they are needed. It is not necessary for the amateur to know all the names of files and grades of cut. The tool salesman is quite used to recognising a customer's requirements by description as easily as by trade names.

A set of miniature files will certainly be required. These should be dead smooth cut, with teeth hardly perceptible to the unaided eye. They are usually about 3″ to 4″ long and can be bought singly or in sets, comprising all the sections shown for larger files. Swiss-made miniature files are as good as can be bought. Cheaper sets are obtainable, but the quality and fineness of cut are usually lacking.

Fit a turned wood handle to each file as it is put into use. These handles are cheap and are obtainable at any tool store. It is a common but risky practice to hold the tang in the palm of the

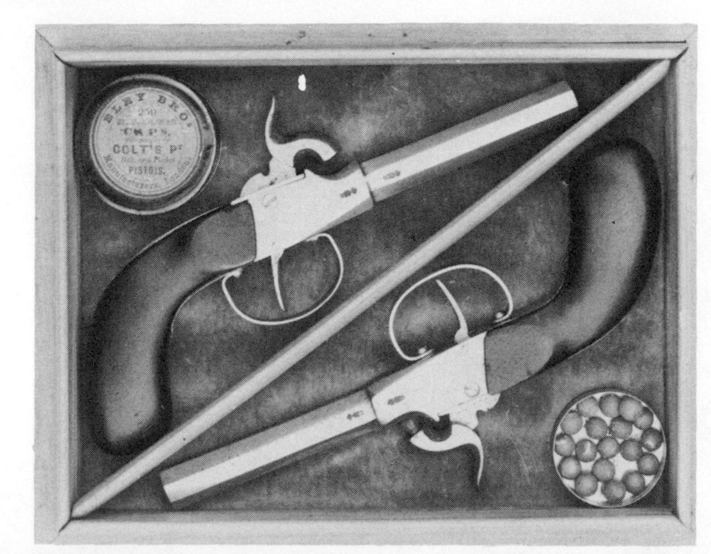

Plate 1.
An auction-room fake. A pair of common pocket pistols with butts restained and polished to imitate ebony, and fitted into a case which originally contained cutlery.

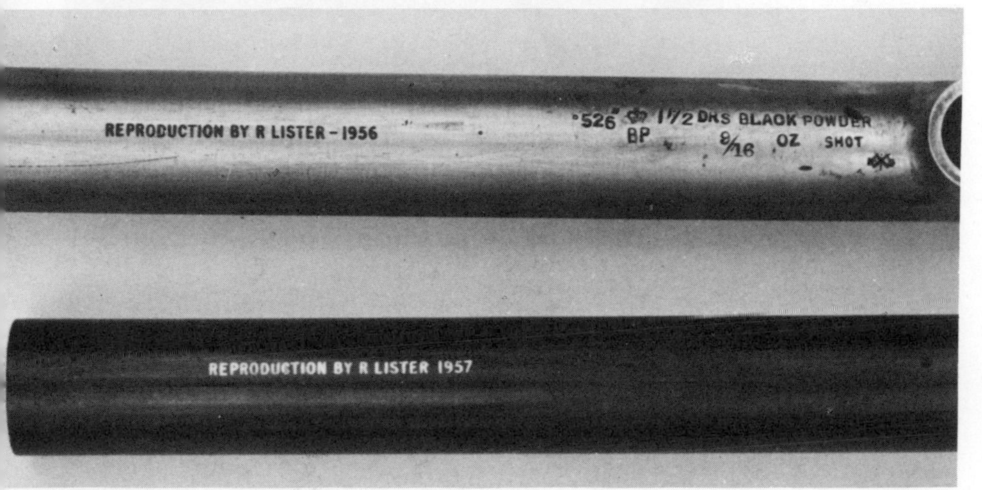

Plate 2. Engraving on barrels of two replicas of antique guns made by the author. Note the Birmingham proof marks on the upper barrel. This gun is a matchlock and is safe to shoot.

Plate 3. Portable three-legged bench. Working top 36 in. by 10 in. with fixed engineer's $3\frac{1}{2}$ in. vice. The small anvil weighs 12 lb.

hand. Many of the miniature Swiss files have an integral handle in the form of a rod instead of a tang.

There is another type of file which is invaluable on occasion. Of 1/16″ round section, about 8″ long, it is held in tension in a hack-saw frame in much the same way as the blade of a fretsaw. It will cut large holes or irregular shapes in sheet metal, which cannot be done with the flat-bladed hack-saw. *Plate 9* shows the hole in a barrel key being made with a tension file of this kind.

A 10″ half-round woodworker's rasp will be required for any work on wood butts or stocks. It is similar in shape to a half-round file, but with a different form of tooth and a much coarser cut.

Steel "bristles" mounted in canvas, known as file-card, are used for clearing the clogged teeth of files. These can be bought by the foot and pieces about the size of a nail brush are cut and tacked firmly to a wood backing.

The file is a precision shaping tool and the file work of a first-class fitter will show an amazing degree of finish and accuracy. Considerable practice is needed to move the file across the work in exactly horizontal strokes. A severe test of filing ability is to take an irregular piece of metal and, with only a steel square and callipers for testing, to file it into a perfect cube with every edge equal, every angle a right angle and every face flat.

Any amateur worker who can produce a 1″ cube in this way, true everywhere to 1/100th of an inch can count himself competent. A highly skilled fitter will work to much finer limits than this. Even today, some of the most accurate and delicate gun-fitting is done with a file.

Drills. In the absence of either a drilling machine or a lathe, one must rely on hand drills. A hand-operated drill is suitable for holes up to ¼″ diameter, while a standard joiner's brace will hold twist drills with square shanks up to ⅜″. Although metal drilling with a brace up to this size is slow, it is quite practical, particularly if a ¼″ pilot hole is drilled first.

The popular pistol-type electric hand drill is good for quick metal drilling up to ¼″ or 5/16″. These three types are shown on *Plate 10.* The makers of these useful electric tools issue a catalogue of accessories, where they list such items as bench clamps for fixing them rigidly to take grinding and buffing wheels, circular wire brushes for de-rusting, etc. There are other fittings to enable the tool to be mounted as a light vertical drilling machine.

Parts are also listed for adapting these portable electric tools to wood turning, but it must be emphatically stated that they are not suitable for metal turning, except perhaps to polish a screw head, or such other light job as can be held in a $\frac{1}{4}''$ chuck.

Drills starting at 1/16″ and increasing by 1/32″s up to the largest size the chuck will take are necessary, and intermediate sizes can be added as required. A 90° countersink bit will also be needed.

Drills require periodical sharpening and in engineering shops, where they are in regular use, an attachment to the grinding wheel ensures that sharpened drills will have all angles correct and be exactly symmetrical. Most amateurs sharpen their drills by hand

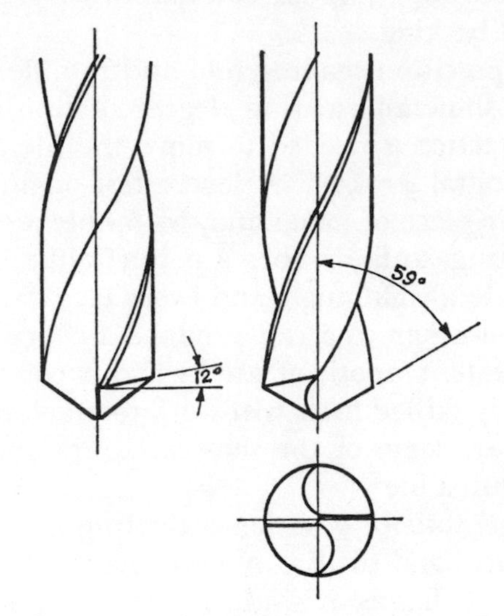

Figure 7. Twist drill, correctly ground.

and *Fig.* 7 shows the correct shape of the cutting end. The accepted theoretical angles are indicated, but a variation of a degree or two will not seriously impair the efficiency of a drill. Like turning, however, drill grinding is difficult to learn from diagrams. In the absence of an obliging engineering friend who will demonstrate the job and patiently supervise practice, it is a good idea to take a new drill and hold it against the stationary wheel, to ascertain the correct angles for grinding the cutting edges and faces. If there is appreciable variation from the angles shown in the drawing, the drill will be much less efficient and, whether the angles are correct or not, if the opposite sides are not exactly symmetrical, the result will be a hole larger than the drill's rated size.

If a drill has a tendency to make an oversize hole, drill a smaller pilot hole so that the larger size will centre itself. The man who finds that he just cannot get the knack and, in his repeated attempts, is grinding his drills away down to the shank, will have to send them out periodically to be ground.

Taps and dies will be required for some jobs and these can be bought singly as required. I have a collection of them in sizes from Nos. 0 to 8, B.A. or, from approximately 6 to 2 millimetres diameter, and, in the coarser Whitworth thread, from $\frac{1}{4}''$ to $\frac{1}{2}''$, rising in sixteenths, together with several external chasers which can be used with the lathe for matching non-standard threads.

A Hack-saw is essential. One with a pistol grip and adjustable back to take blades up to 12″ long will be found satisfactory. High-speed steel blades are comparatively expensive, but more than repay their additional cost in length of service.

A fairly fine blade—say twenty-two teeth to the inch—will be about right, and some people find that they cut down breakages by using 10″ instead of 12″ blades. Remember that provision is made in the frame for the blade to be turned at right angles, which can be convenient in some cases.

A miniature hack-saw of the type having a $\frac{1}{4}''$ x 6″ blade sprung into a light $\frac{1}{4}''$ bent wire frame is extremely useful for light work.

The little 12-lb anvil (see *Plate 3*) is a most useful tool for flattening and bending. A short length (say between 8″ and 12″) of heavy section T-iron about $2\frac{1}{2}''$ to 3″ wide, clamped in the vice by the central web, makes a workable substitute for the flat top of an anvil.

Other metal workers' tools which are likely to be necessary are: a blow-lamp, centre punches, flat-nosed punches, a scriber for marking-out on steel or brass, internal and external callipers, steel dividers, a 6″ steel square, and an engineer's steel rule 12″ x 1″ wide, graduated in inches, eighths, sixteenths, thirty-seconds and sixty-fourths, also in tenths, fiftieths, hundredths and millimetres. This rule will also serve as a straight-edge for setting-out with the scriber.

A number of special pin punches will be wanted to drive out the wire pins which were commonly used to fix barrels, trigger guards, ramrod pipes or thimbles, etc., to the wood stocks. These are merely lengths of hardened steel rod of different gauges, set in handles for hammering. They are sold in sets of three or five, but these, as also nipple keys and mainspring vices, are increasingly difficult to come by, and they may have to be obtained from the mail-order firms who advertise in gun collectors' magazines.

Punches and nipple keys can easily be made, however, if there is any difficulty in obtaining them, and the simple procedure will be described later.

As regards the mainspring vice, the standard hinged hand-vice described earlier will serve just as well and can be bought at any tool shop. It may not be so neat and light as the special-purpose tool designed for one job only, but it will do that job quite efficiently, and others besides.

Wood-Working Tools will occasionally be required, such as cross-cut and tenon saws, chisels and gouges, say, $\frac{1}{4}''$ and $\frac{3}{8}''$ of each, a plane, and a joiner's brace with several bits from $\frac{3}{4}''$ to 1″ for boring wood clamps for gun barrels if breech plugs have to be removed.

This may seem a formidable list of tools but not all of them are needed at the outset—some, perhaps, not at all. Usually they are accumulated as the necessity arises.

I keep at hand a small drawing-board with a T-square, 30°/60° and 45° set squares, a protractor and a 12″ scale graduated in inches and millimetres, along with a pair of 3″ compasses and a smaller spring bow compass. This drawing equipment may seem something of a luxury, but it is useful to be able to make a full-size dimensioned drawing before beginning work on a complicated replacement part.

CONTAINERS

Glass screw-top jars are useful for storing screws and small parts. They are airtight and the contents are visible. Equally useful are the plastic boxes with lids sold in various sizes for kitchen equipment. These, together with a couple of the plastic trays made to take a dozen eggs, will hold parts of dismantled guns. The particular virtue of the egg trays is that while dismantling, say, a lock, each small screw or similar item can be laid in a separate compartment in the order of removal, ready for reassembly in reverse order. An enamel bowl about 12″ diameter x 4″ to 6″ deep will be needed for soaking and cleaning metal parts.

It pays to provide special containers like these, rather than to make do with a haphazard collection of old saucers and miscellaneous boxes.

Other tools will be described as they become necessary for special jobs.

CHAPTER THREE

MATERIALS

FROM time to time the gunworker will require a variety of materials which it is unlikely he will be able to buy casually over the counter. Even such standard articles as brass and steel sheet, rod and tube may not be readily obtainable in small amounts, and screws in the bastard pitches frequently used by the old working gunsmiths are most difficult to find.

For example, he may require a piece of sheet brass 3″ x $\frac{3}{4}$″ x 16s gauge to make a new side plate; a piece of black horn to tip a ramrod; a short length of 3/16″ inside x 5/16″ outside steel tube to make a nipple key; a few inches of $\frac{7}{8}$″ x $\frac{1}{4}$″ steel strip to make a flint top jaw, or some $\frac{1}{4}$″ square rod for sights; various gauges of wire for pins; a square foot of sheet copper or aluminium or lead for vice jaw covers. In fact, quite an extensive list could be made but, with patience and ingenuity, everything one needs can be obtained ultimately, and a useful stock gradually accumulated.

For instance, I once bought a pound of mixed round wire nails from 1″ to 2$\frac{1}{2}$″ long of different gauges from which I can always find something suitable for pins by nipping off the points and heads and trimming to length. The local wool shop would appear to be an unlikely source of stock for gun work, but it was from there that I got some steel knitting needles in various gauges from 15s to 20s for making pin punches. They were so hard that a file would not touch them, so they had to be nicked round on the edge of the grinding wheel and broken into 2″ and 2$\frac{1}{2}$″ lengths. Driven $\frac{1}{2}$″ deep into tight holes in 2″ lengths of brass rod for handles and with the ends ground true and burr polished off, I had a set of five pin punches of the finest quality, and stock left for necessary replacements. In this case, economy was not the main object. I made these five punches in less than an hour after waiting many weeks for a set which I had ordered from a gunsmith. Stainless steel wire meat-skewers sold in sets of assorted lengths and gauges are also excellent for making punches. They are tough and resilient and not so hard as to be brittle.

Shops which cater for model makers can be good sources of supply, particularly for screws, rod, strip and tube, and blacksmiths, working garages or small engineering shops will often supply limited quantities of material.

It is, however, replacement parts such as springs, nipples, triggers, etc., which present the most difficult problem, and making these, which involves forging, tempering or precision lathe work, is generally beyond the capability of the untrained amateur.

Time was when there were gunsmiths who could provide old parts or even complete detached locks. An old-established dealer whom I knew had hundreds of nipples of all sizes and patterns, quantities of old screws, mainsprings, sear and trigger springs, trigger guards, butt plates, locks and so on, all sorted into boxes, but when he retired his successor cleared out all this "obsolete litter". I wish I had been there when he did so! There may be a few gunsmiths who still have some of the old stock left, but they are becoming fewer and less willing to dispose of what they have. If the collector belongs to a gun or arms society, inquiries through fellow-members may reveal some useful supply of parts.

There is, however, another source of supply through the American mail-order firms who advertise in gun collectors' magazines. These firms issue profusely illustrated catalogues and appear to be able to supply almost any antique gun, pistol or revolver part which could ever be wanted. Many finished replacement parts for the more common American flint or percussion guns and revolvers are catalogued down to the smallest screw. Many of these parts are genuine old surplus unused stock; some come from broken-up guns, and others are of the original pattern but of modern manufacture.

It is quite a practical proposition to build a complete shootable flint-lock or percussion gun or pistol, or percussion revolver, from parts supplied by such firms. They supply maple or walnut stocks, either as rough blanks or partly finished, barrels, complete locks or any of their component parts, springs, screws, sights, side plates, butt caps, nipples and keys, flints, cap and patch boxes, ramrods and thimbles, horn and metal tips, frizzens, hammers of almost any description, some finished and squared to fit the tumbler and others in the rough for the buyer to finish and fit. These are but a very few of the parts offered, and at the outset the gun-restorer should send for one of the catalogues issued by such firms.

It is suggested that the first small order for stock might consist of a supply of nipples, nipple keys, flints, a few springs and hammers and an assortment of screws. Nipples were made in several patterns and many sizes and different thread diameters and pitches, some with four flats for square keys and others with two parallel flats. Order a mixed lot of sizes and types and six assorted keys or wrenches, unless you prefer to make your own keys, which is quite a simple job.

When ordering springs or hammers, always send dimensioned sketches of the patterns required, a description of the gun, and, if possible, the name of the maker. If the component cannot be exactly matched, ask for the nearest larger size which would be suitable for filing down.

The "throw", i.e. the distance from the centre of the tumbler screw to the centre of the hammer nose (or, in the case of a flint-lock, to the face of the bottom jaw), of a replacement hammer is important. A slight variation, say 1/16″ in the case of a flint-lock, is permissible, but for the percussion hammer the throw must be exact.

Fig. 8 shows the type of rough sketch which will enable the supplier to understand your requirements.

In the case of fractured springs, send the broken sample. Order hammers without the square hole in the boss. Unless a standard pattern hammer for a specified type of gun is available, it is extremely improbable that the squares of the tumbler and hammer will correspond either in size or angle.

To find the throw for a new percussion hammer, when the old one is missing, measure accurately the distance from the centre of the tumbler screw to the centre of the face of the nipple. The case of a missing flint hammer is not so easy. The proportions of the hammer must be such that, in the "fired" position, the underside of the bottom jaw clears the guard behind the flash-pan by about $\frac{1}{8}$″ to $\frac{1}{4}$″, depending on the size of lock. The dotted positions of the nipple and pan respectively in *Fig. 8* should make this clear.

When sketching the style of hammer, whether slender or massive, swan-necked or with double neck, engraved or plain (if no authentic copy is available through a fellow collector), reference to museum specimens or photographs in collectors' publications will give a reasonably reliable guide to the appropriate type for the weapon and period.

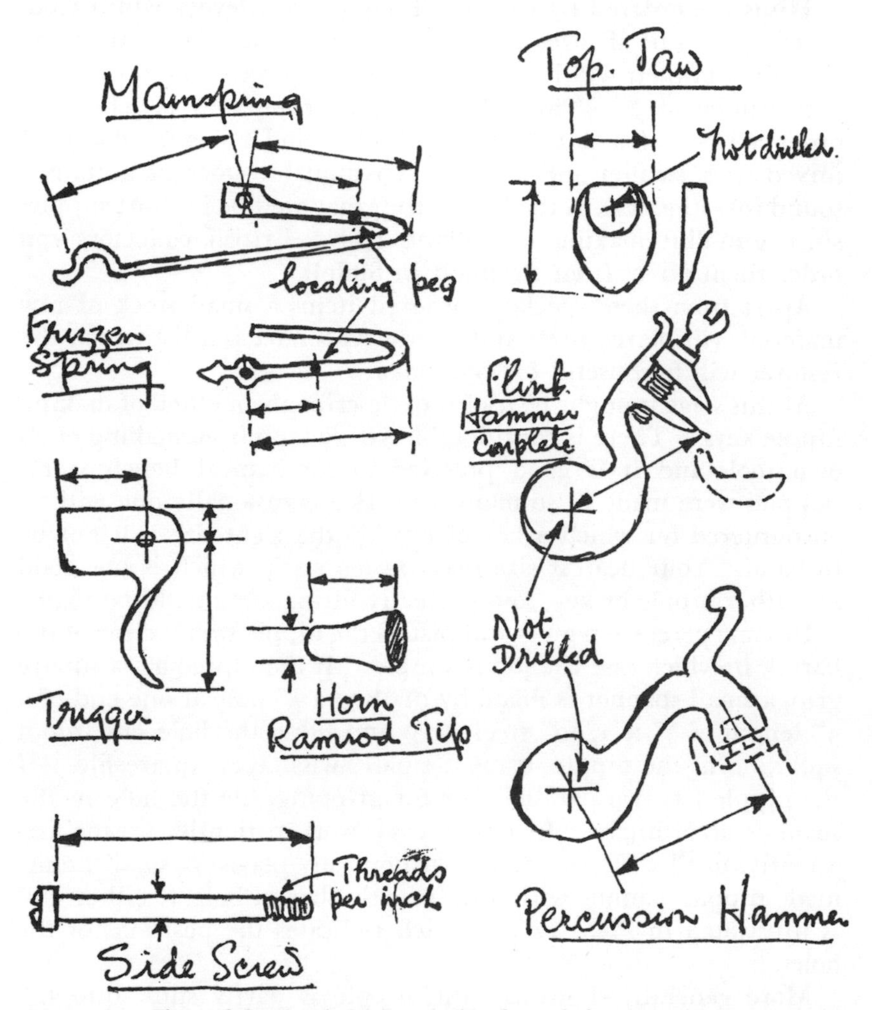

Figure 8. Type of free-hand sketch suitable for ordering parts by post. A few typical items are shown and the arrowed lines indicate the essential dimensions which must be given. Additional dimensions and descriptive notes will be helpful to the supplier.

Include two or three dozen assorted screws suitable for lock fixing and cock or top jaw screws and smaller miscellaneous replacement screws. It is a good plan to collect a sample of every diameter and thread pitch available and keep them together in a separate container.

Flints are ordered by width. They come in every width from $\frac{3}{8}''$ to $1\frac{1}{4}''$ to suit all sizes of locks and are usually classified in size according to their width to the nearest $\frac{1}{8}''$. I have found the most useful to be $\frac{1}{2}''$, $\frac{5}{8}''$, $\frac{3}{4}''$ and $\frac{7}{8}''$. They are comparatively cheap, so order a stock of a dozen of each width, and an extra dozen of mixed sizes, smaller and larger. A reasonable stock of flints is a sound investment as in the future they may well be in short supply, since gun-flint making is a dying craft. British collectors can order them direct from Brandon in Suffolk.

Apart from these specially ordered items a small stock of raw material will be required and in the Appendix is a list which the restorer will find useful for reference.

At this stage it might be useful to describe the method of making nipple keys. There is considerable satisfaction from making one's own tools and it is good practice in mechanical bench work. Nipples were made in so many sizes that occasionally one will be encountered for which a key of exactly the right size will not be to hand. Your nearest size may be too slack, which is not good for either nipple or key, so a perfectly fitting key should be made.

In some percussion guns and pistols the nipple stands clear of the barrel, in which case the job is simple. If the nipple has a square grip, a small spanner is made by drilling a $\frac{1}{8}''$ hole at one end of a 3″ length of $\frac{3}{8}''$ x 3/32″ steel strip and filing the hole out into a square to fit the nipple, using a small Swiss taper square file. If the nipple has two parallel flats for gripping, file the hole in the spanner accordingly. In either case, work patiently, testing frequently, until the spanner fits without any play. A small home-made nipple spanner with a differently shaped hole at either end is illustrated in *Plate 11* (2) which indicates the positions of the holes.

More generally, however, the nipple is partly sunk into the breech block, and a key with a round shank is necessary. *Plate 11* (*1*) shows a home-made key of this kind for a nipple with parallel flats and (*3*) a corresponding key for a squared nipple.

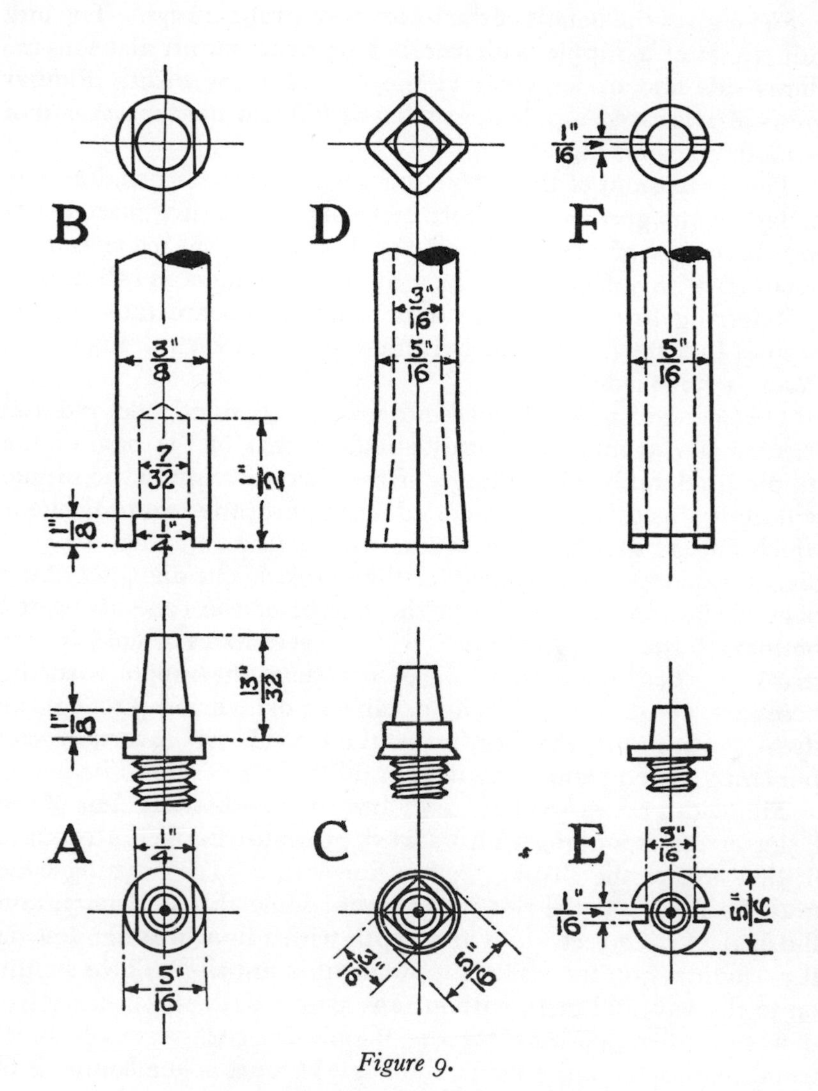

Figure 9.

A. Top and side views of nipple with parallel flats.
B. Side and under views of end of key for A.
C. Top and side views of nipple with square.
D. Side and under views of end of key for C.
E. Top and side views of nipple with slots.
F. Side and under views of end of key for E.

Fig. 9 gives the details of the lower ends of these keys. Top and side views of a nipple with parallel flats are shown at (A). (B) shows side and under views of the end of a key to fit. Similar views of a squared nipple are shown at (C) and the bottom end of a suitable key for this at (D).

The dimensions of the nipple must first be ascertained. It may be fast in the gun and therefore awkward to measure exactly, but the diameters of the base and the bottom of the cone can be obtained with sufficient accuracy by using dividers as callipers.

Referring first to (A), the dimensions given are those of the nipples in a Belgian double-barrelled gun for which key No. 1 on *Plate 11* was made.

The shank of a key of this kind is made of round steel rod and its diameter should be at least equal to that of the base of the nipple (preferably a little larger if the clearance round the nipple will allow), as this will give added strength to the two projections which engage with the flats. The nipple illustrated has a 5/16″ dia. base, so rod $\frac{3}{8}$″ dia. is used for the shank. The diameter of the base of the cone is 3/16″ and the height of the cone above the bottom of the flats is 13/32″, which necessitates a hole in the shank of 7/32″ dia. and $\frac{1}{2}$″ deep to receive the nipple with the necessary clearance. This hole can be drilled by putting the shank vertically in the vice, using the smooth jaw covers, centre-punching the end and using the hand-drill.

The width across the flats is $\frac{1}{4}$″ and the depth of the flats $\frac{1}{8}$″, so a slot of corresponding width and depth must be filed across the drilled end of the shank. A flat file with a 3/16″ cutting edge must be used and the slot roughed out somewhat undersize, and finished off to correct width and depth with a fine Swiss file, testing it periodically on the actual nipple until it just slides down snugly on to the flats and grips without any perceptible play.

A convenient position for the handle for turning a key is 3″ from the nipple, so the shank is made $3\frac{1}{4}$″ long. The handle is of 5/32″ steel rod, 3″ long, and the hole, in which it is a driving fit, is drilled $\frac{1}{4}$″ from the top end of the shank. The handle is tested in a 5/32″ hole in a piece of scrap metal and, if it is an easy fit, the hole in the shank is made with the next smaller diameter drill and enlarged with an $\frac{1}{8}$″ round taper Swiss file until the handle can be hammered in.

The ends of the handle must be rounded off and all corners and edges smoothed and polished with strips of fine emery cloth to give the professional finish.

The construction of a key for a squared nipple is rather different. The nipple (C) for which key No. 3 (*Plate 11*) was made was on a Tranter percussion revolver. The shank (D) of this key was made from steel tube 1/16″ thick, the inside diameter being equal to the side of the square; for a nipple as illustrated with a 3/16″ square, the tube would require to be 3/16″ internal x 5/16″ outside dia. x $3\frac{1}{4}$″ long. If tube of the correct size is not to hand, a hole of the required diameter 1″ deep, drilled concentrically into the end of a piece of round steel, will serve the same purpose.

The next requirement is a piece of $\frac{1}{4}$″ square section steel rod tapering at one end for 1″ of its length down to $\frac{1}{8}$″ square to serve as a former for the socket. There is a type of screw-driver with a tapered square end for screws with square recesses instead of saw cuts, which, being quite true and of the correct taper, is perfect for the job. The 10″ long size has a $\frac{1}{4}$″ to $\frac{1}{8}$″ taper, which will serve for any size between these dimensions. Alternatively, the taper can be filed on a piece of $\frac{1}{4}$″ square-section stock rod.

Firmly clamp the screw-driver or rod vertically in the vice with the taper end upwards. Place the 1-lb hammer and the anvil ready to hand and, holding the shank with a pair of pliers, bring the tubular end up to a dull red heat with the blow-lamp. Put the heated end over the squared taper and drive it down with three or four sharp blows of the hammer. Drop the hammer and pliers on to the bench and, gripping the rod with the left hand, quickly release it from the vice and, laying rod and shank across the anvil, hammer the heated end of the tube against the taper flats, giving a quarter turn between each stroke.

This will loosen the shank, which can be lifted off with the pliers. All this should be done as rapidly as possible before the shank cools. The hole will not yet be big enough to go over the nipple, so heat it again and repeat the procedure until the square is perfectly true, and large enough to receive the square of the nipple. As the hollow squared end of the shank will have a slight taper, it should be filed down until it just fits the square without any appreciable play.

Trim off the top end of the shank where it has received the hammer blows, fit the cross-handle and finish as previously described. *Plate 12* shows a square key shank being made, using the square-section screw-driver included on *Plate 5* as a former.

There is another kind of nipple which has two small slots on opposite sides of the base to receive a key. It was never popular and example (E) *Fig. 9* is from an English transition revolver. Both nipple base and key are inherently weak in design. No doubt this type, when new, was fairly satisfactory but, if these nipples are very stiff in the sockets due to rust or fouling, they will often either break the pegs off the key or the corners off the slots, rather than unscrew. Views of the bottom end of the key to fit the slotted nipple (E) are shown at (F) and the method of construction is obvious from the drawing.

CHAPTER FOUR

DISMANTLING AND CLEANING

OF the early firearms, the common single-barrel, centre-hammer, box-lock, percussion-cap pocket pistol is the simplest to dismantle and reassemble. It is fairly safe to say that all collectors will have at least one example. Consequently it is a suitable pattern on which to start work. *Plate 13* illustrates a typical example, and *Plate 14* shows the same pistol completely dismantled with the parts enumerated.

Assume that the pistol that we are going to dismantle is complete and mechanically sound. Compare it with the photographs. A cursory examination might reasonably suggest that to get at the parts inside the box the cover-plate must first be taken off; that to take off the cover-plate the hammer must be removed; that to remove the hammer the pivot screw must be taken out. It would seem logical, therefore, that the removal of the hammer pivot screw is the first step to take. In fact, however, the removal of the pivot screw at this stage could result in damage from the sudden release of the mainspring tension. The correct sequence of operations is as follows:

Have ready a container for the larger parts and an egg-tray for the nipple, small pins, screws, etc.

First take out the nipple. Next remove the wood butt which is attached by two wood screws, one above through the tang of the box cover-plate, and one underneath through the tang of the frame. (The top screw is nearly always the smaller one and should be taken out first.) Then take out the screw from underneath. The butt should now slide easily from between the tangs, and as this is the only piece of wood in the pistol, it can be laid aside until all the metal parts have been dealt with.

The mainspring and the boss of the hammer are now disclosed inside the box. Leave them where they are for the time being.

Next take out the two small screws at the front corners of the cover-plate, so that the plate is free to slide up the neck of the hammer until stopped by the head.

Now put the hammer at full cock and watch the mainspring while doing so. As the hammer is drawn back, it will force down the top member of the spring which reaches its lowest position at full cock, and this is as far as the spring should ever be compressed. It should be an invariable rule, when removing or assembling the mainspring, that it must never be flexed beyond the position which it assumes at full cock. To do so puts it under unnecessary strain which, with springs a century or more old, may well result in fracture.

Now take the small hand-vice and wind insulation tape round the jaws to avoid marking the metal of the pistol and to prevent slipping. Hold the loose cover-plate out of the way and set the bottom tang and the mainspring between the open vice jaws, with the vice as far up the mainspring as it will go. This position is usually limited by the trigger guard. Close the vice until it grips, but does not compress the spring further (see *Plate 15*). Now press the trigger and lower the hammer. As the spring is held in compression by the vice, the hammer will swing freely on its pivot.

Now take out the hammer pivot screw, and lift out the hammer, which will free the cover-plate. Before opening and removing the vice, measure exactly the gap between the jaws so that the spring can be closed by precisely that amount and no more, when re-assembling the pistol. Remove the vice, and the relaxed main-spring can be lifted off its anchoring hook.

Tap out the trigger pivot pin, using a punch slightly less in diameter than the pin, and draw out the trigger.

The trigger spring, housed in the front of the box, is a little "V" spring, held in position by a small locating peg which fits into a hole in the box. After the trigger has been removed, this spring can be drawn back and lifted out with slender-nosed pliers or strong tweezers.

The trigger guard is held in position at its front end by an integral stud, which screws into a tapped hole in the underside of the box, and at the rear end by a screw inserted from the inside of the box into a tapped hole in the trigger guard. Take out this rear screw and detach the guard by rotating it round the front screw.

Plate 4. Hinged hand-vice mounted in bench-vice for fine work. A cock-screw is being slotted with a miniature hacksaw.

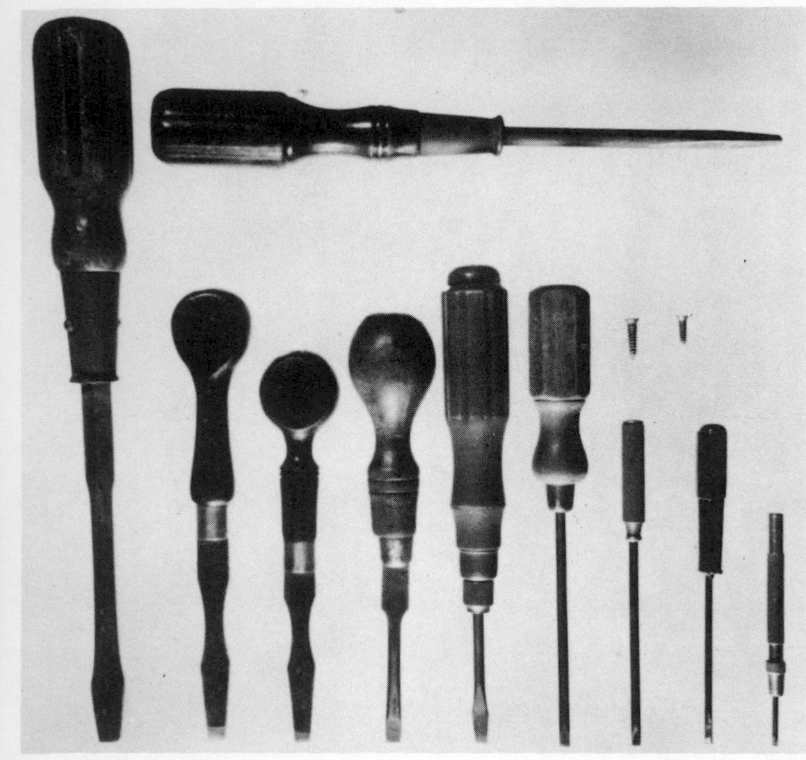

Plate 5. Miscellaneous collection of screwdrivers used by the author. Widths—3/8 in., 5/16 in., 1/4 in., 7/32 in., 3/16 in., 5/32 in., 1/8 in., 3/32 in. and 1/16 in.

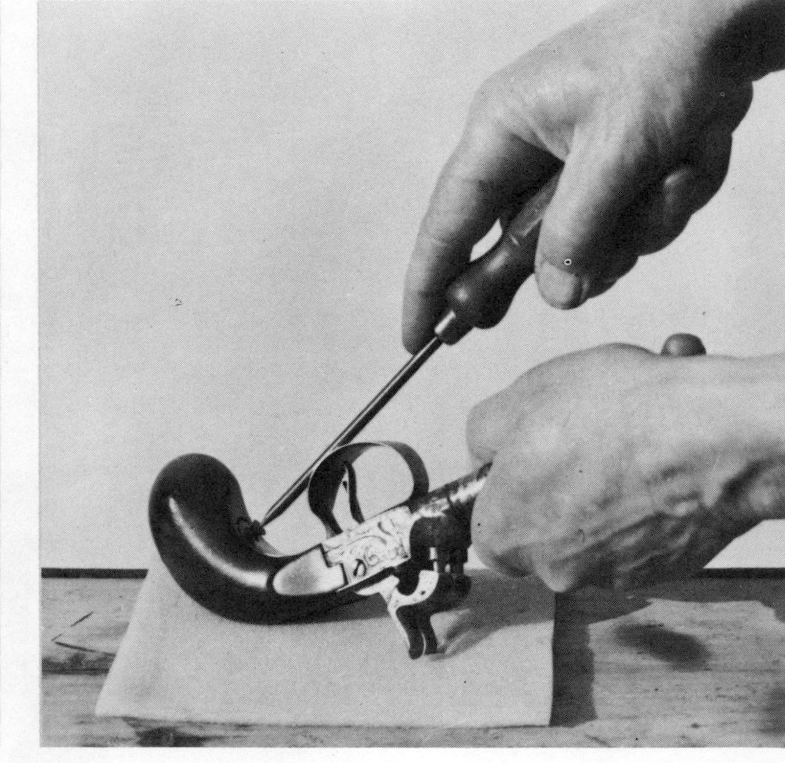

Plate 6. Illustrating the advantage of a long, round-shank screwdriver. A short screwdriver would bring the hand into contact with the trigger-guard and a flat-shank screwdriver would foul the trigger-guard at each half turn.

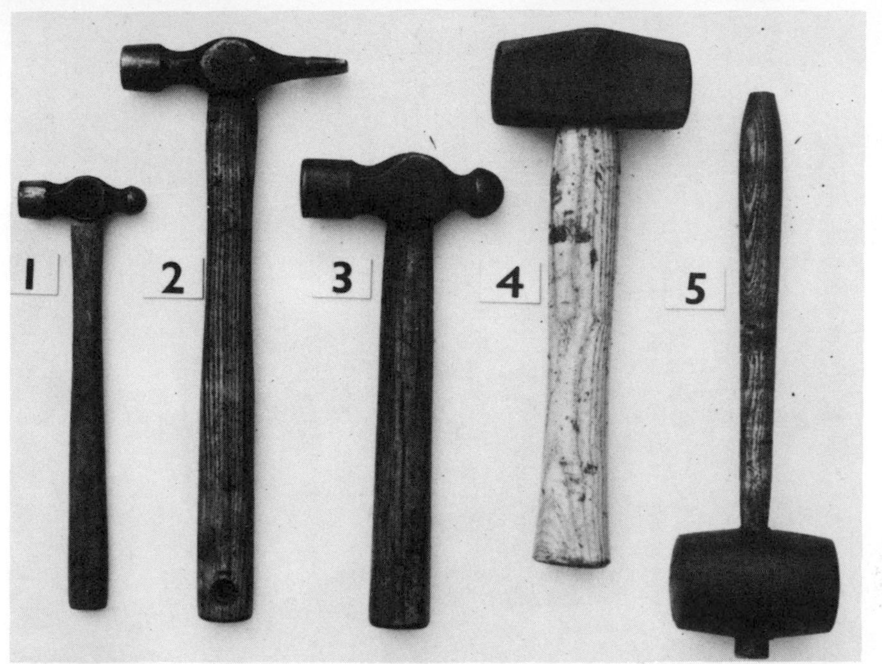

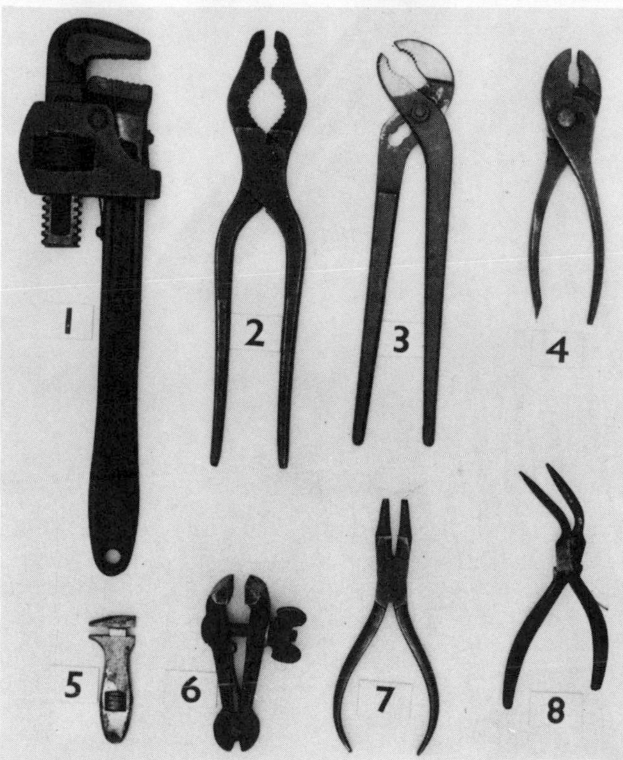

Plate 7. HAMMERS

1. 4 oz. ball peen. The size most frequently used in gun-work.
2. ½ lb. cross peen.
3. 1 lb. ball peen.
4. 4 lb. hammer. Very seldom required.
5. Hard rubber mallet, weight about 8 oz.

Plate 8.

GRIPPING TOOLS.

1. 12 in. wrench.
2. Large flat pliers.

3 and 4. Adjustable pliers.

5. Small adjustable spanner.
6. 1¼ in. hinged hand-vice.
7. Round-nosed pliers.
8. Long-nosed off-set pliers.

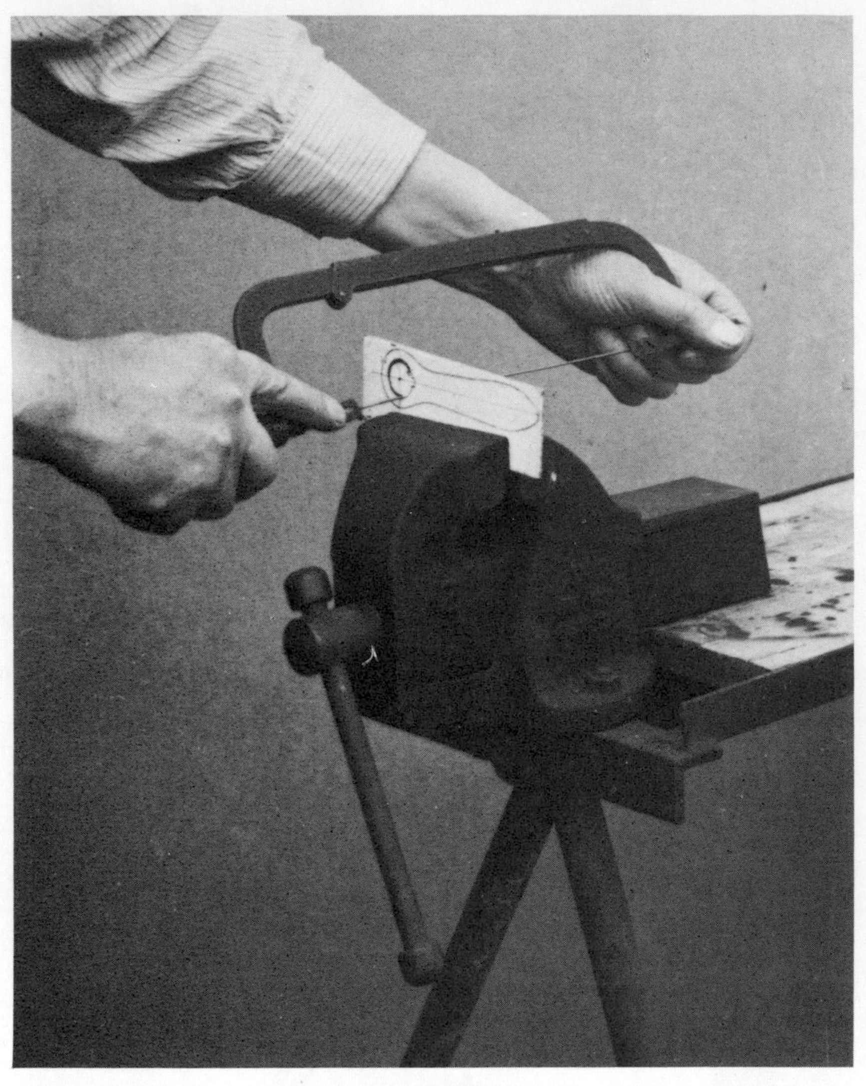

Plate 9. Cutting out the large hole for a barrel key with a wire file in a hacksaw frame.

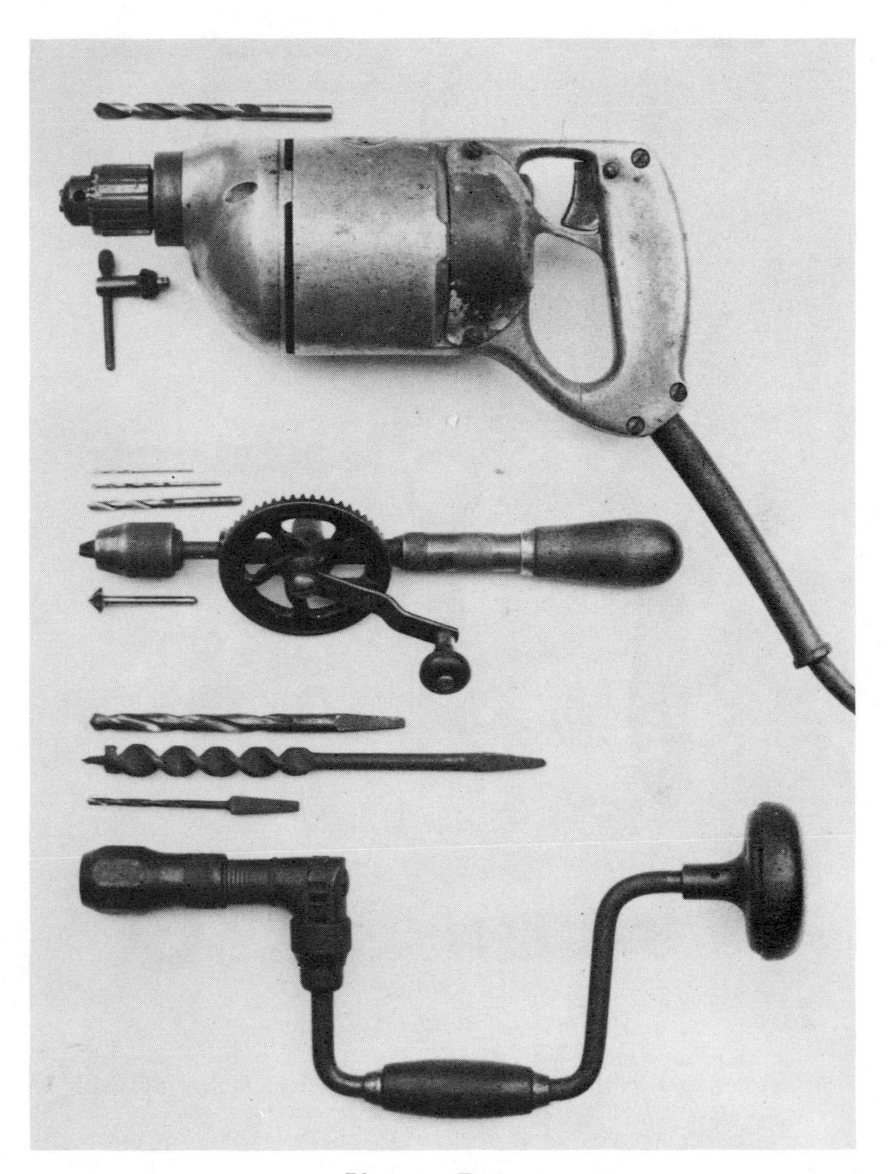

Plate 10. DRILLS.

Top: Electric drill. *Middle:* Hand drill. *Bottom:* Joiner's brace. Of these drills, the hand drill is the most useful to the amateur gun restorer.

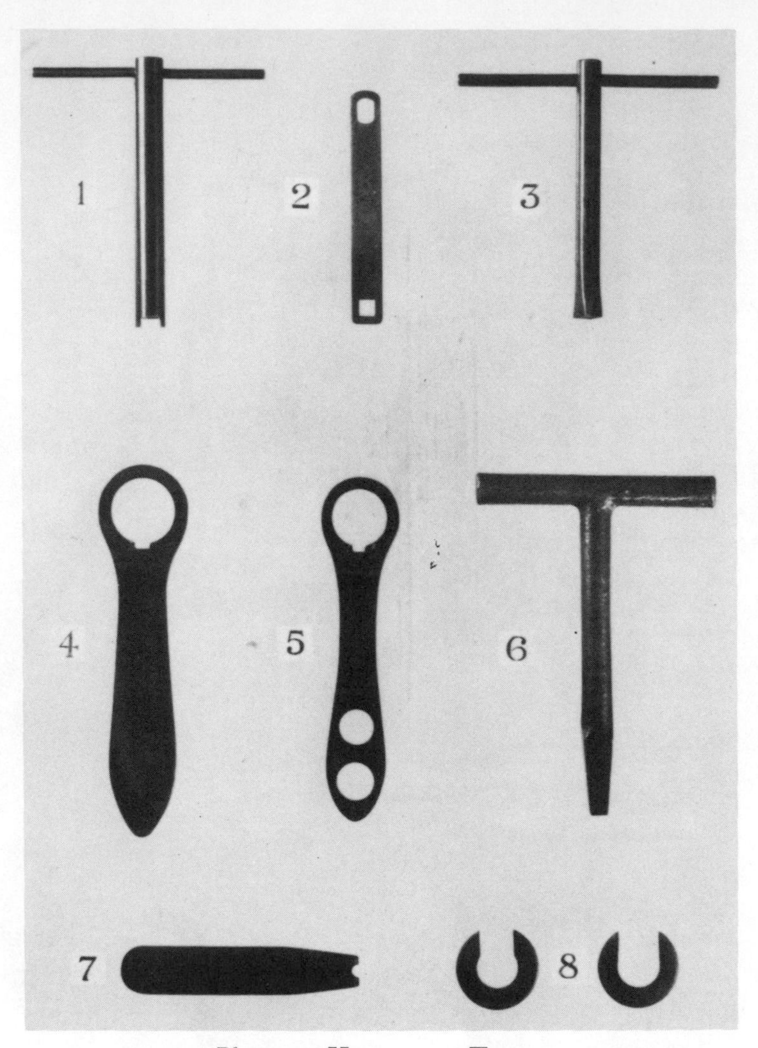

Plate 11. HOME-MADE TOOLS.

1. Key for nipples with parallel flats. 2. Key for nipples with either parallel flats or with squares. 3. Key for nipples with squares. 4. Barrel key for turn-off pistol. 5. A similar key with 'stop-or-pass' gauge for bullets. 6. Barrel key for internally grooved barrels. 7. Key for slotted nut. 8. Grips for mainsprings.

This leaves only the barrel and breech block which, in the pistol illustrated, are permanently screwed together. The pistol has now been reduced to its component parts.

The important thing to remember, when taking down a box-lock pistol, is that the hammer pivot screw must never be removed until the hammer has been relieved of the pressure of the mainspring. What happens if this is attempted? The pivot screw comes out quite nicely for about 3/16", when its screwed end disengages with the thread in the far side of the box. Instantly the upward pressure of the mainspring lifts the hammer and its pivot screw as far as the clearance in the near bearing hole will permit. The pivot screw is now jammed at an angle in its hole and, as it is out of alignment, it cannot be screwed back. The hammer is canted over at a similar angle and is jammed in the slot in the cover-plate.

In this predicament the first reaction is to grip the projecting head of the screw with pliers and pull it out by force. This will almost certainly scar the head, score the smooth bearing part of the screw and damage the threaded end. Moreover, as the screw comes out, the freed hammer, with the force of the mainspring behind it, will either fly into the air and disappear behind the bench, or, more probably, wedge itself firmly in the front of the box with the end of the triumphant spring above the spur on the boss, instead of underneath it. The only thing to do then is to remove the butt and cover-plate, so that the hammer and spring can be released.

To deal with the situation where the hammer pivot screw has been partly withdrawn and jammed, place the pistol in the vice, using the smooth jaw covers. Press the hammer sideways with the left thumb to overcome the pressure of the spring, until the hammer is again vertical. In this position it should be possible to re-engage the pivot screw with its threaded hole and screw it home. A fresh start can then be made in the correct sequence.

To return to the dismantled pistol. Put all the metal components in paraffin to soften solidified grease and dirt. Brush them thoroughly clean, paying particular attention to screw threads. A toothbrush is excellent for this, with a twisted wire brush for cleaning the inside of the barrel and a pipe-cleaner for the blind screw holes.

If there is a hard residue of fouling inside the barrel, try boiling in water for an hour or two. This was the traditional method of removing black-powder fouling and is always worth trying. While it may not be fully effective on deposits of many years' standing, it will have a useful softening effect. In stubborn cases, scrape the inside of the barrel with a piece of $\frac{1}{8}''$ dia. brass rod filed at 45° to give a chisel effect at the scraping end. The final smoothing can be given by wrapping fine emery cloth round a piece of wood dowel, working it up and down the bore while slowly rotating the barrel.

After cleaning, thoroughly dry all the parts and leave in a warm place to allow any traces of paraffin in screw holes and corners to evaporate. Examine all ferrous parts for traces of rust and, where necessary, treat with a commercial rust-remover. They may safely be immersed in this for a whole day but not longer. Some of these preparations will attack the metal itself, leaving a slight frosted effect on the polished surface if the treatment is too prolonged.

Blued or browned surfaces must never be immersed in solutions of these compounds. Instead, pick off any rust with a strand of stiff sharp-pointed wire or the small blade of a pocket knife. Then carefully paint rust-remover on the affected spots only. All parts which have received this rust-solvent treatment must be thoroughly washed and dried.

There is an extra finish which requires considerable patience, but which gives a much improved appearance to the pistol when it is finally assembled. The iron or steel parts of an old gun which have been preserved from rust, but which have lost the original blue or brown finish, or which were originally bright, will, in the course of time, acquire an attractive dark patina. This is seldom uniform. It may be greyish in the places which have received most handling and cleaning, but much darker where the surface is protected or inaccessible—for example round the nipple and the hammer, and behind the trigger and guard. This somewhat patchy appearance is not obtrusive, but there is a very noticeable improvement if all these parts are brought to a uniform tone.

To achieve this I use ordinary brass metal polish. Too prolonged rubbing would ultimately remove the patina on iron but, by carefully working over the darker patches on the dismantled components, these can be lightened without destroying the patina to give a uniform grey effect. A similar result can be obtained by using the very finest grade of steel wool sold for burnishing. On no account should emery cloth be used, as even the finest grade will destroy the patina.

If any of the screw slots or pin ends have been burred or marked by careless handling in the past, clean them up with a flat Swiss file and give all the parts a wipe with oil ready for reassembly.

The only other part requiring attention is the butt, which may be of walnut, rosewood or other choice wood. Always try to preserve the original polish or finish. A stock or butt which has been sanded to remove every dent and scratch, and re-polished, tends to look too immaculate and unconvincing on a gun which bears elsewhere the honourable signs of age. Merely clean the butt with a soft nailbrush in tepid, soapy water and, when thoroughly dry, finish with a good wax polish.

While the pistol is in pieces, make a note of proof stamps, makers' marks and serial numbers, some of which may be hidden when the pistol is assembled.

Reassembling should be an easier job than dismantling, as all parts should go together smoothly and without trouble. Assemble in this order:

Screw on the trigger guard and fix it with its rear screw.

Using tweezers, place the trigger spring in position, making sure that the locating peg is in its hole.

Insert the trigger, lining up its pivot hole with the holes in the box sides. Tap in the pin.

Set the mainspring on its anchoring hook and place the hand-vice in exactly the same position as before, tightening up the vice until the mainspring is closed to the predetermined full-cock position, as noted at the time of dismantling.

Thread the hammer boss through the top plate and put it into the box; manœuvre it until the pivot holes line up; insert and tighten up the pivot screw.

Put the hammer at full cock and remove the vice. Release the hammer by pressing the trigger and then cock and half-cock it a few times to make sure that the lock is functioning correctly. It should hardly be necessary to say that no hammer should ever be allowed to fall with its full force on the nipple. As the trigger is pulled, ease the hammer down with a finger of the left hand.

Fasten down the cover-plate by its front corner screws, after freely oiling the moving parts inside the box. Slide the wood butt into position and fix it with its two wood screws, putting in the lower one first.

Finally screw in the nipple and the pistol is complete again. Wipe off surplus oil and your specimen will be as good in appearance and mechanical condition as it is possible to make it.

VARIATIONS IN BOX-LOCK PISTOLS

So far we have dealt with only the simplest type of pocket pistol. The earlier flint-lock patterns have a few more parts in the ignition system, but these present no special difficulties.

Plate 16 shows a pocket flint pistol with centre hammer and frizzen. Instead of the nipple in the breech, there is an oval flash-pan with a vent connecting to the powder chamber and a frizzen hinged to a lug which is integral with the breech forging.

The frizzen is held in the open or closed position by a short flat spring on top of the breech block. To remove this, use the small hand-vice to close the spring slightly, which will allow the hinge screw to be taken out and the frizzen to be lifted off. To reassemble, the procedure is reversed. A worker with a strong hand can hold this light spring down with the thumb while taking out or replacing the hinge screw.

The method of dismantling and reassembling the hammer top jaw which grips the flint is obvious.

The pistol illustrated has an additional feature in the form of a safety catch which will occasionally be found on better-class pocket pistols. By sliding the trigger guard forward about $\frac{1}{8}$" the hammer is locked until the guard is slid back. An additional spring inside the box holds the guard in either the "safe" or free position. Its operation and method of fixing will be apparent after the mainspring and hammer have been removed, and it can be taken out and replaced without any detailed instruction.

Plate 17 shows another pattern of centre-hammer flint-lock pocket pistol with a different form of frizzen spring. Here the spring is attached to the hinged cover by a screw which only needs to be taken out to release the spring. As the screw is turned, the tension on the spring is progressively relaxed and, when the screw comes out, the spring comes with it, leaving the frizzen free on its pivot screw, which may now be withdrawn.

To replace the frizzen, reverse the procedure and adjust the spring screw which, as well as fixing the spring, allows the tension to be set to the correct degree to permit the pan cover to open and close smartly.

This specimen has also a safety lock which in this case consists of a sliding member which lies along the top plate, terminating at the front end in a small bolt. When the slide is pushed forward, the bolt enters a hole at the base of the closed frizzen and prevents it from opening, and an internal claw also locks the hammer until the slide is drawn back by the thumb.

When dismantling a pocket pistol of this type, the safety catch should be drawn back and left *in situ* until the top plate has been removed in the manner previously described. The method of its attachment to the top plate will then be apparent. Remember to fit it again before the top plate, hammer and mainspring are assembled.

The same pistol incorporates a further variation in that, instead of a trigger guard, it has an automatically folding trigger which normally lies in a recess under the breech block and swings down into position when the pistol is cocked. On being released after firing, or if the hammer is lowered, the trigger returns into its recess. This was a not uncommon device and, as its mechanism is simple and visible inside the box after the other parts have been removed, it should present no difficulties.

Plate 19 illustrates another variety of percussion box-lock pistol. Instead of the central hammer with the half- and full-cock notches in its boss, there is a separate tumbler in the box with squared axial extension through the side of the box on which a side hammer is mounted. The nipple is carried on a projection on the same side of the breech block, so that the top of the barrel and breech are unobstructed, and sights are fitted. As the method of stripping this type of pistol is somewhat different it is shown completely dismantled on *Plate 20*.

Begin by taking out the nipple and removing the butt. The top plate can next be taken off as it is not obstructed by the hammer. The tumbler is now exposed within the box.

Set the hammer at full cock and, with the mainspring restrained by the hand-vice, let down the hammer. Next take out the tumbler screw which fixes the hammer and take the hammer off the squared end of the tumbler projection. It is likely to be a tight fit, so make a couple of brass wedges and lift it off in the manner shown on *Plate 29*. The details of these wedges and their method of application are described in the text which accompanies the photograph.

As the tumbler has a bearing on each side, the near side of the box (that is, the one opposite the hammer), is made detachable. To remove this, take out the small screw which will be found underneath the box on the near side, close to the rear of the trigger guard. Draw the loosened side slightly backward to disengage the small locating stud at the front, after which the side can be removed and the tumbler lifted out.

Open the vice, after noting the gap between the jaws, and lift the spring off its hook. Tap out the trigger pin and remove the trigger and its spring, and take off the trigger guard as previously instructed.

We are now left with the barrel tightly screwed on to the breech block. In this type of pistol the barrel has a projection on the underside which allows it to be screwed off by means of a special key, and the method of making keys for this and other kinds of "turn-off" barrels is described later in this chapter.

Everything is now ready for cleaning and oiling, and the pistol is reassembled by reversing all the above operations.

Box-lock pistols were frequently made double-barrelled and, although the working parts are usually merely duplicated, like two single-barrel locks lying side by side and working independently, a slightly different procedure is necessary to take out the mainsprings.

After the butt has been taken off, the top plate loosened by removing its front screws and the hammers cocked to compress the springs, it will be found that the hand-vice cannot be positioned to hold both of them simultaneously. As a single pivot screw is used for both hammers, this is necessary before the screw can safely be removed. Proceed as follows. With the left-hand hammer at full cock, adjust the hand-vice to hold the compressed spring and the tang. Take a piece of 1/16" thick sheet steel 1" square and file a recess into one side of it of the same width as the distance between the vice jaws. Trim off the sharp external corners and bind the sides of the opening with a turn of insulation tape to prevent slipping. You now have a grip to hold the spring in the full-cock position. Slip this over the spring and tang immediately in front of the hand-vice and let down the hammer. Remove the vice and the spring is left firmly held in the grip at full-cock position.

Again, with the right-hand hammer at full cock, set the hand-vice on its spring and let down the hammer. Both hammers will now swing free and the pivot screw can be taken out and the hammers removed. Open the hand-vice and lift off the right-hand spring. Transfer the vice to the left-hand spring close behind the grip and tighten up just sufficiently to allow the grip to be taken off; finally, open the vice and lift off the left-hand spring. The dismantling can then be continued in the usual way.

All this may sound rather complicated but, apart from the few minutes spent in making the grip, the whole operation is performed quite quickly and easily. Home-made grips for main-springs are illustrated in *Plate 11, item 8.* These were made from steel washers 1″ outside diameter (which happened to be at hand), the shape of them being, of course, immaterial.

To put back the springs when reassembling, place them on their hooks and close the left-hand spring with the vice until the slotted grip will just fit on in front of the vice jaws and release the vice, leaving the grip to hold down the spring. Transfer the vice to the right-hand spring and close it to the same position. Put back the hammers and the top plate and insert the pivot screw. Put both hammers to full cock and remove the grip and the vice so that the springs can take over their work and the hammers can be lowered and the top plate screwed down. *Plate 18* shows a double-barrel pistol partly dismantled with springs held down by the vice and grip.

BARREL KEYS

Instead of having barrels permanently screwed on to the breech block, many box-lock pistols, both flint and percussion, are fitted with "turn-off" barrels for breech loading. The "turn-off" barrel is threaded at the breech end to fit a screwed boss on the front of the breech block. The powder chamber is bored in the breech block and the bore of the barrel is slightly enlarged at the breech to receive the ball.

The barrel can be screwed on by hand, but the final pressure must be applied with a key giving sufficient leverage to ensure a gas-tight joint. The key will consequently be necessary to loosen the barrel for removal.

No doubt originally these "turn-off" pistols were provided with keys, but it is very exceptional to find a pistol complete with its key and I have never seen loose keys included in any catalogue. This is not surprising, as barrels were of octagon or circular section of so many sizes that usually every pistol required its own key, and the collector should make one for each "turn-off" pistol in his collection.

Round barrels usually had a small projection near the breech, and a key to fit is made as follows. With the callipers and steel rule measure the diameter of the barrel. If the barrel is tapered, measure at the centre of the projection as shown in *Fig. 10 (A)*. The key (B) shown on this drawing and also on *Plate 11, item 4*, was made for a barrel 13/16″ diameter and the overall dimensions are suitable for this size of barrel. Keys with larger or smaller holes can have their dimensions modified in proportion.

To make a key for a 13/16″ barrel, a piece of sheet brass $4\frac{3}{4}''$ x $1\frac{1}{4}''$ x $\frac{1}{8}''$ thick is required. Give one side a coat of light colour wash and, when this is dry, set out the outline of the key in pencil. A light centre-pop will give a convenient hold for the compasses when setting out the hole and outside radius.

Now drill a $\frac{1}{8}''$ hole within the 13/16″ circumference and, using the lead jaw covers, clamp the job in the vice. Thread the tension file through the $\frac{1}{8}''$ hole, fix it in the hack-saw frame and cut out the inside of the circle, just leaving the pencil line showing. Finish the hole accurately with a smooth half-round file.

Plate 9 shows a key set out and the hole being made. The projection on the barrel is tapered with the narrow end towards the muzzle, so file the slot to a width that will pass only half-way along the projection. Roughly shape the key with a hack-saw and trim off with a file. Wash off the coat of colour, and smooth and polish the whole key with emery cloth.

The key for an octagonal "turn-off" barrel necessitates a little more patience in filing and fitting. It is very unusual for an octagonal barrel to taper, so that, in setting out, the muzzle end can be used as a template. A slot will still be required if the pistol has a front sight (see *Fig. 10 (C)*).

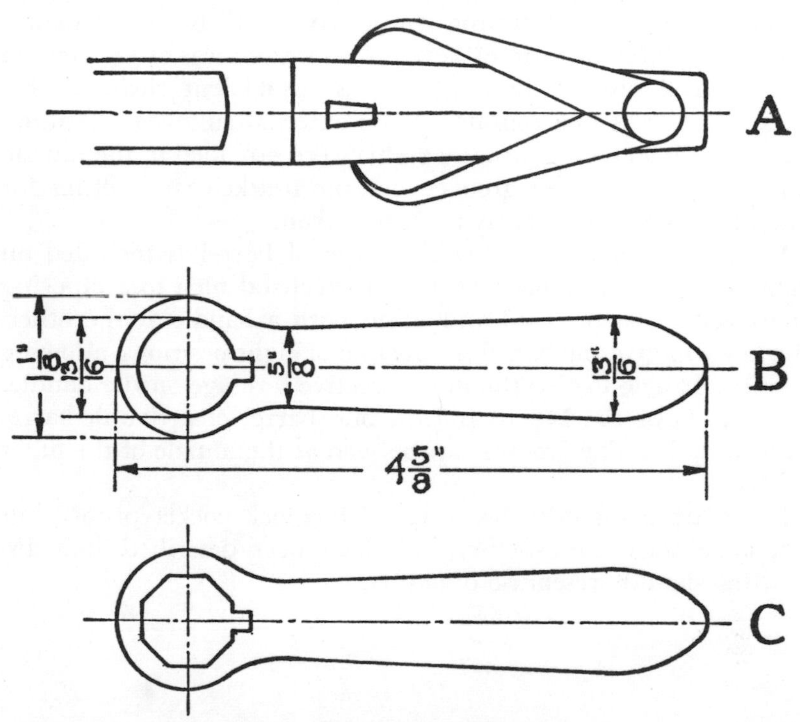

Figure 10. Making barrel keys.

A. Underside of round taper barrel showing projection and position to measure for size of hole in key.
B. Suggested dimensions for key for barrel 13/16" diameter.
C. Key for octagonal barrel with slot to pass over front sight.

To detach a stiff "turn-off" barrel which hand-pressure on the key will not move, hold the pistol firmly by the butt, distributing the grip as much as possible. Give the end of the key a few smart taps with the rubber mallet, and the barrel should begin to turn.

Plate 21 shows the correct grip and angle of striking the key. When the threads have been cleaned and oiled, it should be easy to screw the barrel on and off by hand, the key being used for only a fraction of a turn to lock or unlock.

A brass key will not mark a steel barrel, but in the case of a brass barrel it is a good plan to make the hole in the key just sufficiently oversize to allow a turn of insulation tape to be wrapped round the barrel to protect it where the key grips.

Another system of gripping round "turn-off" barrels demands an entirely different form of key. This system was often used on double-barrel pistols where there was insufficient clearance between the barrels to accommodate an external ring key. A number of tapering grooves (usually eight) were provided in the muzzle end of the bore. These grooves look not unlike coarse rifling, for which they have occasionally been mistaken.

A suitable key for turning this type of barrel is included on *Plate 11* (*6*). It was made of $\frac{3}{8}''$ dia. steel rod filed to a tapering square section at one end and fitted with a handle at the other. The key will grip the barrel in any one of eight positions, allowing a choice of angle to give the most effective leverage on the handle. *Plate 22* shows the key in use on one barrel of a double-barrel pocket pistol. The grooves can be seen at the muzzle of the other barrel.

There are many other varieties of box-lock pocket pistols, but after some practice on such types as have been described their dismantling should present no difficulty.

CHAPTER FIVE

SIDE-LOCK GUNS

APART from box-lock pistols and early revolvers, the majority of antique guns of the flint and percussion periods were fitted with detachable side locks. The method of attaching the lock varied. Usually two long screws were passed through the stock and engaged with threaded holes in the lock plate. Sometimes, instead of a rear screw, the lock plate had an internal claw which hooked into a slot in the stock, and which was invisible when the lock was in position. To protect the stock from damage by the screw heads there was either a plain or ornamental side plate, or individual metal cups were sunk in the stock to act as washers.

Barrels and furniture might be of iron or brass, with occasionally some of the fittings of silver. Metal parts were attached to the stock by pins, keys or screws.

Some pistols had receptacles for percussion caps or nipples, and shoulder guns often had spring-lid boxes let into the side of the stock to hold greased patches, etc. Ramrods could be of metal or wood, detachable or linked to the stock. Notwithstanding the apparent similarity of a group of flint or percussion guns, considerable variation in detail will be found in different specimens.

Plate 23 shows a heavy flint horse pistol and *Plate 24* the same pistol dismantled with the exception of the components of the lock which, for the time being, will be considered as a self-contained unit.

A pistol or gun of this pattern is dismantled in the following order. Withdraw the ramrod. See that the hammer is in the "fired" position and unscrew for about two turns the two side screws which hold the lock, and tap the heads of the screws with the mallet to push the lock plate out of the recess in the stock.

Take out the screws and lift off the lock. There might be a slight difference in the length of these screws. If so, note their relative positions. Put the lock to one side to be dealt with separately.

Lift the side plate out of its recess in the stock. In this particular case, the side plate was sunk flush with the stock and was a tight fit. It could not be sent out from the lock side as the holes in the plate and the lock were the same size. A tapered piece of softwood pushed with a twisting motion through one of the holes in the plate gave sufficient grip to pull the plate out. In a similar case, if this method was not effective, the point of a $\frac{1}{4}''$ fine-cut taper round file could be used. The teeth of round files are arranged spirally and act like a screw thread, and a few clockwise turns will make the file grip in the hole, and similarly, counter-clockwise turns will release it.

Take out the screw at the front of the trigger guard. The trigger guard can now be detached by raising the front end and unhooking the rear claw from its slot in the trigger plate.

Take out the barrel tang screw and the one at the back of the butt plate. Both these screws pass through the stock and screw into the trigger plate. The trigger plate can now be detached with the trigger complete with its housing and pivot screw.

Take out the pivot screw and draw out the trigger.

Take out the remaining butt cap screw and lift off the butt cap.

Take out the screw which fixes the barrel band. The brass barrel band is a taper fit and is likely to require the hammer to remove it. To do this without damage, measure the diameter of the barrel immediately behind the barrel band. Take a piece of close-grained hardwood about 2″ wide by $\frac{1}{2}''$ thick by 8″ long and, with a joiner's brace and bit, drill a hole of the measured diameter near one end. If you have not a bit of the exact diameter, use the next smaller size and open the hole by the necessary amount with a half-round wood rasp. Saw off the end of the wood leaving only half the hole as in *Fig. 11.*

Next cut a piece of wood dowel about 4″ longer than the barrel and of the largest diameter which will drop loosely into the bore, and set up the gun as shown in *Plate 25*. With the front of the dowel pressing against some solid object, place the semi-circular notch in the wood slat over the barrel against the band and, holding it firmly in place, strike with the mallet at a point near the barrel. After a few strokes the band will start to move and then quickly come off, and free the barrel from the stock.

The gun is now stripped down with the exception of the ramrod

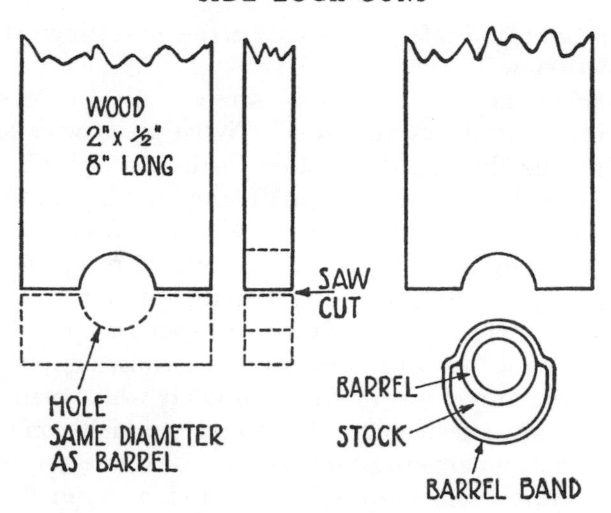

Figure 11. Wood block for removing barrel band.

pipe which is riveted over inside the stock. This should not be removed unless absolutely necessary, say, to repair a damaged pipe.

The brass fittings of this gun are the side plate, trigger guard, barrel band and butt cap and ring, and all can be brought to a high polish with household brass cleaner.

Treat any iron parts with rust remover if necessary and finish them as previously described. Clean all screw threads and wipe all parts with an oily rag. Wash the polished parts of the stock using a mild soap. Allow it to dry thoroughly and finish with a good wax polish.

Reassemble the gun in the reverse order, starting with the barrel, leaving only the lock to be dealt with. *Plate 26* shows the lock of this pistol dismantled with the various parts enumerated.

The original names of some of the flint-lock parts have changed over the years and to avoid confusion it might be useful at this stage to review our nomenclature.

In flint-lock days the falling member carrying the flint, which we now call the hammer, was known as the cock, the term hammer, or sometimes "battery", being given to what is now called the frizzen or pan cover.

With the advent of the percussion cap system the cock became a true hammer, although we still speak of "cocking" even a hammerless gun, and refer to the cock screw to distinguish it from the tumbler screw.

Some makers applied the term "screw" only to wood screws which were threaded into the stock. What are now called metal screws with fine threads, they called "nails" or "pins". For example, the tumbler screw was originally the tumbler "pin", and the side screws fixing the lock to the stock were called the side "nails".

Although I must acknowledge a sentimental regard for the old names, to avoid misunderstanding I shall, throughout this book, use the modern terms in accordance with popular practice.

Before taking a lock to pieces, study its construction carefully and observe the correct way to grip it in safety whilst manipulating the hammer. A detached flint-lock, and especially one of large size, is definitely a dangerous mechanism to handle carelessly. A hammer carrying a sharp flint falling on to a finger or thumb will cut to the bone and, as the tail of the sear which releases the hammer stands out from the detached lock and can easily be inadvertently knocked, the very first thing to do, before cocking the hammer, is to take out the cock screw and remove the top jaw and flint. The sharp front edge of the bottom jaw of the hammer can still inflict a nasty cut, so handle the lock with respect.

Screw the front side screw into its threaded hole in the lock plate. With the hammer still in the "fired" position and the frizzen fully open, grip the front end of the lock behind the frizzen with the left hand with the side screw lying between the second and third fingers. The position is shown in *Plate 27*. With this grip it will be seen that, even with the flint in place, the hand is out of reach of the hammer which can now safely be put at half or full cock with the right hand. To let the hammer down also requires a certain knack, so practise it from the half-cock position first. Hold the lock in the safe grip in the left hand and with the thumb and first finger of the right hand draw back the hammer sufficiently to release the nose of the sear from the half-cock bent or notch. Press the tail of the sear against the bench and, still controlling it with the right hand, lower the hammer to the "fired" position.

To lower the hammer from full cock requires a little more skill as the initial pressure of the mainspring is increased, the arc of fall is greater and the sear has a lighter pull-off. However, so long as the left hand is kept in the position illustrated, no harm will be done even if the hammer gets out of control, and it requires strong fingers to hold the hammer of a big lock with a powerful mainspring.

If one is nervous of manipulating the hammer of a detached lock it can be lightly screwed into the stock and cocked and released by the trigger in the normal way.

With the flint removed, the first operation in taking the lock to pieces is to extract the mainspring. Put the hammer at full cock and set the hinged hand-vice on the compressed spring. Pressure on the tail of the sear will release the hammer and it will swing free, leaving the mainspring held by the vice. The mainspring can now be lifted off and, after noting the width between the jaws to enable the spring to be compressed to the correct degree when reassembling, released from the vice (see *Plate 28*). Remember to cover the vice jaws with insulation tape to avoid marking the spring and to prevent slipping.

Remove the tumbler screw and, before taking the hammer off, lightly centre-punch tumbler and hammer at one corner to facilitate reassembly. The hammer will be a tight fit and will have to be forced off. Cut two pieces of brass strip about 2″ long and file one end of each to a tapering wedge like a joiner's chisel. Insert the wedge ends between the hammer boss and lock plate on opposite sides and tap them in with the 4-oz hammer, striking each alternately. This will force off the tightest fitting hammer without leaving a mark (see *Plate 29*). The common practice of levering off the hammer with a screw-driver will almost certainly scar both boss and plate.

To remove the frizzen spring, set the frizzen in the intermediate position when the spring is at its maximum compression. Apply the hand-vice and close the frizzen, which will then swing loose on its pivot screw. Withdraw the pivot screw and lift out the frizzen. Release the spring from the vice and take out its fixing screw and detach the spring.

The sear spring is on the inside face of the lock plate and is light enough to be taken off without the use of the hand-vice. It is fastened by a screw at the fixed end and by a small peg between this screw and the bend of the spring, which engages with a recess in the lock plate.

Loosen the sear spring screw about a couple of turns and insert the blade of a knife under the bend of the spring and lever it upwards. This will lift the peg out of its recess and allow the spring to open. Take out the screw and remove the spring.

Next take out the sear pivot screw and slide the sear out from under the bridle. Finally, remove the remaining two screws and lift off the bridle, which will allow the tumbler to be withdrawn from its bearing in the lock plate.

Clean and oil all parts and reassemble in reverse order. When you come to inserting the sear spring, screw it on loosely and with the left thumb press the spring against the sear until it closes sufficiently to allow the peg to snap into its locating recess and, holding it in that position, tighten up the fixing screw.

When replacing the frizzen or feather spring it should first be screwed on firmly before being compressed in the hand-vice, just so much as is necessary to get the frizzen into place in the closed position, and insert the frizzen pivot screw. Open the frizzen to the intermediate position, remove the vice and let the frizzen spring take over its work.

When putting the hammer back on to the tumbler square, see that the two centre pops are together and, using the rubber mallet, tap it down on to its seating.

The mainspring is closed in the hand-vice to full-cock compression and inserted with the hammer in its lowest position. The hammer is then put at full cock and the vice taken off. Replace the top jaw, flint and cock screw. The reassembled lock can now be attached to the stock and the gun is complete again.

Occasionally a hammer is too slack a fit on the tumbler square and it is not difficult to tighten it up, by reducing the size of the square hole. The method is described in detail in Chapter 11 where, amongst other things, the fitting of a new hammer to an existing tumbler is dealt with.

Plates 30 and 31 show another flint-lock holster pistol, not dissimilar in general appearance to the previous specimen, but differing in several respects in its constructional details.

This example is also typical of many flint pistols and shoulder guns. The barrel is attached to the stock by two flat keys, and the ramrod pipes and trigger guard are fixed by round wire pins; also the trigger is pivoted in a different manner.

Plate 12. Forming the square hole in the shank of a nipple key, using a square-tipped screwdriver.

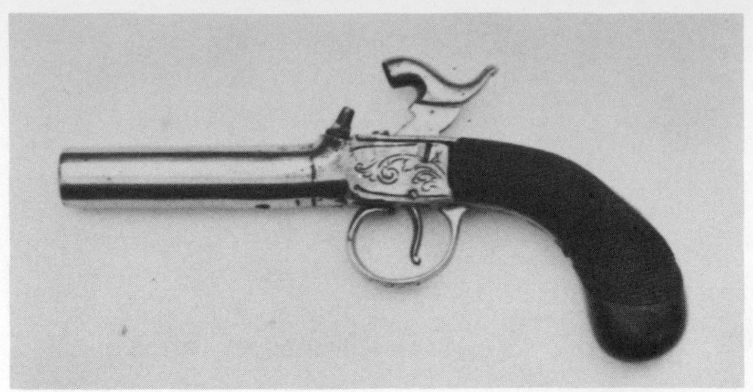

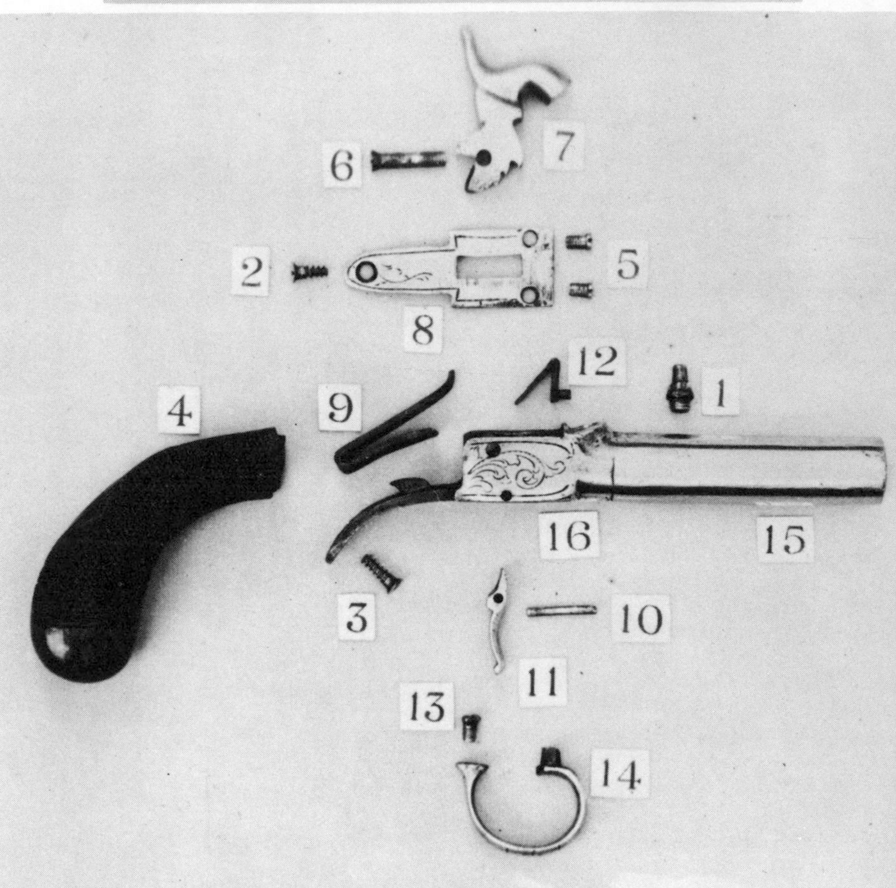

Plates 13 and 14. Common box-lock pocket percussion pistol. The lower picture shows the pistol dismantled, the parts numbered in the order in which they are removed. 1. Nipple. 2. Upper butt screw. 3. Lower butt screw. 4. Wood butt. 5. Front screws for cover plate. 6. Pivot screw for hammer. 7. Hammer. 8. Cover plate for box. 9. Mainspring. 10. Pivot pin for trigger. 11. Trigger. 12. Trigger spring. 13. Screw fixing trigger guard. 14. Trigger guard. 15. Barrell 16. Breech block.

Plate 15. Hinged hand-vice applied to mainspring of flint pocket pistol. Note the tape wrapping on the vice jaws to prevent slipping and marking the pistol.

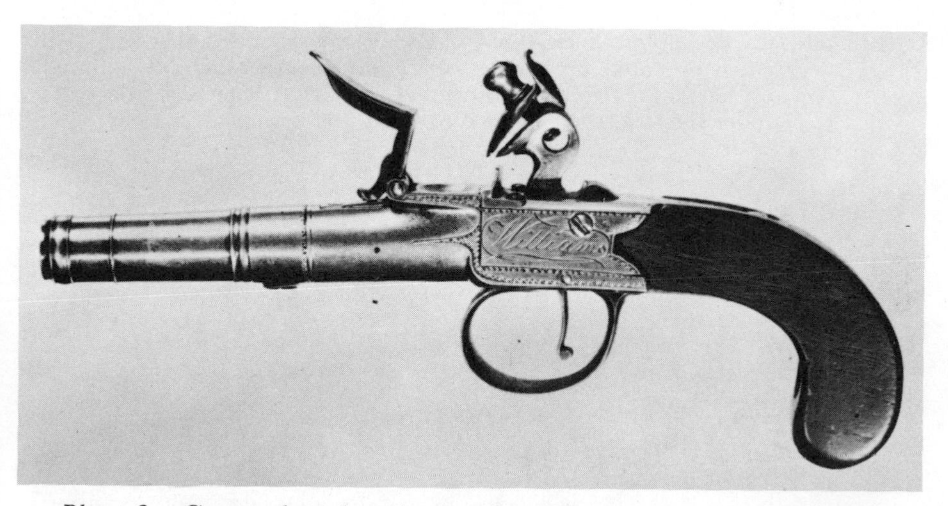

Plate 16. Cannon-barrel pocket box-lock flint pistol by Williams, with safety catch operated by sliding trigger guard. Screw-off barrel for breech loading.

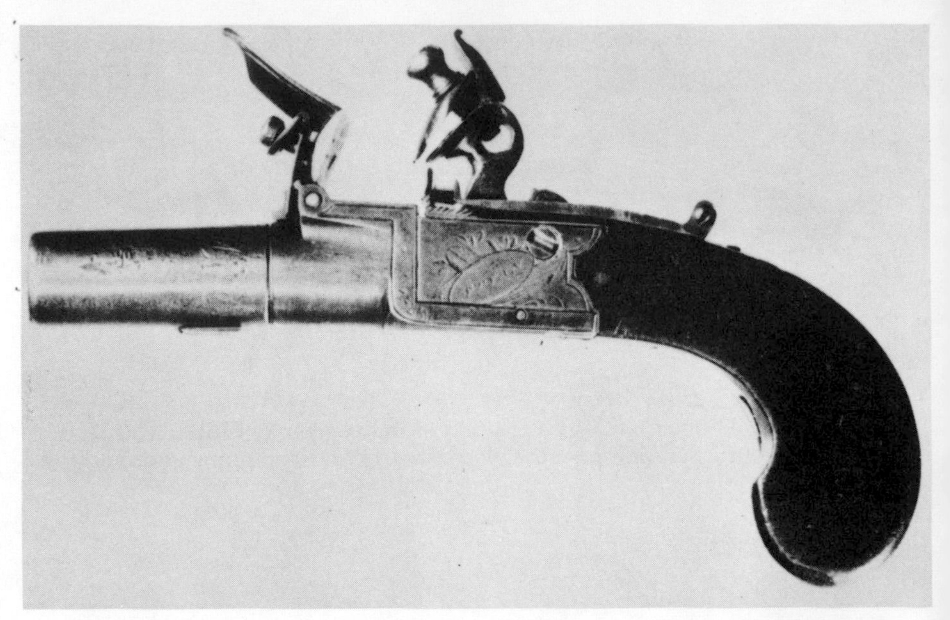

Plate 17. Pocket box-lock flint pistol by Styan of Manchester, with safety catch operated by thumb on sliding member behind hammer. Screw-off barrel for breech loading. The folding trigger lies in a recess under the lock and swings out when the hammer is cocked.

Plate 18. Hinged hand-vice and slotted grip applied to both mainsprings of a double barrel box-lock percussion pistol. Note the tape wrapping on vice jaws and grip.

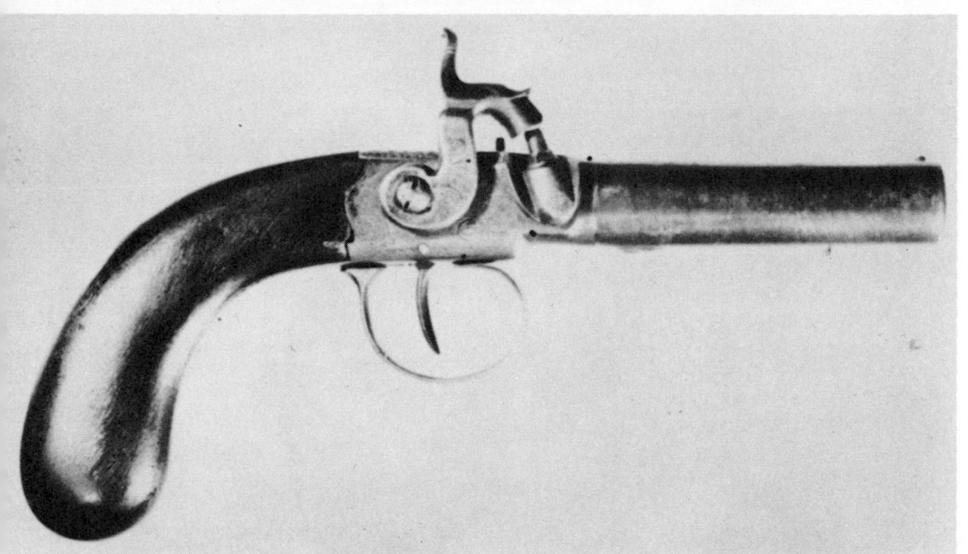

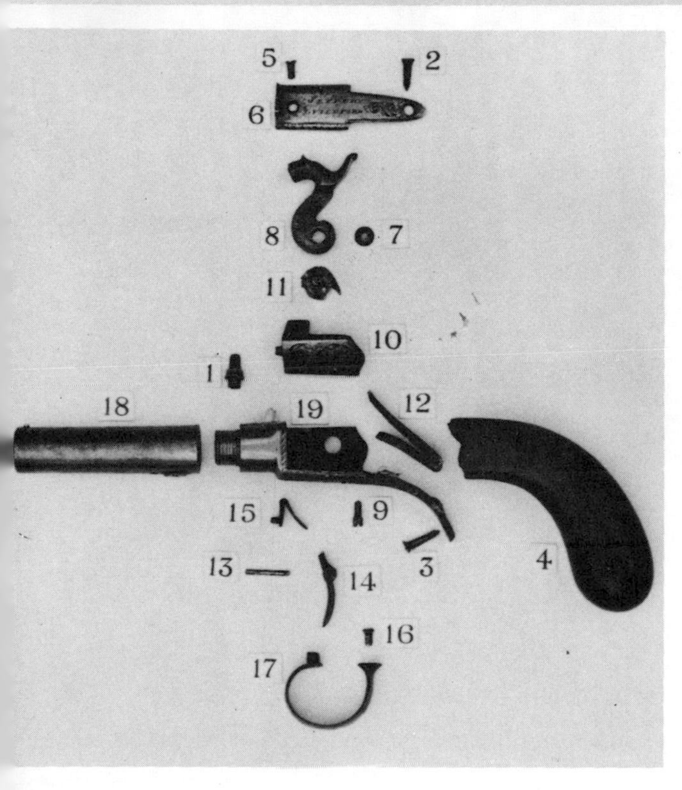

Plates 19 and 20.
Side-hammer percussion box-lock pistol by Jeffery of Guildford. Turn-off barrel for breech loading. The parts illustrated in the lower picture are numbered in the order in which they are removed.

1. Nipple.
2. Upper butt screw.
3. Lower butt screw.
4. Wood butt.
5. Cover plate front fixing screw.
6. Cover plate.
7. Tumbler screw.
8. Hammer.
9. Screw fixing detachable side of box.
10. Detachable side of box.
11. Tumbler.
12. Mainspring.
13. Trigger pivot pin.
14. Trigger.
15. Trigger spring.
16. Screw fixing trigger guard.
17. Trigger guard.
18. Barrel.
19. Breech block.

Plate 21. Loosening a stiff turn-off barrel, showing correct grip of pistol.

We will now dismantle this pistol and note what are the deviations.

Draw out the ramrod and take off the lock. Instead of a side plate there are two sunk, cupped brass washers. If these are tight in the stock, remove them in the manner previously described. Detach the ramrod pipes by driving out the wire pins which fix them to the stock, taking extreme care to avoid damaging the surrounding wood. Too often we see the polished surface of a gun stock scarred round the pins where the punch has not been accurately centred or has slipped off the pin.

If you have any doubt as to your ability to drive out the pins cleanly, take a piece of softwood about 3" wide by 1" thick and about 12" long, and a dozen 1½" round wire nails. Drive the nails through the wood at intervals, nip off the heads and points and file them flush with the surface of the wood. Using the smallest diameter punch and the 4-oz hammer, drive out the nails, leaving a series of clean 1/16" holes with the surrounding wood unmarked. When you can do this every time, you will have the knack and confidence to deal with the actual gun.

The stock, of course, is of hardwood, but the pins were driven into pre-drilled holes so that they grip to about the same degree as nails hammered direct into softwood.

It is essential that the axis of the punch be accurately in line with that of the pin. More often than not the pin enters the curve of the stock at an angle but, as only the flush end is visible, the assumption that the hidden pin runs at right-angles to the surface of the wood might result in the punch being applied at an angle to the pin as shown in *Fig. 12 (A)*. This is likely to damage both pin and stock, so carefully determine the direction of the pin by noting the position of each end before applying the punch. With the axis of the gun set horizontal and the punch held vertical, the position will be correct.

When punching out the pins, prop the gun firmly on two supports protected by rubber packing, leaving a narrow gap to accommodate the pin as it comes out. *Plate 32* shows the arrangement. When the pins are removed the ramrod pipes will come away.

The pin securing the front of the trigger guard and that on which the trigger is pivoted, go through the stock only as far as

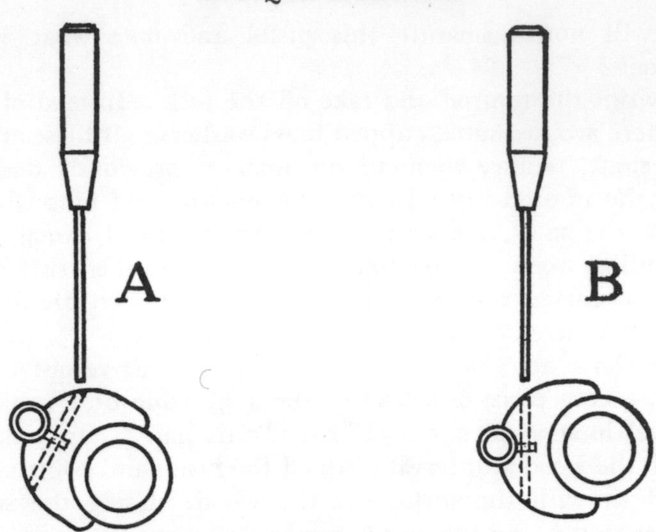

Figure 12.

A. Punch and pin out of line.
B. Punch and pin in line.

the recess which accommodates the lock, and they both can be punched out from the recessed side.

When the trigger, trigger guard, trigger plate and butt cap have been detached by the methods with which we are now familiar, we are left with the stock and barrel.

The flat keys which hold the barrel to the stock engage with slotted lugs on the barrel and can be driven out only so far. They are permanently anchored to the stock by concealed pins which it is unnecessary and undesirable to remove. When driving these keys out, take care not to damage the stock.

A screw-driver (with a tip slightly narrower and thinner than the end of the key) lightly tapped with the rubber mallet will start them for the first $\frac{1}{8}''$ of movement. Using a strip of softwood about $\frac{1}{4}''$ to $\frac{1}{2}''$ thick, to protect the stock and to act as a fulcrum, the screw-driver can then be used as a lever under the heads of the keys to withdraw them sufficiently to release the barrel. I was taught that it is considered to be bad workshop practice to use a screw-driver as a punch or lever, but the light work involved in this case does not the slightest damage to the tool or the work.

The removal of the barrel from the stock has, in both cases, been left until the last. The reason for this is that the side walls of the wooden stock, particularly near the muzzle, are thin and comparatively fragile. With the barrel in position, the stock is reinforced along its length while work is being carried out on the rest of the gun.

Before driving back the pins when reassembling, run a fine Swiss file round the circular edge at each end to remove any burr. This will prevent the leading end of a pin pushing a splinter off the stock as it comes level with the surface.

Make sure that the fittings are properly seated down and all holes in line before driving the pins through. As a check, sight through the holes or feel the run of the holes with a punch or piece of wire a shade less in diameter than the pin.

It sometimes happens that, owing to slight shrinkage of the wood stock over the years or from other causes, pinned parts such as the muzzle end of the barrel, the ramrod pipes, or trigger guard may develop a degree of play or slackness which should be put right. The easiest way is to cut a paper packing to fit out of sight between the stock and the fitting. Using brown paper of a shade to match the stock, give the groove in the stock a coat of transparent varnish and, when this is tacky, press the paper into position, press the fitting firmly down and insert the pin. If it is still too slack, take the packing out and use thicker paper.

Paper makes a perfectly satisfactory packing but some workers may prefer to use a shim of copper or brass foil. I keep a small stock of copper foil about 3/1000″ thick and have used it for this purpose.

Before leaving the flint-lock it will be useful to consider the flint itself. The "mystery" or craft of flint-knapping has been carried on unchanged from prehistoric times to the present day. At Brandon in Suffolk today the knappers use the same inherited knowledge of how and where to strike the chalk-encased virgin nodule of flint to make it fall apart in a particular way and thereafter to strike off flakes which precisely resemble those of the Stone Age. It is from these flakes that gun flints are struck.

In the flint-lock period knapping was a thriving trade and gunflints were produced in millions. Today in England there are left only two or three who still practise this craft.

As the flints are shaped by using the natural cleavage planes of the stone they are all somewhat irregular in form and no two are exactly alike. A typical gun flint has two parallel faces, one flat for the whole area and the other smaller, giving a bevelled edge all round. The front or striking edge is an acute angle, the side and back edges having a slight bevel. Occasionally the angles at front and back are similar, in which case the flint has two striking edges and is therefore reversible.

Plate 33 shows a flake before being separated into individual flints and a range of flints from $\frac{3}{8}''$ to $1\frac{1}{4}''$ wide. The two larger flints are reversible.

The question is often asked which is the correct way to clamp the flint in the hammer. Should the flat side be above or below? The answer is that the correct way is the one which gives the best strike, and this largely depends on the proportions of the particular flint being used and can best be determined by experiment.

The correct way to fit a flint is to enfold the back part in a piece of soft leather about 1/16″ thick. The fine teeth on the inside of the hammer jaws will grip the leather, which in turn will grip the flint. Sometimes sheet lead was used as a packing medium. A flint should never be clamped direct in the jaws without packing, or the teeth will be flattened.

Open the pan cover and see that the hammer is down. Choose a flint of the same width as the frizzen. Insert the flint with its leather packing between the hammer jaws, flat side up, until it stops against the cock screw, and lightly clamp it up. Put the hammer at half cock and close the pan cover. Adjust the flint so that its striking edge is parallel to the face of the frizzen. If there is about 1/16″ to $\frac{1}{8}''$ clearance between edge of flint and frizzen, we are all right, but it may be found that the edge of the flint comes in contact with the frizzen and prevents the pan cover fully closing.

In this case the flint can be turned over with the flat side underneath, which will cause it to strike the frizzen at a lower position. If this still does not allow clearance when the frizzen is closed, a shorter flint must be fitted.

On the other hand, a flint with the flat side below may give excessive clearance and strike too low and possibly not run right off the face of the frizzen to throw it over at the bottom of the stroke. Turning the flint over may correct this, especially if it is a thick one; if not, a longer flint is required.

Assuming that a flint has been fitted with the flat side up, an observation of the action of the lock will make it apparent that, other conditions remaining the same, the thinner the flint, the lower it will strike the frizzen and the more clearance there will be at half cock; the thicker the flint, the higher it will strike and give less clearance.

With the flat side down, whether the flint is thick or thin will not affect the position of the striking point or the amount of clearance.

When testing the setting of a flint, it is recommended that the fall of the hammer should be controlled by a finger hooked round the cock screw. It is fascinating to see the shower of sparks generated when the released hammer is unchecked, but the metal of old hammers can crystallise and become brittle, and it seems foolish to risk a fractured neck.

It might well be questioned whether, in cleaning a mechanically sound gun or pistol which has obviously been reasonably cared for, it is really necessary to dismantle it so completely. Personally, I do so once with almost every new acquisition. In the case of the pistol which has just been discussed, the barrel and all the furniture are brass which was brightly burnished when I bought it. The stock was highly polished and the weapon might fairly have been described as in very fine condition. However, when dismantled, it was apparent that internally it had not had any attention for many years. The barrel and vent contained quite a lot of fouling, the lock was dry inside and showed signs of rust, and the underside of the barrel and butt cap and other brass fittings had patches of verdigris. Not only were these faults remedied and deterioration checked, but brass parts such as the side screw washers and trigger plate, which previously had been inaccessible for cleaning, were polished and all the old oil and wax which had accumulated over the years in the joints between the parts was removed. The barrel and other bright brass furniture met the polished stock in a clean fine line of demarcation and the general improvement was really gratifying. If one of a pair of pistols is fully treated before starting on its fellow, the difference will immediately be appreciated.

CHAPTER SIX

FLINT AND PERCUSSION SIDE LOCKS

THE original patent for the use of fulminating salts as a method of ignition for firearms was taken out by the Reverend Alexander Forsyth in 1807. Various mechanisms were designed to utilise the invention, all of which were ultimately superseded by the copper percussion cap.

The story has been told in detail in many collectors' books, but we are concerned only with the mechanical aspect from the restorer's point of view.

The lock was considerably simplified by the elimination of the flint with its clamping mechanism, the flash-pan and the moving frizzen.

It was common practice to convert locks from flint to percussion. The vent was drilled out and the enlarged hole threaded to receive a boss bored and tapped to carry the percussion cap nipple, and a plain hammer to detonate the cap was substituted for the elaborate flint cock.

Such conversions can generally be recognised by the traces in the lock plate of the screw holes for the feather spring and frizzen and, even when these have been filled, they can be detected on the reverse of the lock plate.

Many collectors rather despise flint-to-percussion conversions and, admittedly, whilst the original unaltered piece would be preferred, a good conversion is an interesting specimen to possess. Re-conversion back to flint is difficult and, in my opinion, should never be attempted.

For a time the mainspring continued to be placed in front of the hammer, but in later designs it was fitted behind the hammer. This was known as the back-action lock and, apart from developing a neater and more streamlined appearance, one of its advantages was that the position of the recess farther back in the stock, away from the barrel channel, did not weaken the wood to the same extent as in the case of the old flint-lock.

Plates 35 and 36 show external and internal views of a number of typical flint and cap locks. They illustrate the transition from flint-lock, through the conversion stage, to front-action percussion lock, and later to the back-action design. Although they are functionally similar, each of these locks has minor constructional differences.

No. 2 is the lock which was discussed in detail in the previous chapter and illustrated in *Plate 26*.

No. 1 is a very massive lock from a bell-mouth swivel gun. The hammer has a ring neck for strength and the fixed end of the mainspring is attached to the lock plate by a cheese head screw, instead of a peg.

No. 3 is a smaller pistol lock which also has a ring hammer and the mainspring fixed by a screw.

No. 4 is from a Customs Officer's holster pistol. Instead of a slot in the back of the top jaw engaging with a narrow comb on the hammer to prevent it turning, this top jaw has a straight back which slides on a wide flat comb. The feather spring has a small anti-friction roller fitted at its moving end which gives a smooth and quick action to the frizzen. This lock is a good example of a well-designed action which, according to the old test, should "shut slow and open fast".

Where the other locks have the head of the frizzen pivot screw on the outside, the pivot screw in this case is inserted from the inside with the head countersunk so as to be almost unnoticeable. The end of this slender screw is visible on the outside and could be mistaken for a pin and an attempt made to punch it out.

Also, the feather spring screw, instead of passing from the outside through a hole at the fixed end of the spring and screwing into the lock plate, has its head on the inside of the lock plate and is screwed into a tapped hole in a boss in the spring.

No. 5. This lock from a very ornate carriage pistol also has the feather spring fixed in a similar way to *No. 4*.

No. 6 is from a duelling pistol by Tow and, like *No. 4*, it has a feather spring roller. Pollard says that these rollers appeared about 1790,[1] which is worth remembering when considering the

[1] *The Book of the Pistol*, by H. B. C. Pollard, p. 31.

age of a gun. Whilst the presence of a roller would indicate a date subsequent to 1790, its absence gives no help as this refinement was not universally adopted.

No. 7 bears the name Peyton & James and is from a blunderbuss. It has been converted from flint to percussion and the holes in the plate for the frizzen and feather spring can be seen.

The attachment of this lock to the stock is unusual. It will be seen that the forward end of the plate terminates in a bevelled, concave recess. This fits under the head of a screw permanently fixed in the stock and, when it is placed in position, a single side screw through the stock secures the lock.

No. 8 is an exceptionally fine percussion lock from a heavy pistol of high quality by Thomson of Edinburgh. The internal mechanism is superb and, although normally hidden, every part, including springs and screw heads, is polished to a mirror finish. When taking a lock of this quality to pieces it is particularly important that the jaws of the hand-vice should be well wrapped with insulation tape to protect the springs.

The lay-out of this lock is similar to the flint type with the mainspring in front of the tumbler. A link which eliminates sliding friction is introduced between the moving end of the mainspring and the tumbler, giving a smooth, quick fall of the hammer. The lock is attached by one side screw.

No. 9 shows a back-action percussion lock. This design was the logical arrangement when frizzen and flash-pan were no longer required. The mainspring, instead of pushing the tumbler downward at the front, pulled it upward at the back through a short link. There is no separate sear spring. A slender extension at the fixed end of the mainspring controls the sear and the whole design is extremely compact. The lock is fixed by one side screw.

Nos. 10, 11 are a pair of right- and left-hand back-action percussion locks from a double-barrel gun. The lock plates have claw-like projections at the inside of the rear tips of the plates which hook into concealed slots in the stock, both locks being secured by a single screw passing through one plate, through the stock, and screwing into the opposite plate.

These examples describe a few of the many variations in the design of side locks.

One important difference between the flint and the percussion lock should be noted. The fall of the hammer of a flint-lock had to be arrested at a point after the flint had run off the frizzen and before it could strike the flash-pan. The neck of the hammer, therefore, was formed with a shoulder which met the top of the lock plate, stopping the hammer at the correct position. That is why a flint-lock should always be set at half cock before taking off the hammer.

The hammer of a percussion lock had to be stopped by impact with the cap on the nipple, yet here again, if the nipple was removed, it was necessary to prevent the nose of the hammer striking the nipple seating. This was generally done by limiting the movement of the tumbler by means of a projection which, at the appropriate position, was stopped by contact with the bridle. A percussion hammer, then, may be removed from its stopped position without losing control of the sear. Furthermore, if the hammer of a detached percussion lock is inadvertently released, it is less likely to trap the fingers since the nipple and its seating remain on the barrel.

Apart from the lock, the stock, barrel and furniture of many percussion guns closely followed flint-lock practice.

Stripping down a percussion lock presents no new difficulties and there is no frizzen and feather spring to deal with. The simplicity of the percussion lock permitted workable and fairly reliable guns to be produced to a lower standard of workmanship than was essential for flint ignition. To operate at all satisfactorily, a flint-lock had to be well designed and constructed of good-quality materials to accurate dimensions. With the percussion system all that was required was a nipple screwed into the breech block to receive the cap and a hammer to fall and explode it. It did not much matter if the hammer had a certain amount of play, or did not strike the cap quite centrally. For this reason the collector is likely to come across cheap-quality weapons in the percussion group, as workable guns of this type could be turned out in back-street workshops by mechanics of limited skill.

Of course, the leading makers produced percussion guns of the very highest quality and *Plate 34* (*a*) shows a high-class percussion holster pistol. This weapon has a heavy octagonal barrel, quickly detachable for cleaning, and a linked metal ramrod, both features which were frequently found on percussion cap guns. *Plate 34* (*b*) shows the same weapon with the barrel detached.

A barrel of this type has no fixing tang, but instead the breech plug projects in the form of a heavy claw which hooks into a secondary or false breech block which carries the usual tang screwed to the stock.

It will be seen from the illustration that the assembly is almost indistinguishable in appearance from, and might easily be mistaken for, the more usual arrangement. The fitting of the guns of this type is invariably meticulously accurate, though the fine line where the actual barrel breech butts against the secondary breech can be detected on close inspection.

As the secondary breech is secured by an additional screw from below, it cannot be removed with the barrel even after the tang screw has been taken out. This is sometimes puzzling until one has located the second screw.

To detach the barrel the hammer is put at half cock, the fixing key midway along the stock is tapped out, the ramrod is withdrawn and allowed to hang free and the muzzle end of the barrel is lifted until the claw is disengaged at the breech. The barrel carrying the ramrod can then be withdrawn, the whole operation taking only a few seconds, which must have been a boon in black-powder days when the barrel required scouring in hot water after every few shots.

The linked, or stirrup, ramrod is detached from the barrel by taking out the screw which passes through the links and the fixed boss under the muzzle of the barrel. The links are usually riveted to the swivel and the detached ramrod assembly can be cleaned and adjusted without further separation of the component parts.

Plate 37 illustrates a heavy double-barrel under-and-over percussion pistol and *Plate 38* shows it dismantled. The barrels and breech block are permanently built into a unit. The steel barrels are rifled, requiring extra care in internal cleaning, the method being to boil in water and scour with a cylindrical brass brush.

The special feature of this type of firearm is the manner of attaching the barrels to the wood butt which has no extension of the stock past the breech.

The forward end of the butt terminates in a flat face which meets the flat rear face of the breech block. The upper barrel has the usual tang projecting from the breech block, fastened by a screw which passes vertically through the butt and engages with a threaded hole in a boss on the trigger guard plate.

The back-action locks are inset into each side of the butt, with extensions at their forward ends dovetailed into recesses in the breech block. The forward end of the trigger guard projects beyond the butt and terminates in a circular extension which fits into another recess on the underside of the breech block and is secured by a screw.

Lock plates, trigger guard and tang are tightly fitted into their recesses and the removal of the barrels demands considerable thought and care. This particular gun affords a good illustration of how to approach the problem of dealing with an unusual weapon without previous experience of the type.

The design of this gun was new to me when I acquired it and, in line with my usual practice, I prepared to dismantle, clean and oil it. Careful examination indicated that to release the barrel tang from the butt it must be lifted upward or drawn forward but, with the lock plates dovetailed into the breech block, neither of these movements was possible. Obviously then the first thing to do was to take off the locks. These both appeared to be secured by only a single side screw at the extreme forward end of the lock plates.

I had handled locks with one-screw fixing before, but the screw had always been approximately central in the lock plate—the obvious mechanically efficient position. The assumption was, therefore, that the rear ends of the locks were attached internally, since there was nothing visible externally.

The hammer of a back-action lock in the "fired" position projects beyond the front end of the lock plate and, after the side screw has been removed, it will usually serve as a convenient handle to give sufficient leverage to allow the lock to be eased out of its recess.

These particular locks, however, with the forward ends of their plates dove-tailed into the breech block, and which probably had not been disturbed for years, remained firmly in position. I replaced the side screw and then loosened it two or three turns so that the head projected. A few smart taps with a hammer through a piece of wood on the head of the screw dislodged the front of the lock plate.

After again removing the side screw, the front of the lock could be eased out of its recess. This movement revealed a steel claw-like projection at the rear inside end of the lock plate, clearly visible in the illustration, which fitted into a slot in the butt and which could only be disengaged after the front end of the lock had been lifted well clear.

The remaining lock, with its smooth clearance hole, required a different approach. The hole being quite near the hammer boss, the blade of a knife was inserted until it wedged itself in the space between the hammer and lock plate so that the hole was covered. A short length of $\frac{1}{8}''$ diameter brass rod was passed through the butt and used as a punch against the knife blade until this lock, in its turn, was loosened sufficiently to be lifted out.

The screws in the barrel tang and the trigger guard extension were next taken out, and the pistol held upside-down by the butt over the rubber mat on the bench, with the muzzle resting lightly on the mat and the breech just clear. A few light blows with the rubber mallet on the breech block immediately in front of the trigger guard loosened both joints and detached the barrels. The two barrels, permanently screwed to the breech block and joined by fillets along their full length, form a single inseparable unit.

The remaining parts of the pistol were removed in the manner previously described. Traces of rust were found on the inside of both locks and under the butt cap and trigger guard, which showed that attention had previously been given to the visible parts only. After cleaning and oiling, the weapon assembled smoothly and easily.

CHAPTER SEVEN

PEPPER-BOX PISTOLS AND REVOLVERS

ALTHOUGH flint-lock firearms had been made in multi-shot form it was not until the advent of the percussion cap, which eliminated priming with loose powder for each shot, that revolvers became a really practical proposition.

The earlier ones were generally of the familiar "pepper-box" type where a group of barrels revolved round a central spindle. The barrels were usually bored out of a solid cylinder, but some had separate barrels screwed into a large rotating breech block. Every barrel had a nipple at its breech and they were loaded and capped individually.

The number of barrels ranged from three upwards and, although a few revolving multi-barrelled shoulder guns and some pistols with a fantastic number of barrels were made, considerations of weight limited both size of weapon and number of barrels. In consequence, the six-shot pepper-box pistol is the type found in most collections.

The pepper-box mechanism was simple but effective and reliable. The hammer was usually above the barrels but sometimes below, acting on the lowest barrel.

The revolving barrel block had a ratchet ring at the breech and at each pull of the trigger a claw turned the next loaded barrel into the firing position, cocked the hammer and released it at the end of the trigger movement. There were no locking notches to locate precisely the barrels such as are necessary to align chamber and barrel on a modern revolver. The barrel block was just pushed round against the braking action of a friction spring on the spindle until the nipple was in line with the hammer.

Plates 39 and 40 illustrate an under-hammer, ring-trigger pepper-box pistol by Cooper, complete and dismantled.

To take down a pistol of this type, first remove the wood grips which fit in the butt strap after taking out the fixing screw. If they are found to be too tight a fit to be easily taken off, replace the fixing screw and loosen it off by a turn or two and tap the projecting head. This should push off the opposite grip. The other one can then be pressed out from inside.

If, as is possible, this method, instead of dislodging the grip, merely pushes the nut out of its recess, remove both nut and screw and insert a large-size pin punch through the hole which accommodated the nut and, holding it at a slight angle to bear on the wood of the opposite grip, tap it lightly with the 4-oz hammer until the grip comes off.

Alternatively, after removing the screw, one can sometimes lever off a tight grip by delicately inserting the thin blade of a knife between the wood and the metal butt strap, taking care not to mark the wood. The counterbored washer which receives the head of the screw and the threaded nut on the opposite side are recessed into their respective grips and are usually a tight fit in the wood and, unless they come out easily, there is no need to disturb them.

Next take off the side plate which covers the lock mechanism. It is sometimes difficult to detect by eye which is the detachable side as the fitting is so accurate that only the merest hair-line is visible at the junction of plate and frame and usually the other side is engraved with lines to match; but, either underneath or in the side of the plate, a flush fixing screw will be found which will indicate which side is removable.

This screw should be examined carefully. It enters the metal at a considerable angle and, after the initial fitting, the head has been ground down to conform to the curved profile of the body of the pistol. Should the screw-driver be applied, as is usual, at right angles to the face of the metal, it is probable that its tip will not enter the slot sufficiently to get an efficient grip and will slide sideways as turning pressure is applied. Reference to *Fig. 13* will make this point clear. Generally it is fairly easy to recognise sunk screws which have been put in on the slant as, on close inspection, the heads look slightly oval and the cuts appear to be not quite at right angles to the face of the head.

Figure 13.

A. Screw-driver and screw out of line.
B. Screw-driver and screw in line.

When the screw is taken out, the loose plate can be slid back to disengage the locating stud at the front, and lifted away to disclose the trigger and hammer mechanism.

Before proceeding further the trigger should be operated and the action studied until the function of each part is understood, but always protect the nipples with a piece of cardboard when snapping the hammer.

Now take out the mainspring. In this case no vice is required as the spring is tensioned by its fixing screw and as this is withdrawn it allows the curved mainspring to relax before finally releasing it.

Remove the screw which fixes the trigger spring. This will allow the spring to relax and to be lifted out. As the heads of both these spring-fixing screws are within the butt strap they cannot be reached with a screw-driver. They therefore have square heads and are turned with a small spanner. Trigger and hammer will now hang free.

Behind the trigger will be seen a flat slotted member whose function it is to advance the barrels at each pull of the trigger. A screw passes into the frame through the slot at the rear of this member allowing a combined pivoting and sliding action. The tapered front end passes through a slot in the frame and engages with the ratchet ring on the breech of the barrels. A projecting screw on the neck of the trigger passes through a slot midway along this member and lifts it by the amount necessary to bring another barrel in front of the hammer each time the trigger is operated. A light spring at the rear keeps the tip of the member pressed against the ratchet ring.

The action of this member is an ingenious arrangement of sliding and swinging which is not easy to describe but simple to observe; before it is taken out the set-up should be memorised for reassembly.

Continue to dismantle by taking out the sliding member which rotates the barrels and the slender spring which controls it.

Take out the screw from the front end of the centre spindle. The barrel block will now slide off and the nipples can be extracted. A small screw holds the friction spring in a recess in the spindle.

Take out the hammer pivot screw and hammer and trigger can be drawn out. Finally, the hammer catch spring is removed from the trigger. The pivot pin of the swinging catch which cocks the hammer is in the form of a rivet, so it is left in place during cleaning.

In their time pepper-boxes were popular and fairly efficient weapons of defence. The collector will meet with a variety of designs. A few had spur hammers which could be thumb-cocked, but more often the under or top bar-type hammer was automatically cocked and released at each pull of the trigger, which might be of the ring type, as illustrated, or the normal type with guard.

The principle of the revolving group of barrels persisted into the breech-loading, metallic-cartridge period, and small pinfire pepper-boxes were produced, but, broadly speaking, it was a percussion-cap weapon.

The pepper-box type of pistol was soon superseded by the revolver with a single barrel served by a multi-chambered cylinder of just sufficient length to accommodate the charge and load, which saved a great deal of weight. The revolving shoulder arm became a more practical proposition but in the main the percussion-cap revolver was a hand gun.

It was developed as a highly reliable and accurate personal weapon by Samuel Colt, whose patents for a time gave him a monopoly of the first really satisfactory revolver design; this was

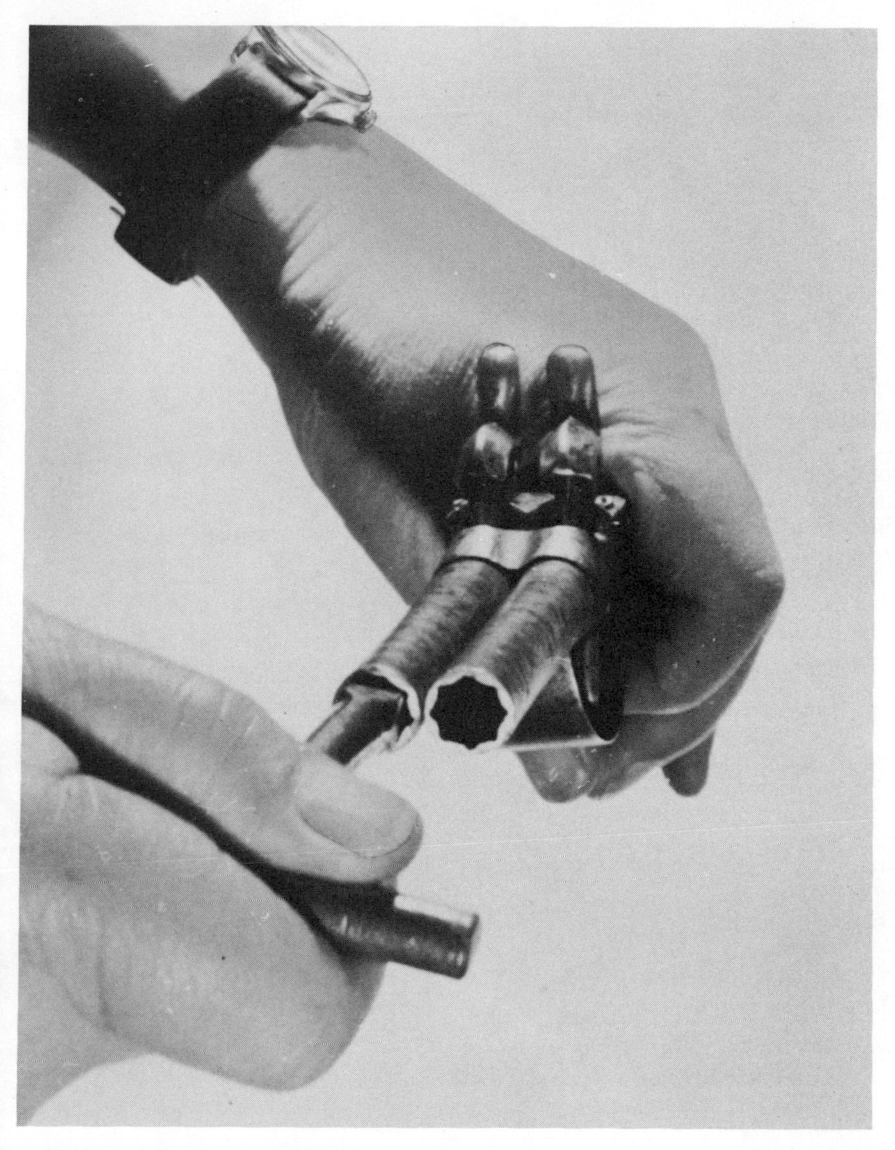

Plate 22. Square barrel key in position in one barrel of a double-barrel pistol. Note the grooves in the other barrel.

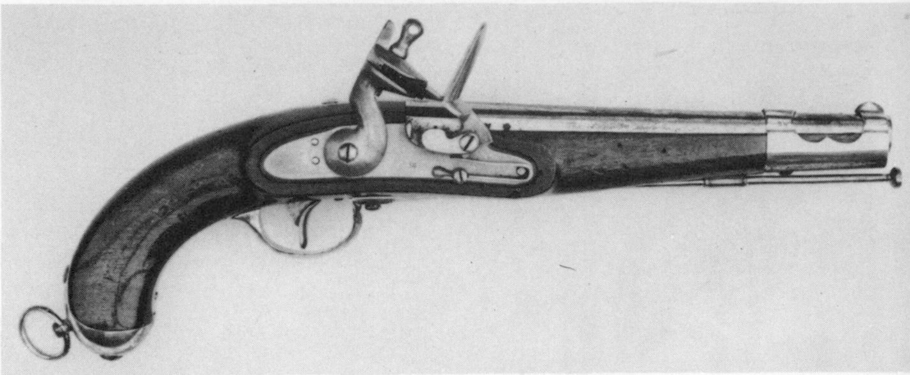

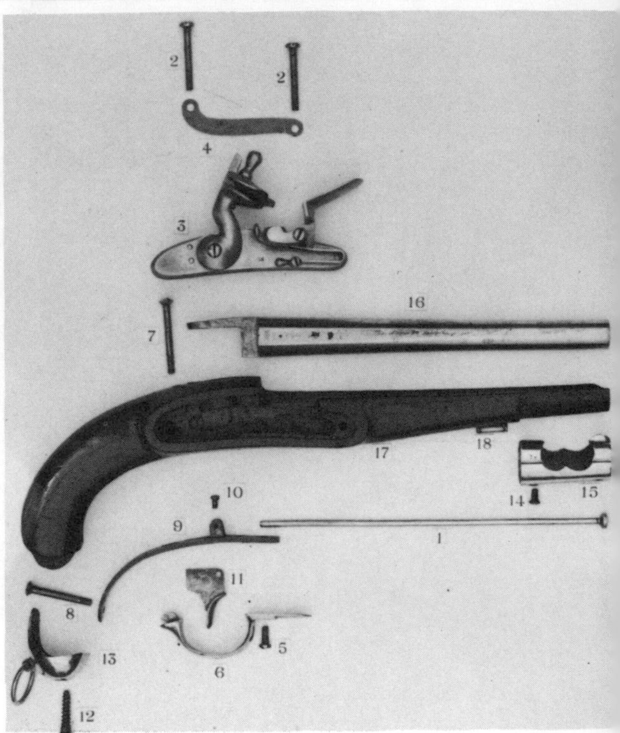

Plates 23 and 24.

Flintlock holster pistol by G. Bentz. The parts in the exploded view are numbered in the order in which they are removed.

1. Ramrod.
2. Side screws which fix lock.
3. Lock.
4. Side Plate.
5. Trigger guard fixing screw.
6. Trigger guard.
7. Barrel tang screw.
8. Trigger plate screw.
9. Trigger plate.
10. Trigger pivot screw.
11. Trigger.
12. Butt cap fixing screw.
13. Butt cap and ring
14. Barrel band fixing screw.
15. Barrel band.
16. Barrel and breech plug.
17. Stock.
18. Ramrod pipe.

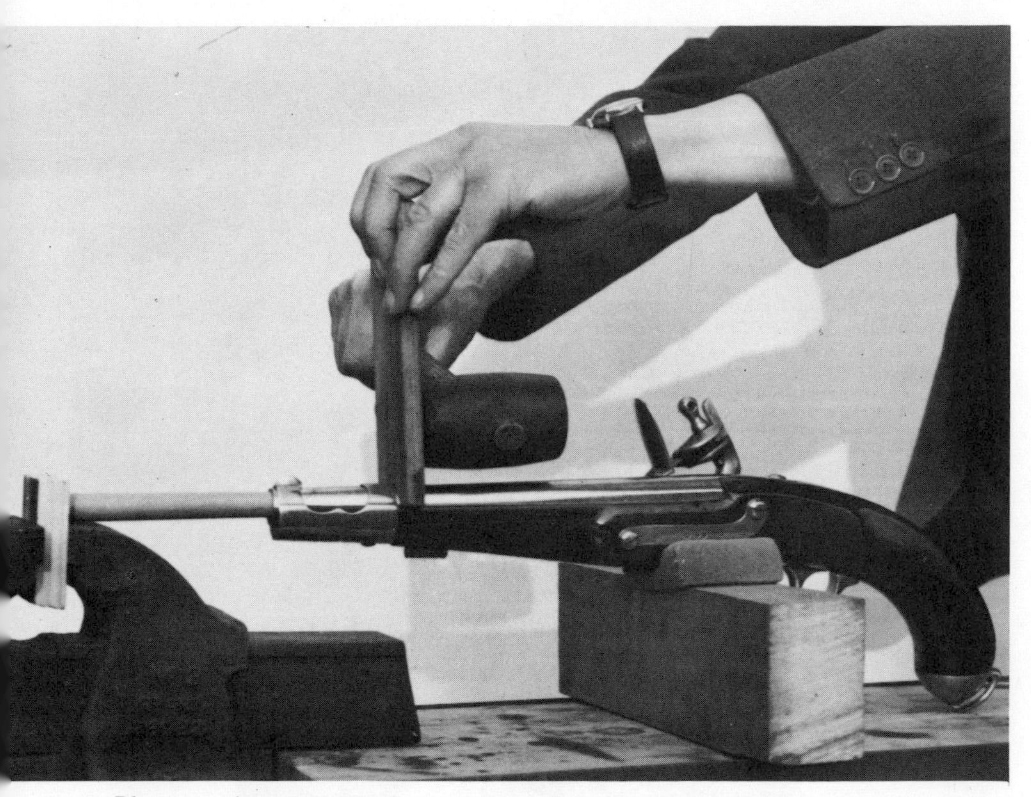

Plate 25. Arrangement for removing barrel-band from pistol or gun.

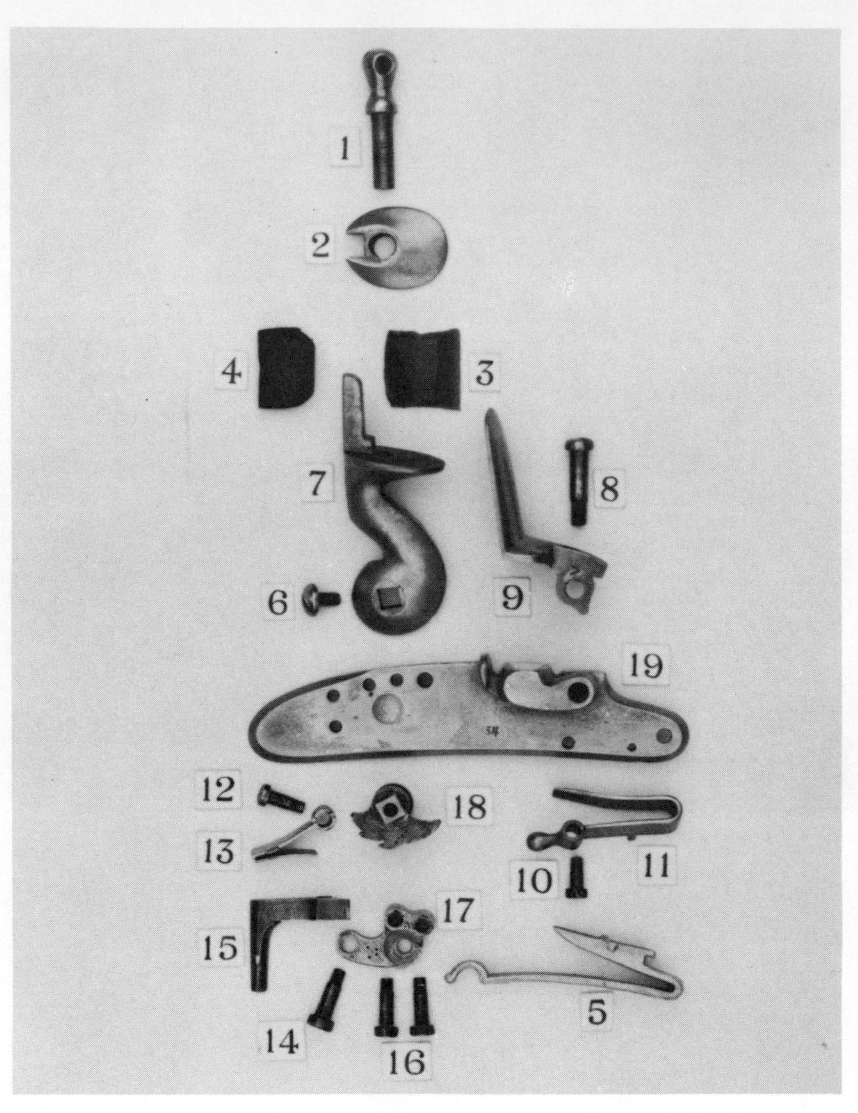

Plate 26. Lock of the Bentz pistol (*Plate 23*) dismantled. Parts are numbered in the order in which they are removed.

1. Cock screw. 2. Top jaw. 3. Flint 4. Leather packing for flint. 5. Main Spring. 6. Tumbler Screw. 7. Hammer (or Cock). 8. Frizzen pivot screw. 9. Frizzen. 10. Frizzen spring screw. 11. Frizzen spring or Feather spring. 12. Sear spring screw. 13. Sear spring. 14. Sear pivot screw. 15. Sear. 16. Bridle screws. 17. Bridle. 18. Tumbler. 19. Lock plate.

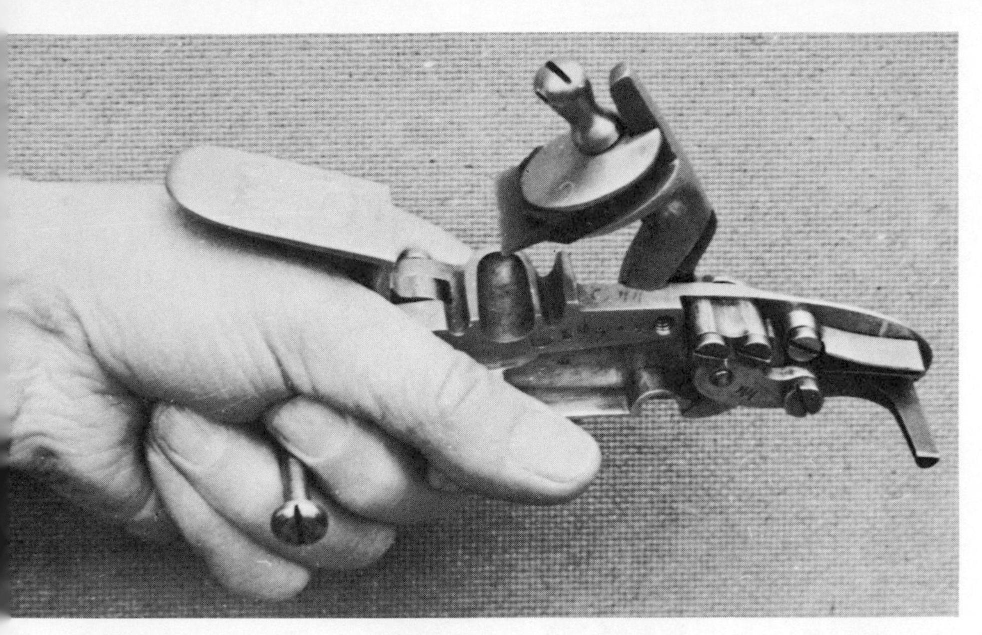

Plate 27. Safe way to grip a detached lock. Held in this manner the fingers cannot be trapped by the hammer shown here at the bottom of its stroke.

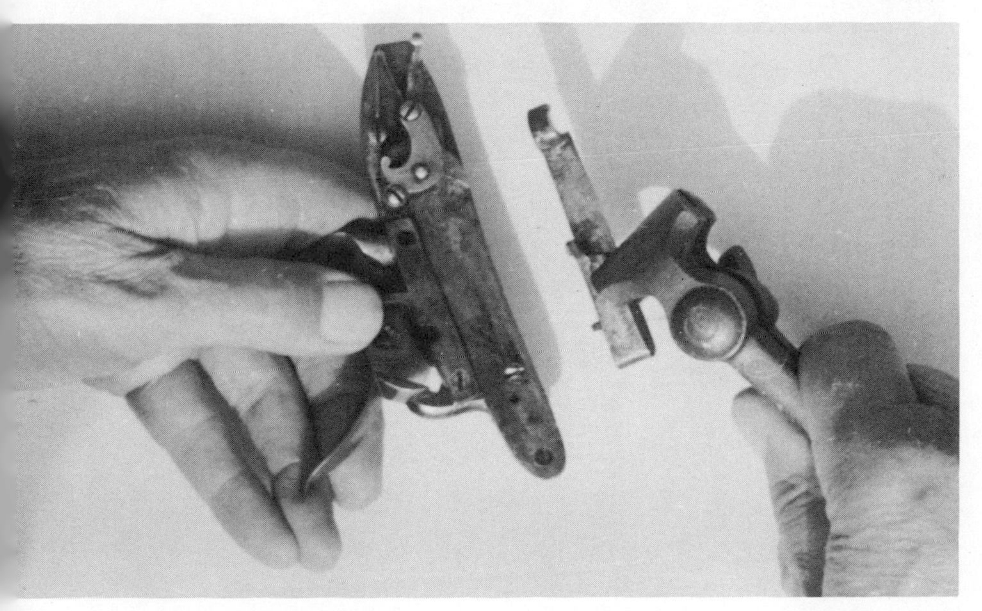

Plate 28. Removing mainspring from lock with hinged hand-vice.

Plate 29. Brass wedges being used to take off a tight hammer.

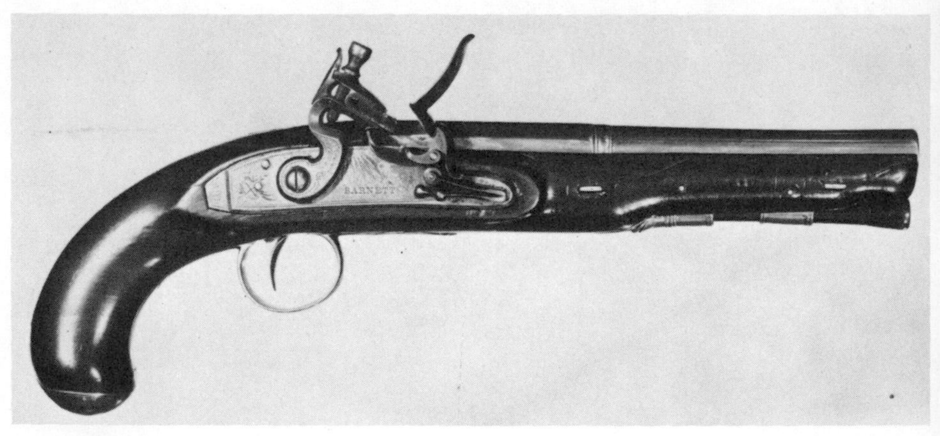

Plate 30. Brass barrel flint-lock holster pistol by Barnett of London.

widely copied in its basic principles when the patent protection expired.

In the meantime revolvers were produced by retaining the pepper-box action, fitting a chambered cylinder and screwing a barrel on to a shortened spindle. These rather makeshift weapons are frequently called transition revolvers, presumably because they embodied some features of both the earlier pepper-box and the later fully developed percussion revolver. Like the pepper-boxes, they were usually cocked and fired by one pull of the trigger.

Plate 41 shows a typical six-chamber transition revolver complete and partly dismantled. It is not considered necessary to show every part taken down. They are largely similar to those already described in the pepper-box action, except that the lay-out of the mechanism is modified to suit the top bar-type hammer. The only extra item in the lock itself is a sliding bolt actuated by the trigger which locks the cylinder in position as each chamber in turn comes into alignment with the barrel.

The barrel of this revolver is rifled and provided with a foresight, the bar hammer having a slot through which the foresight is visible when the hammer is cocked.

There is a butt cap which has a spring lid giving access to a small metal box for carrying spare caps and nipples. If it should be found necessary to remove this, it will be seen that butt plate and box are attached by a single screw through the butt strap.

To detach the barrel and cylinder, first take out the small locating screw on the underside of the boss at the breech of the barrel. This frees the barrel and enables it to be unscrewed from the centre spindle, which in turn allows the cylinder to be drawn off the spindle. The nipples are set radially and are of the rather fragile type shown in *Fig. 9* (*E*).

The trigger guard is of conventional type, and is detached by removing a screw at the back from inside the frame, and then unscrewing the front stud by rotating the guard itself as described for box-lock pistols.

Transition revolvers varied greatly in quality and, while some excellent pistols of this type were turned out, in general they were not very successful. Usually the only connection between barrel and butt was the spindle, an inherently weak design and quite inadequate to withstand rough usage. I once knocked one off the bench. The muzzle struck the wood floor first with the result that the spindle was bent and the cylinder would not revolve freely until the barrel was taken off and the spindle reset.

The inability to cock and take deliberate aim before firing was not conducive to accurate shooting. The chambers were awkward to load and the barrel had a tendency to develop play on the thread of the spindle. However, despite its shortcomings, the transition revolver has its own points of interest.

Every collector is familiar with the Colt revolver. Its introduction marked an epoch in the development of hand guns and it played an important part in American wars and history.

When Colt's patents expired, other equally fine and, in some cases, even superior revolvers appeared, but in practically all cases the rivals were a copy or a development of the basic Colt design.

In addition to the initial advantage conferred by the patent protection of his ingenious design, Colt pioneered the idea of arms manufacture by mass production of machine-made identical interchangeable parts, in place of the traditional individual craftsmanship previously considered essential to the making of guns.

Apart from very early and rare examples, the Colt percussion revolvers found in most collections are of calibre ·44, ·36 or ·31. There will be many variations in section and length of barrel, shapes of trigger, etc., but the general construction was the same.

Plates 42 and 43 show a Colt pocket pistol, calibre ·31, complete and fully dismantled. With their cased pistols Colts issued instructions for taking to pieces, cleaning and oiling and the following is copied from the original.

DIRECTIONS FOR CLEANING

Set the lock at half cock; drive out the key that holds the barrel and cylinder to the lock-frame then draw off the barrel and cylinder, by bringing down the lever and forcing the rammer on the partition between the chambers. Take out the nipples. Wash the cylinder and barrel in warm water, dry and oil them thoroughly; oil freely the base-pin on which the cylinder revolves.

TO TAKE THE LOCK TO PIECES, CLEAN AND OIL

First. Remove the stock by turning out the bottom and two rear screws that fasten it to the guard and lock-frame, near the hammer.

Second. Loosen the screw that fastens the mainspring to the trigger-guard, and turn the spring from under the tumbler of the hammer.

Third. Remove the trigger-guard, by turning out the three screws that fasten it to the lock-frame.

Fourth. Turn out the screw, and remove the double sere spring that bears upon the trigger and bolt.

Fifth. Turn out the screw-pins that hold the trigger and bolt in their places.

Sixth. Turn out the remaining screw-pin, and remove the hammer with hand attached, by drawing it downwards out of the lock frame. Clean all the parts and oil them thoroughly.

TO PUT THEM TOGETHER

Replace the hammer with hand-spring attached, then the bolt, the trigger, the sere-spring, the trigger-guard, the mainspring, and finally the handle; returning each screw to its proper place, the arm is again fit for use.

In the above instruction the term "bolt" refers to the rocking member whose front end rises through the frame and locks the cylinder when chamber and barrel are in alignment. The term "hand" denotes the member which is pivoted to the hammer boss and advances the cylinder as the hammer is cocked.

The instructions do not cover the dismantling of the rammer as the procedure is quite obvious, all parts being visible. The spring locking-piece at the end of the lever which engages with the catch under the muzzle of the barrel is held by a rivet which should not be disturbed unless really necessary, say, to replace a broken spring.

The only piece of advice I offer is that, as the parts are removed from the inside of the lock, they shall be carefully and slowly lifted out with tweezers, and their exact position noted to facilitate re-assembly. A reminder about the usefulness of the twelve-compartment egg tray for keeping parts in consecutive order will not be out of place here. To remove screws and let the freed parts fall out will mean spending a considerable time later finding, by trial and error, in which order, which side up, which way round and which end first, the parts are assembled.

I recall an instance of a revolver being bought at an auction which consisted of the butt and frame and trigger guard to which a linen bag was tied containing a number of small lock parts which the bidder hoped would be a Colt revolver when he had put everything together.

When working on a Colt revolver one cannot fail to be impressed by the simplicity, ingenious design and precise fit of every screw and component part. A contemporary description of Colt's London factory tells how unskilled girls assembled the revolvers with parts straight from the machines.

It was no wonder that the advent of Colt revolvers spread consternation amongst the craftsman-gunsmiths who were accustomed to the traditional methods of file-fitting and individual adjustment during assembly. Of course, factory tooling for the machine-made gun involved great capital outlay, but once production was in progress, the reduced manufacturing costs, speed of output and the facility with which interchangeable spare parts could be replaced from stock, marked a new era in the manufacture of firearms.

As a matter of interest, I dismantled the Colt revolver shown on *Plate 42* (with the exception of the nipples) in less than three and a half minutes, and reassembled it in under seven minutes. No attempt was made to rush the job and the only tools used were two screw-drivers and a pair of tweezers.

Each Colt revolver was factory-marked with a serial number, which was stamped on all main component parts. The collector, therefore, can check whether all parts are original. The Colt revolver illustrated is numbered 3951 on the cylinder, and the same number is stamped on the frame and also on the barrel lug where they join, on the trigger guard, on the strap under the stock, on the underside of the barrel wedge and on the lever of the rammer.

Colt percussion-cap revolvers were of open-frame design and single-action; that is, the hammer had to be thumb-cocked for each shot. When at last Colt's patents expired, his competitors immediately copied the best of the Colt features, such as automatic revolution and locking of the cylinder by cocking the hammer, setting the nipples axially instead of radially and isolating them from each other by dividing partitions on the cylinder, which eliminated the danger of setting up chain-fire by an exploding cap detonating its neighbours.

Some of them also further developed the design by incorporating a solid frame carrying the barrel, and providing double-action locks which permitted the hammer to be cocked with the thumb, or raised and released by the trigger action alone.

Plate 44 (*B*) shows a typical English five-chamber percussion revolver by Adams with a solid frame and double action.

In this and similar solid-frame revolvers, the cylinder is released by sliding forward the centre spindle, which is normally held in position by a small wing screw or spring peg. The rammer lever is at the side and exerts its pressure by a sliding cam action instead of a simple lever as on the Colt, but it is just as simple to detach. The double action added a few parts to the lock, but they present no particular difficulties.

The Lefaucheux revolver (A) on the same plate is really outside the scope of this book as it is a breech-loading, pin-fire, metallic-cartridge type. It does, however, show how the open-frame design was still being used after the percussion period.

(C) is another variation of the percussion revolver. This is a Tranter double-trigger gun which was popular for a time in England. What looks like a spur on the trigger guard is, in fact, a secondary trigger which extends through a central slot in the guard. This was operated by the second finger to cock the hammer, which has no spur for thumb-cocking. The gun was then fired by light pressure of the first finger on the primary trigger within the guard. It was claimed that this system was more rapid than thumb-cocking and did not disturb the aim.

The fitting screwed to the frame behind the cylinder is a spring, shaped somewhat like an inverted letter "Y", which normally holds a steel bolt between hammer nose and nipples, the bolt being automatically withdrawn when the hammer is fully cocked. This takes the place of the usual half-cock catch and forms a very effective safety device.

In this type of revolver the cylinder is detached in a second by pressing a stud on the frame which allows the spindle to be drawn out, when the cylinder falls out of the frame into the hand. The mainspring is not tensioned by a screw and the hinged vice may be required to release it.

When dismantling the side lock of a flint or percussion pistol or gun there is the great advantage of each part being on view whilst it is being dealt with. In the case of most revolvers, some of the lock parts lie hidden within the frame, and I repeat the advice previously given, to remove these slowly and carefully with tweezers and, if one has any misgivings about reassembling them, to make notes or a sketch of their relative positions.

As the worker's experience accumulates he will meet with all kinds of interesting details. For instance, the Colt revolver illustrated has a small anti-friction roller set in the hammer on which the mainspring works. In the Tranter model, a small link between hammer and spring serves the same purpose; some sights are fixed, others are adjustable; small springs may be riveted or screwed, and so on. Some guns will have sliding safety catches, belt hooks, patch boxes and other fitments, but these variations and additions present no particular problems.

Escutcheon plates and similar embellishments inlaid in the wood butt without visible fixing pins or screws should be left undisturbed and carefully cleaned in position.

CHAPTER EIGHT

SCREWS, PINS AND NIPPLES

SO far it has been assumed that the guns which have been dealt with are complete and in such condition that they have not presented any real difficulty. After experience in cleaning a number of specimens by following the methods described, one should now know how to dismantle and reassemble almost any antique firearm. Some guns, however, are not going to take down so easily. Problems will be encountered which will be a challenge to patience and ingenuity, but there is much satisfaction in devising one's own techniques to overcome them.

Stubborn screws are a difficulty most frequently met with. Previous attempts to remove them, even if they have been successful, may have rounded the slots or caused other damage to the screw-heads.

Suppose, for example, we have a side-hammer flint pistol, complete, but rather neglected and rusty, to be taken down, cleaned and adjusted. The first job is to take off the lock fixed by its two side screws.

With the gun on the bench, packed with pieces of wood to keep the lock clear and to prevent it turning over under pressure, we try both screws, but let us assume that neither will move. If the slots in the heads are worn, we cannot exert maximum force without risking the screw-driver riding out of the slot and damaging the stock or side plate.

Most side screws are of the cheese-head type and the heads either stand clear of the plate, or are only partially sunk, leaving the bottom of the slot above the face of the plate. In such a case, with the gun held in the vice, protected by sheet rubber packing, and with the side plate horizontal, the bottoms of the slots can be reshaped and squared up by the hack-saw, using a fine-pitch blade held perfectly horizontal, and dead in line with the original cut. Practise first on one or two old screws until you are sure that you can make a clean, true cut. Using an unworn, properly fitting screw-driver, it is almost certain that the screws can now be undone.

If the screw-heads are deeply sunk with the slots below the surface of the side plate, where they cannot be reached with the hack-saw, the slot must be cleaned out and trimmed as square as possible by scraping. A sharp-edged, small-size screw-driver and a fine-pointed steel scriber are suitable for this job.

With the screw-driver held vertical in the left hand, press the blade end into the slot, grasp the blade as near the end as possible with the fore-finger and thumb of the right hand and move it back and forth in the slot. At each stroke cant the screw-driver over with the left hand so that the leading corner of the blade scrapes the bottom of the slot. The corners of the slot can be scraped in the same way, using the point of the scriber. This method is laborious and, even when the knack is acquired, very little metal is removed but it usually cleans out the rust from the corners sufficiently for the screw-driver to take hold.

If the screws cannot be moved after this treatment, apply a drop of penetrating oil between the heads and the side plate and at the threaded ends where they come through the lock plate. The end of the rear side screw is often hidden under the hammer boss. Putting the hammer at full cock may fully or partially expose it to take the oil. If not, the hammer should be taken off its tumbler square (see *Plate 29*). Leave the gun for a day for the oil to penetrate and, if the screw still cannot be moved, apply more oil and leave for another day.

Sometimes a stubborn screw can be loosened by applying the turning pressure alternately clockwise and counter-clockwise, or again, by smartly striking the handle of the screw-driver as if it were a punch. This, I have found, is more effective with wood screws. Have patience and, in the end, the screws should come out. They can then be cleaned and, held in the lead jaws in the vice, the slots made good with the hack-saw.

The various screws in the lock mechanism can be dealt with in similar fashion, but, being protected behind the lock plate, the heads are likely to be in better shape than those that are more exposed.

Should these internal screws be rusted up, however, their head slots can be restored in the same way, with the advantage that the whole lock can be immersed in oil and left until the lubricant has penetrated. It may take a day or a week, or even longer, but it is seldom that the screws and other moving parts will not finally loosen up.

Metal screws in other parts of the gun may be similarly treated; the smaller the screw, the more are patience and delicacy of touch necessary. The worst offenders are screws with countersunk heads where rust has formed between the faces of the countersunk holes and the underside of the screw-heads, as well as on the threads.

A red-hot poker or length of rod held against the head will sometimes help to free a stiff screw. The screw is expanded slightly as it takes the heat and contracts again as it cools, and several expansions and contractions will tend to loosen the thread. If the screws are so rusted in as to require this treatment, it is unlikely that the general finish of the surrounding metal will be marred by the application of a red-hot poker.

Oil should not be applied to the heads of wood screws such as are generally used to attach barrel tangs, trigger guards, patch boxes and butt plates and caps to the wood stock. If the oil seeps down the screw, the surrounding wood will swell and grip the screw even tighter than before. Clearing the slots, tapping on the screw-head, carefully applying heat to the head and using a screw-driver which is a perfect fit are all we can do, but ninety-nine times out of a hundred the screw will come out.

In dealing with difficult screws it is worth while again stressing the importance of setting the gun firmly in position, either in the vice or on the bench so that it cannot turn or slip under the hardest pressure. Every time a screw-driver slips out of a worn slot it rounds the edges a little more, to say nothing of the risk of damage to other parts of the gun.

Let us now consider the hundredth screw, that will not respond to any of our efforts. If its removal is not absolutely necessary (for example a countersunk wood screw which secures a butt plate which it is not essential to remove), I would recommend that it be left.

Suppose, however, it fixes the trigger guard, which must be taken off to effect a necessary repair; then it will have to be drilled out, and it must be drilled out without cutting into the metal surrounding the screw.

Fix the gun, properly protected, in the vice with the face of the screw-head horizontal. The diameter of a screw-head is usually twice the diameter of the shank of the screw and, in the case of screws with countersunk heads, the angle of the sides of the countersunk hole is usually forty-five degrees to the axis. I say "usually" because the old gunsmiths often adopted their own standards, but the proportions given are reliable as a working rule.

If the head measures 5/16″ diameter, it may be safely assumed that the shank where it joins the head will be approximately 5/32″ diameter. Fit a 5/32″ twist drill in the chuck of the hand-drill and start to drill as nearly in the centre of the screw-head as possible. The slot will usually keep the hole central in one direction, but the drill will almost certainly start slightly nearer to one end of the slot than the other. As soon as this is apparent, slant the drill steeply and guide the point back to the centre. A magnifying glass is useful to judge the positioning of the hole. A little practice should enable one to bring the drill as nearly concentric with the head as can be judged by the eye.

With the hole exactly central and the drill of the same diameter as the shank of the screw, when the drill reaches the shank the head will become detached and lift out on the point of the drill. When this happens, one can congratulate oneself on performing a nice piece of work.

More often the head will remain attached by a thin shell of metal at one side, but a short length of the slot will be left on each side of the hole and a turn with the screw-driver should easily twist the head off. If not, open the hole a little with a drill 1/64″ larger, which will detach the head and free the fitting which it held.

We still have the body of the screw left in the metal or wood and, if any of the shank protrudes, it can be gripped in the pin vice and unscrewed. With the head off and the tension in the shank relieved, the threads lose some of their grip and unscrew more easily.

In the case of a metal screw, if the shank does not project enough to be gripped, drill a central hole a little way down depending upon the length of the screw, and slightly less in diameter than the core, that is, the diameter at the bottom of the threads of the screw. The tapering, hardened end of a small screw-driver very lightly hammered into this hole will nearly always bite sufficiently to turn out the piece of screw. If it still refuses to move, increase the size of the hole until it just reaches the female thread, when the remains of the male thread can be picked out with the point of a scriber.

A screw left in the wood of the stock is a different matter. The thread of a wood screw is so deep that the central core of metal is too small to attempt to drill it out. The piece of screw must be loosened and drawn out.

Drill a ring of holes all round the shank with a 1/16" drill; then drill into each hole on the angle to break it into those adjoining; work round the screw with the point of a scriber or a joiner's bradawl, scraping the fibres of the wood away until a narrow channel is left all round sufficiently wide to receive the jaws of the fine-nosed pliers, and turn the screw out. If it won't come, drill your ring of holes a little deeper until the screw loosens.

Extracting rusted and broken screws is a job requiring patience, persistence and practice, and before attempting to work on any firearm I suggest that some screws for both metal and wood with countersunk heads be firmly screwed into scrap material and then removed in the manner described. The aim must be to get a metal screw out without damaging the countersunk hole or the thread into which it fits, or, in the case of a wood screw, to leave a hole less or, at most, no larger, than the diameter of the head of the screw.

This hole must be filled to receive the new wood screw and for this purpose I normally use a plastic wood which I make with sawdust and a good brand of tube glue. Saw a few thin sections with a fine tooth saw off a piece of scrap walnut and catch the sawdust on a sheet of paper. With the blade of a knife mix about a teaspoonful of this with a squeeze of glue, adding more sawdust or glue to make it into a fairly stiff paste. Pack the plastic wood into the hole, working it down with a match stick or a piece of rod until the hole is full and let the filling stand proud of the surrounding wood to allow for shrinkage on drying. Then leave the job for a week. The surface may be dry and hard by next morning, but the middle of the mass will not thoroughly dry out for many days. A screw inserted too soon will not only fail to cut a thread, but it will adhere to the glue and if it is removed in the future it will come out with its thread full of hardened plastic wood leaving a stripped hole. When the filling has had ample time to set and finish shrinking, level off the surface of the plastic wood, taking care not to mark the polish of the surrounding wood.

Although the filling will not show when the parts are reassembled, take that little extra trouble to match the wood of the stock. Plastic wood will take stain quite well.

When inserting new screws into hardwood, particularly those which need to be removable at intervals, it is important that holes of a suitable size to receive them should be drilled to accommodate both the screwed and plain portions of the shank. Piercing a leading-hole with a bradawl and letting the screw rive out its own hole and thread may be satisfactory enough in softwood where screws are put in to stay, but it will not do for gunwork.

Use a drill of the same diameter as the solid core of the threaded part of the screw. The diameters may easily be matched by holding them together against the light. Measure the length of screw which has to enter the wood, add $\frac{1}{8}''$ or so for end-clearance, make a chalk mark on the drill to indicate the depth of hole required and drill the hole to that depth.

That part of the hole which takes the plain part of the screw shank will need to be enlarged by a second drill about 1/64″ larger in diameter than the shank. Again make a chalk mark on the drill to indicate the depth necessary for the enlarged part of the hole and drill precisely to that depth.

A new screw fitted to a hole prepared in this way will cut a clean thread for itself, the plain part of the shank will not bind in the hole and it can be taken out and replaced many times without damage.

The wood screws found in many older guns differ from the modern type in that they were threaded for their full length and tapered from point to head. Naturally the original old screws should be retained wherever possible. The faces of the countersunk screw-heads were often slightly domed and, where these have to be replaced, dome-head screws should be used. They can be obtained from the larger hardware dealers.

To burnish a flat screw-head, take a couple of pieces of wood about four or five inches square and about a quarter of an inch thick and in one of them drill a group of half a dozen holes just large enough to pass the screw-head. Put a piece of emery cloth between the pieces of wood with the abrasive side toward the holes and clamp them vertically in the vice with the holes toward you. Fix the screw shank in the chuck of the hand-drill and, using one of the holes as a guide, spin the screw-head against the emery cloth. Move the work from hole to hole at intervals as the emery cloth wears smooth. By using progressively finer grades of emery one can, if desired, obtain a mirror-like finish, though this is seldom necessary. A domed head can be burnished in the same way by putting thin sheet rubber behind the emery cloth which will allow it to assume the curved contour of the head. To keep the drill steady while burnishing the sides of a cheese head, make some notches in the edge of the wood to act as guides.

Personally, for this and nearly all work on firearms, I prefer the hand-operated drill to the electric tool. The control is more sensitive. If a high-speed power-driven drill should happen to slip or run off centre it can do a lot of damage in a very short time before it can be stopped. It is a convenient tool and a time and labour saver for many jobs in the workshop but, for work on the gun itself, I recommend the light hand-operated drill.

Occasionally in old guns one will find wood screws which turn indefinitely, having stripped the threads in the hole in the stock, so that they can neither be tightened nor withdrawn. The heads are usually such an exact fit that it can be quite a problem to extract a wood screw from a stripped hole. A useful little tool called a "screw-holder" is invaluable for this purpose. Its primary use is to hold and start wood screws into awkward positions where they cannot be manipulated by the fingers.

The tool consists of a metal rod about the size of a pencil, knurled at one end for holding, and furnished at the other with a projection made to fit into the slot of a screw-head. The middle section (about a third) of this projection is separate and is controlled by an internal spring. By inserting the projection in the slot and pressing the tool against the screw, the spring is released and twists the middle section out of line. This grips the sides of the slot in the screw-head sufficiently tight to turn and draw out most wood screws in stripped holes. This tool will not deal with very small screws, or those with badly-worn slots. *Plate No. 45* shows a screw-holder of this kind engaged in a wood screw from which a walnut gun stock is suspended. Actually it will maintain its hold against a considerably greater weight.

Failing this special tool, which may not readily be obtainable at some tool shops, one must try some other method of drawing out the screw without damaging the area around the head. Two very small screw-drivers, say 1/16″ or 3/32″ wide inserted side by side in the length of the slot and twisted in opposite directions might transmit enough pull on the screw to coax it out.

Another trick is to file a piece of strip steel so that the end will be a push-fit in the slot. Sideways pressure on the strip will temporarily bind it in the slot to give a useful grip.

If the extracted screw is the original, always use it again in preference to fitting a modern one.

It is worth mentioning that there is another and more popular type of screw-holder which must not be confused with the one I have just described and which would be useless for the purpose of extracting a screw with a sunk head. It is an attachment for the end of an ordinary screw-driver. It holds the screw under the head and is only effective for inserting screws.

For a stripped wood thread, leaving a clean round hole, I do not use plastic wood. I drill the hole about 1/16″ larger and fill it with a wood plug. Shape the plug to a slight taper with a chisel or a coarse file and see that both the plug and the sides of the hole are completely covered with a film of glue. Tap the plug into place and leave it for a day; then drill a new hole and replace the screw as previously described.

The reason for enlarging the stripped hole is that the original diameter will be exactly the same as the overall diameter of the screw thread. Therefore, merely to plug this hole and insert the screw would bring the thread to the surface of the plug and cut it into a spiral. It would then be liable to strip again if it was screwed up tightly.

Metal screws with stripped threads present a more serious problem, but fortunately this does not often happen. When it does, it is more often the male thread that strips, and there are several ways of dealing with such cases. With a little luck it might be possible to obtain a modern standard screw of the same diameter and pitch, and then to alter the head to match the original pattern.

An alternative is to make, or have made, a new screw to the old pattern and this is not a difficult job to one accustomed to lathe work.

A heavy long screw could be lengthened by welding, so bringing a new part of the thread into use. *Fig. 14* shows how a cheese-head side screw was lengthened in this manner. The screw was $\frac{1}{4}''$ diameter and about 2″ long, the last $\frac{1}{2}''$ being threaded. The

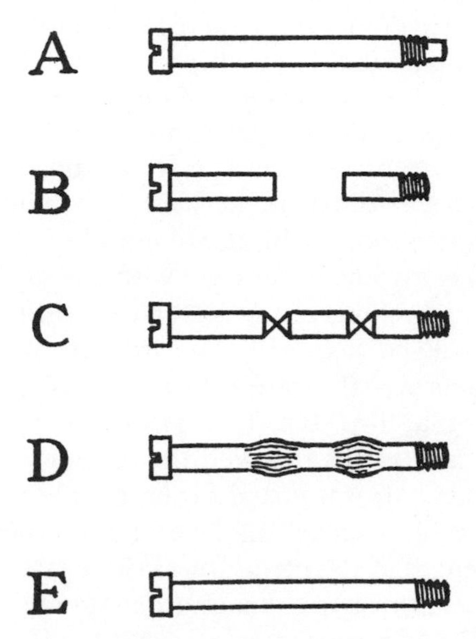

Figure 14. Lengthening a damaged screw: sequence of operations.

A. Screw with end of thread stripped.
B. Stripped portion of thread cut off and piece cut from middle of screw.
C. New piece inserted to bring screw to its original length with ends filed for welding.
D. The three parts welded together.
E. Finished screw.

lock plate was $\frac{1}{8}''$ thick, and the thread in the tapped hole was sound, but the first 3/16″ of thread on the screw was stripped clean, as shown at (A).

The stripped end was sawn off and trimmed by filing, leaving 5/16″ of good thread, but the screw was now too short by $\frac{1}{4}''$. A piece $\frac{3}{4}''$ long was cut out of the middle of the shank as at (B) to be replaced by a piece of $\frac{1}{4}''$ rod 1″ long to bring the screw to its original length. The ends to be joined were filed conical, ready for welding as at (C) and the pieces welded together as at (D).

The scale was hammered off and the protruding rings of metal filed away, leaving a sound strong screw of the original length (E). Any welder would join up the pieces in a few minutes.

If an original screw is missing it may be necessary to find the pitch of the thread from the tapped hole before a new screw can be provided. To do this, cut a chip of softwood a few inches long and shave and sandpaper one end to a diameter a little larger than the clear-way through the threaded hole, and taper the end to act as a lead. Apply a little oil to the wood and screw it backwards and forwards several times for at least $\frac{1}{2}''$. The thread will impress itself on the wood, enabling the number of threads per inch to be measured easily and accurately with the steel rule.

No general instructions can be given for dealing with a stripped threaded hole. Each case will pose its own particular problem, but here are some actual examples which have come my way.

The first was a flint box-lock pistol where the thread was stripped in the hole which received the hammer pivot screw on the far side of the box. It is unusual for both male and female threads to fail together. It is generally one or the other, depending on the relative strength of the metal, but in this case the thread on the pivot screw also was nearly gone, and I could obtain no stock screw of the type and size required to replace it. However, I found a long round-head wood screw of the right diameter to fit the clear side hole and the hole in the hammer boss, with sufficient length of plain shank for the whole job, and I made a new screw in the manner indicated in *Fig. 15*.

By comparison with the usual proportions the cheese head of a box-lock hammer screw is small and thin because of the limited depth of the counterbore in the box side. Careful filing will turn a round head into a suitable cheese head but there is very little, if any, margin for error.

The screw was fixed vertically in the vice with the head about $\frac{1}{4}''$ clear of the jaws. The round head was first filed down to nearly the same thickness as the depth of the counterbore. This left a circular flat on the head and the edge of it was then filed,

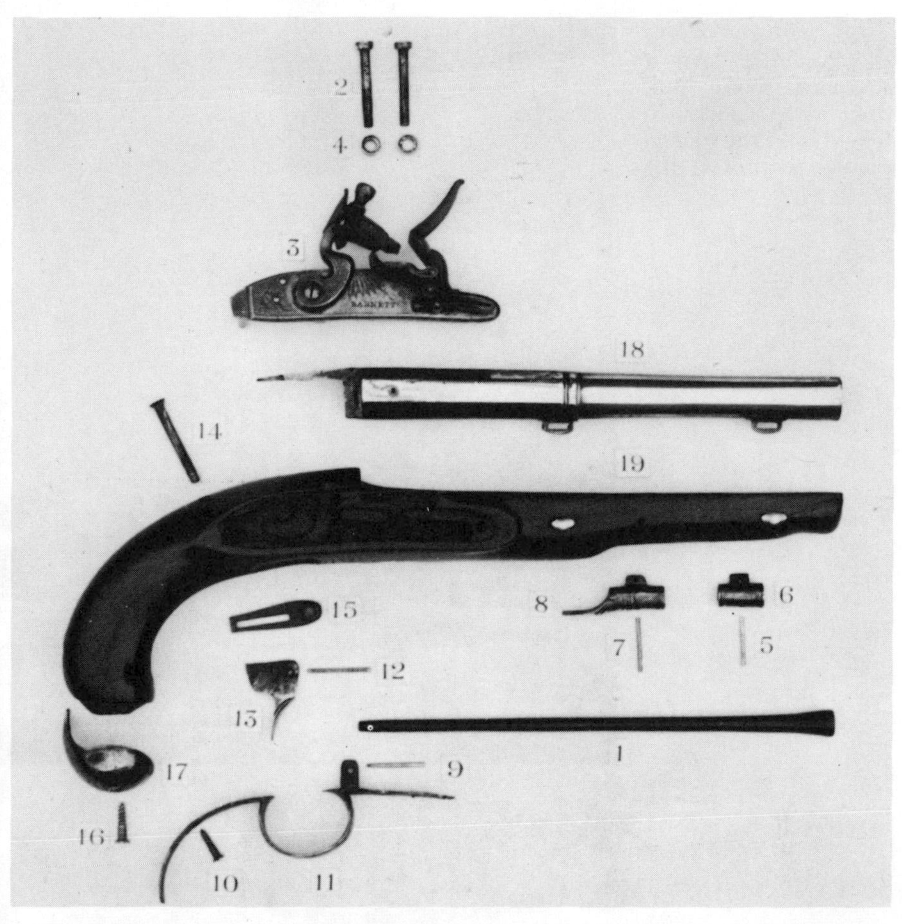

Plate 31. Exploded view of Barnett pistol (*Plate 30*). The parts are numbered in the order in which they are removed.

1. Ramrod. 2. Side screws which fix lock. 3. Lock. 4. Cupped washers for side screws. 5. Pin for fixing front ramrod pipe. 6. Front ramrod pipe. 7. Pin for fixing back ramrod pipe. 8. Back ramrod pipe. 9. Pin for fixing front of trigger guard. 10. Screw for fixing back of trigger guard. 11. Trigger guard. 12. Trigger pivot pin. 13. Trigger. 14. Screw for fixing barrel tang and trigger plate. 15. Trigger plate. 16. Screw for fixing butt cap. 17. Butt cap. 18. Barrel. 19. Stock with keys for fixing barrel.

Plate 32. Punching out a trigger guard fixing pin. Note the wood blocks to raise the gun and the sponge rubber pads to protect the stock.

Plate 33. Gun and pistol flints from $1\frac{1}{4}$ in. wide down to 3/8 in. Above them is a flake of flint before being divided.

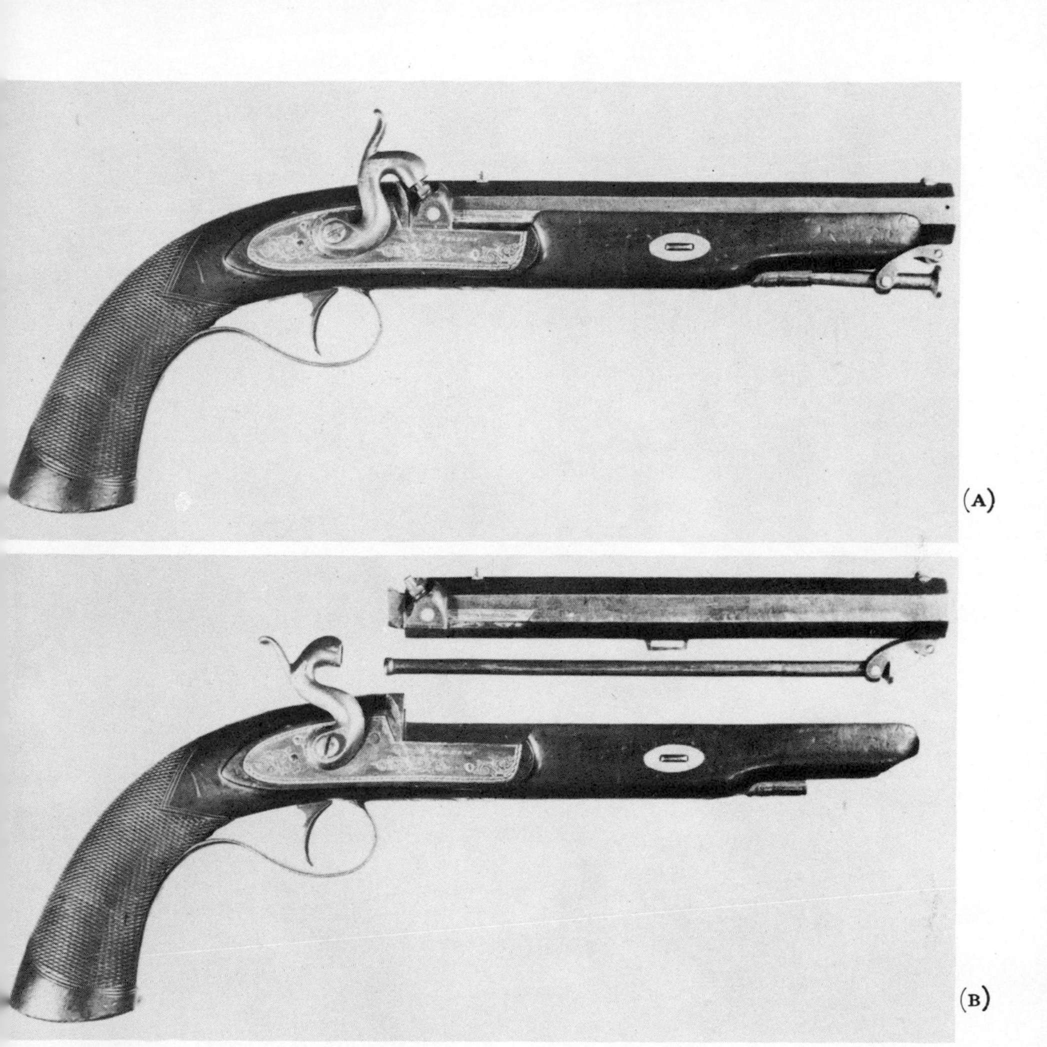

(A)

(B)

Plate 34. *Top:* Percussion pistol by Thomson of Edinburgh. *Bottom:* Thomson pistol with barrel detached.

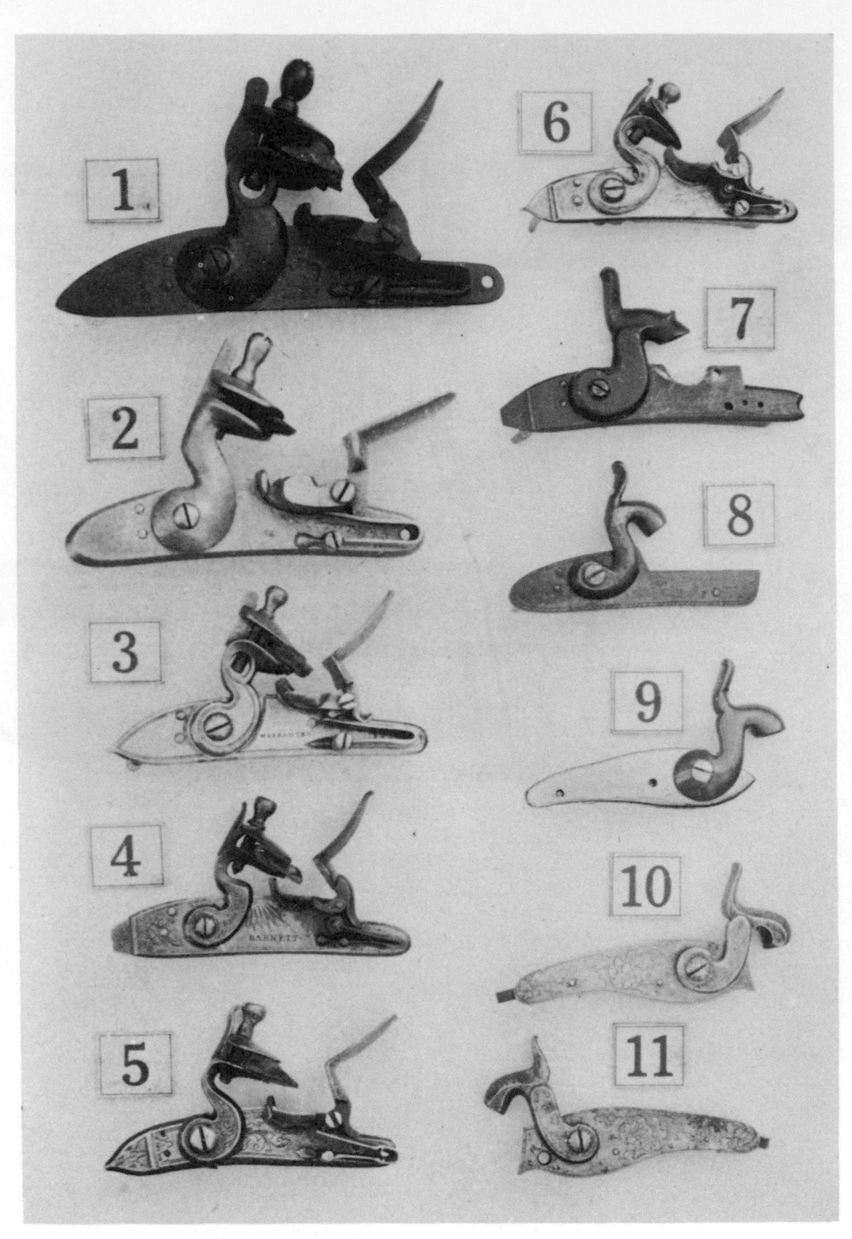

Plate 35. Exterior views of flint and percussion locks.

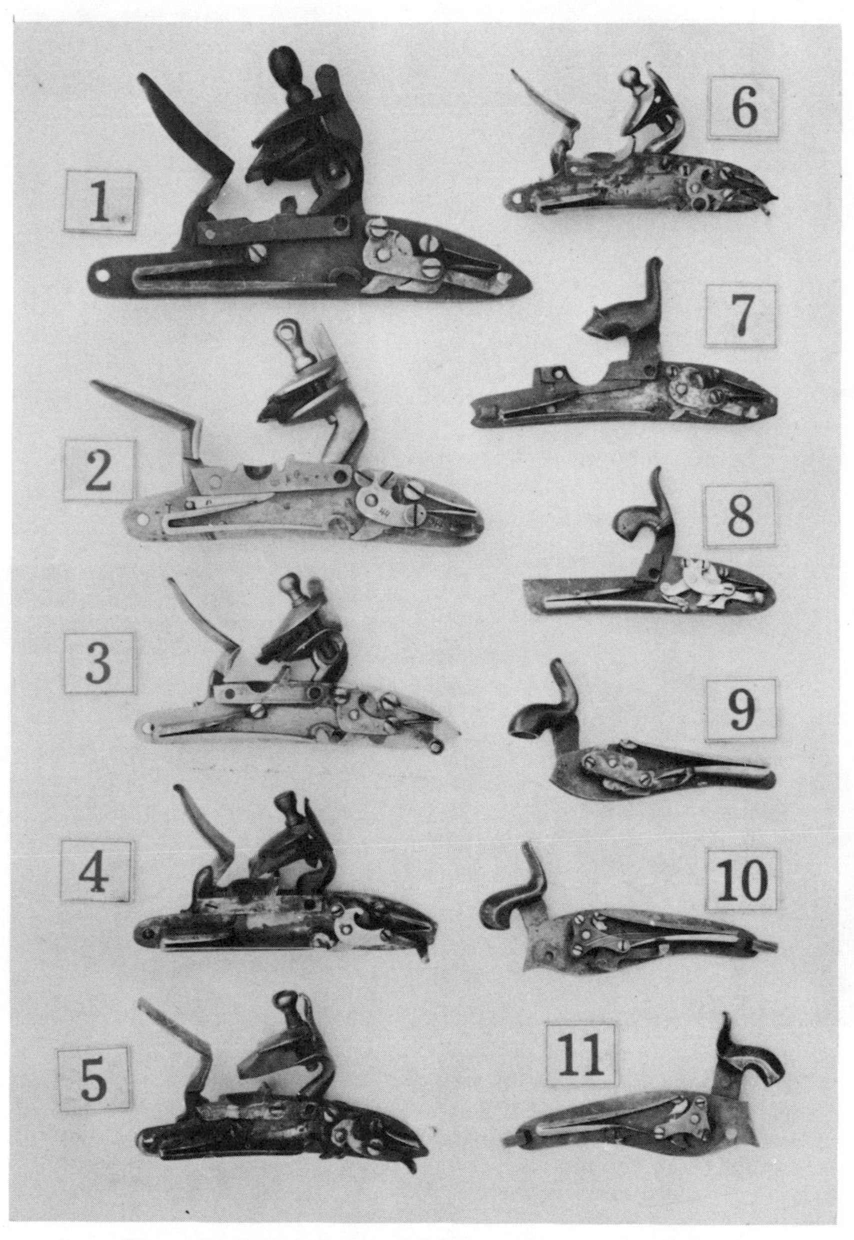

Plate 36. Interior views of flint and percussion locks.

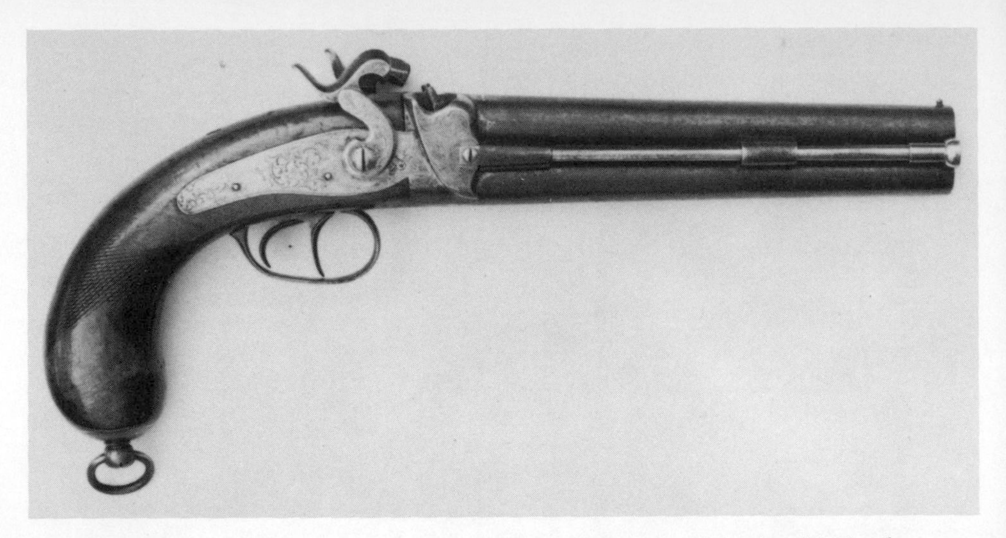

Plate 37. Under-and-over double-barrel percussion pistol with back-action locks.

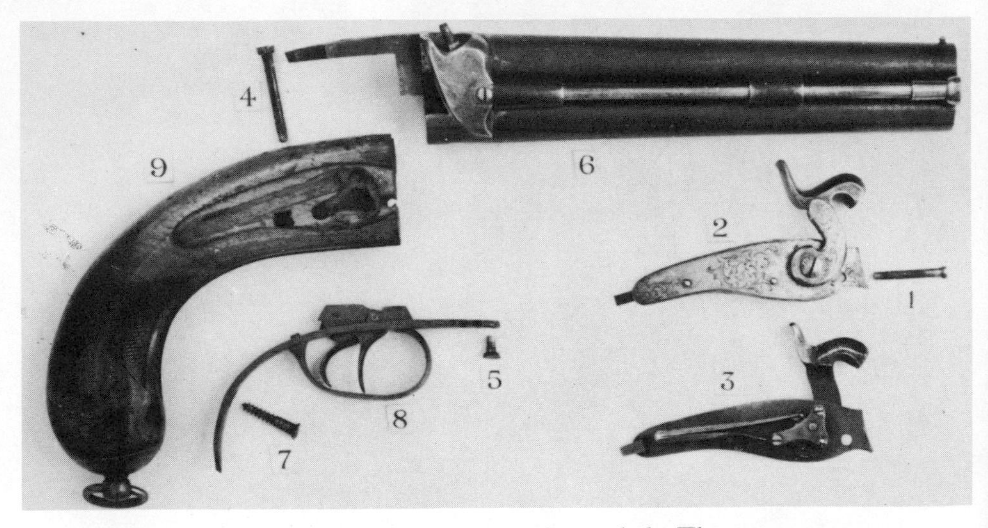

Plate 38. The pistol in *Plate 37* partly dismantled, The parts are numbered in the order in which they are removed.

1. Screw fixing both locks. 2. Right-hand lock. 3. Left-hand lock. 4. Barrel tang screw. 5. Front trigger plate screw. 6. Barrels and breech block assembly. 7. Back trigger plate screw. 8. Trigger plate, guard and triggers assembly. 9. Stock.

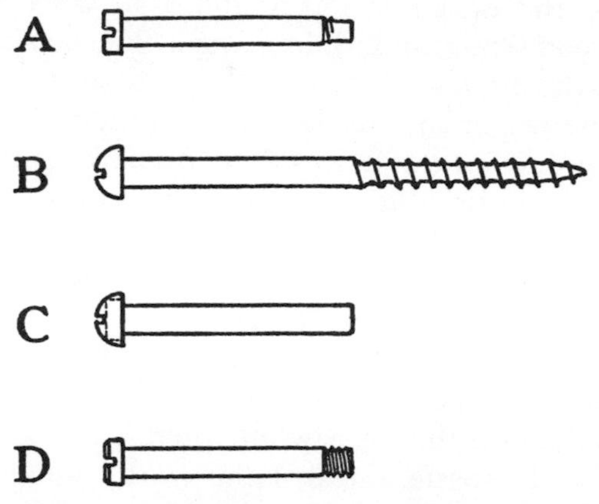

Figure 15. Making metal screw from wood screw.

A. Original cheese-head screw with stripped thread.
B. Round-head wood screw with plain shank of sufficient length.
C. Screw cut to length required.
D. End threaded and head re-shaped.

working round evenly to keep it circular, until it fitted the counter-bore.

A large washer was dropped over the head of the screw and allowed to rest loosely on the vice jaws to act as a guide for the bottom edge of the file and to prevent scoring the faces of the jaws.

The final finishing to fitting size was done with a fine file and the face and edges were smoothed by spinning in the hand-drill against emery cloth as already described.

The stripped hole in the box side was filled by welding, the outside filed flat and polished and a new hole set out and drilled ready for tapping. The nearest standard thread to suit the diameter of the shank was found to be No. 2 B.A. and taps and a die of this size were bought and the screw and the hole threaded.

With a precision lathe one could, of course, modify a screw-head with considerably less labour, but the filing process is quite a practical proposition and if one or two screws are spoiled no harm is done—you just go on until you succeed.

Another box-lock percussion pistol with a similar defect could not be welded without destroying the fine engraving and original finish around the screw hole, so this time the screw hole was tapped out to the next size larger and a new screw made, also from a long wood screw, and again using a B.A. standard thread.

Obviously, the new screw had to be of slightly increased diameter, necessitating enlarging the holes through the hammer boss and side of the box on the head side. By making the head to fit the existing counterbore, the outside of the pistol remained unaltered on that side.

Occasionally one finds the thread in the cock-screw hole stripped in a flint-lock hammer, due to excessive tightening. If there is enough clearance between the screw and the comb of the hammer, the hole can be tapped out to the next screw size, a new cock screw made and the hole in the top jaw enlarged. If the worker is not equipped for and experienced in lathe work, the screw will have to be ordered.

The reason for choosing the B.A. standard when re-tapping is that it is a comparatively fine thread but sufficiently strong for our purpose. It has the advantage that, for a given size of tapping hole, the diameter of the screw shank is less than would be the case with a coarser and consequently deeper thread of, say, Whitworth standard. This may often be the deciding factor as to how a job can be done.

If it can be avoided, I prefer not to weld-fill, plug or bush holes but, where there is insufficient clearance to make an oversize re-tap, one of these methods may be necessary unless the defect is to be left.

Dealing with damaged screws and stripped threads, especially of metal screws, is not the most attractive side of gun renovation. It demands a good deal of ingenuity and patient work, often with nothing to see for it; but we have the satisfaction of knowing that we have improved a weapon which was deteriorating.

The manipulation of pins or keys which were used to attach barrels, trigger guards, ramrod pipes and other fittings to the stock is usually fairly straightforward, but sometimes they can need a little extra coaxing.

To take the flat barrel keys first, prolonged light tapping with a suitable punch will usually move them. In ordinary circumstances I have suggested using a screw-driver for this purpose, but if the key is stubborn the end is liable to be spread by the hardened tip of the screw-driver, and a punch of softer metal should be used.

This can be merely a short length of mild steel strip a fraction less in width and thickness than the end of the key. If the end of the punch begins to spread, file the burr off the edges and continue, and ultimately the key will come free.

Remember to drive the keys only so far as is necessary to free the barrel. As previously explained, their movement is limited by fine pins in the stock which are out of sight beneath the barrel, and which will be sheared off if the keys are driven right out. When the barrel is removed, the heads of these pins and the slots in the keys through which they pass can be seen.

Again, hardened pin punches could distort the ends of the wire fixing pins which pass through the stock if these are so rusted or tightly fixed as to require hard and persistent tapping. In such cases it is preferable to use round wire nails slightly thinner than the pins and with the points filed off. They are much easier on the pins and new ones are ready to hand if they bend or begin to spread.

Above all, take care that the punch is applied in the direction of the axis of the pin and that it does not slip off sideways and dig into the stock. If at some time the wood of the stock surrounding a pin has been damaged, fill the cavity on one side with plastic wood after the pin has been removed. When it is dry, sandpaper it smooth and stain and polish it to match the stock.

Then from the other side, using a drill which is a push fit into the pin hole, drill through the wood filling. Treat both sides in the same way if necessary.

Fine emery cloth will remove rust from the pins so that they can be used again but, if the ends are badly rusted or spread with previous hammering, I usually make and fit new pins from my stock of various gauges of round wire nails. The appearance of clean pin ends in smooth wood is, in my opinion, preferable to rusty ends sunk in rather sore-looking holes in the stock.

If a pin is too tight to pass into the stock without undue force, reduce its diameter with file or emery paper. Never, on any account, apply oil to the pin with the idea of reducing the friction. The surrounding wood will swell and hold it immovably in a vice-like grip.

Occasionally one may find a pin so loose in the stock that it will almost fall out. If the pin is very slightly bent before it is replaced it will have to spring straight as it is tapped in and will bind in position quite tightly.

Percussion-cap nipples which resist normal pressure on the key may be something of a problem. To external rust is often added the binding effect of old powder-fouling deposited internally at the junction of nipple and barrel. If this spot can be reached with a pointed wire scraper at, say, the bottom of revolver chambers, pick away as much as possible of the fouling and apply penetrating oil.

With suitable protective packing, most guns can easily be held in the vice while extracting nipples, but in the case of a pepper-box or revolver the barrels or cylinder must be removed and hand-held. The comparatively large and fluted barrel of a pepper-box generally permits an efficient grip, but the smaller smooth cylinder of a revolver tends to turn in the hand. Wrapping the cylinder with insulation tape and wearing a rubber glove will give a surer grip.

If the nipples still refuse to move, the cylinder or barrel block must be held in the vice and *Plate 46* shows how to hold a revolver cylinder firmly without risk of marking. Two pieces of round iron rod slightly less in diameter than the chambers and of sufficient length to reach their full depth, plus a good clearance above the vice jaws, are clamped vertically in the vice, the distance apart being such that when the cylinder is placed over them they enter two of the chambers. The cylinder is now firmly held, whatever pressure is applied to the nipples. A wrapping of insulation tape round the pegs will prevent marking the chambers.

I have seen cylinders marked with the imprint of vice jaws on their opposite sides. In one case, the cylinder of a revolver had been placed in the vice at some time. Although packing pieces or soft jaws had apparently been used, the cylinder had been so set that the thin outer walls of two opposite chambers took the squeeze, instead of the solid web separating the chambers. The disastrous result was a compressed flat on each side of the cylinder.

If, with the gun or cylinder rigidly held and fairly strong pressure applied to the key, any of the nipples still refuse to move, I would be inclined to leave them. Excessive pressure may round off the corners of the square or flats, or break the head off the nipple, leaving the screwed piece embedded flush in the seating. The experienced worker can usually judge how much force he dare safely apply but, if you are unfortunate enough to shear the body of a nipple, or if you acquire a specimen where someone else has already done this, there is nothing for it but to drill and extract in the manner described for decapitated metal screws.

Here is a minor point which is worth remembering. If a broken nipple screw which has been drilled resists the counter-clockwise turning pressure of a screw-driver pushed into the hole from the outside, try inserting it through the chamber, tapping it well in to get a grip, and turn it clockwise to send the screw out from the inside.

The difference is that, when turning the screw counter-clockwise, it has to rise against the pressure that is being applied, but when turning it clockwise, the screw will move in the same direction as the pressure with appreciably less resistance. I have found this idea effective on several occasions.

CHAPTER NINE

RUST REMOVAL, SPLIT STOCKS AND RE-POLISHING

NEGLECT an antique gun, hang it on a wall in an unheated room, leave it in a damp cupboard, and, before one realises what is happening, the steel and iron parts are attacked by rust. Many of our old weapons carry the scars of such past abuse. An interesting or rare specimen may come into your hands red with present rust, or clean, but roughened or pitted from earlier ravages of this plague.

If the gun is clean and bright and shows no active rust patches, one must generally be prepared to accept any old traces or, when actual rust is present, to clean it down to the unaffected metal.

Proprietary rust-removing solutions are quite effective for this purpose and the affected parts should be brushed with a fine wire brush to remove as much surface rust as possible, and then immersed in the solution until every particle of rust is removed. The pitted surface is not what we would like, but it must be accepted until a better example of that particular gun can be obtained.

While I cannot suggest any effective way of removing deep rust pitting, I am strongly averse, except in special circumstances, to the too-common procedure of working over the affected parts with emery cloth. We all have seen the unhappy result of this treatment when inexpertly applied.

To me, the clean pits of old rust are usually more acceptable than a surface treated with emery cloth leaving untouched patches around sights and in inaccessible recesses, octagon barrels with the corners radiused and the sharp edges of revolver cylinders and other fittings rounded, often enough with the rust pitting still apparent.

The only time emery cloth might be used to deal with rust pitting on a gun is when the traces are slight and the surfaces simple, and then time and patience must be given, working progressively through several grades of cloth to give a uniform polished finish. I have cleaned rust patches off several round barrels from box-lock pistols, the octagon barrel of a revolver, and, in one case, starting with a coarse file and finishing with the smoothest emery, restored the very rusty iron barrel of a blunderbuss to its original appearance.

A round barrel can be wedged on to a piece of round wood dowel to overhang the vice and worked on with strips of emery cloth applied in a crosswise or circular direction, as shown in *Plate 47* (*A*).

On an octagonal barrel, the strokes must be longitudinal and the emery cloth tightly wrapped round a flat strip of wood which must be held perfectly parallel to the face which is being worked (see *Plate 47* (*B*)). Before working on an actual octagon barrel, it is advisable to practise on a piece of hexagon rod until the polished faces are left true and flat. Finally, the acute sharp corners may be taken off the edges of the octagon barrel by a few light longitudinal strokes with the finest grade of emery. In the hands of an experienced worker, emery cloth may occasionally be employed safely on this kind of work but, as has been said, it must always be used with discretion.

The blueing or browning of steel parts seen on some antique guns is, in my opinion, beyond the capacity of the ordinary amateur to achieve to the old professional standard of perfection, and I do not recommend making the attempt to re-finish in this way. Materials for the work with instructions for its application are obtainable from gun shops and the worker can try them out if he likes, but I have yet to see such an applied finish which could be mistaken for the original. My advice is, if there is any of the original colour left, try to preserve it; if it has all gone, leave the metal in the "white".

These remarks refer to a complete re-finish. It is not difficult to heat-treat a small part to match up with original blueing and, as one becomes expert with practice, larger parts can successfully be attempted. The bigger and more irregular-shaped the work, however, the more difficult it is to get uniform temperature and colour.

Start with a steel screw-head. Bring it to a high polish all over and do not touch it with the fingers afterwards, as the slightest trace of grease will spoil the finish. Grip the screw by its thread in a pair of pliers and hold the head over, but not actually in, the flame of a gas jet or blow-lamp and heat it fairly slowly. The bright surface will first go dull and then yellowish, passing through straw-brown, yellow and purple to clear blue, and then begin to turn pale again.

The art is in heating at the correct speed, raising the temperature uniformly and stopping at the right time. Experiment on a piece of polished $\frac{1}{4}''$ diameter steel rod. Apply the flame an inch or two from one end and watch the colours form and travel along to the end.

If the work is overheated and passes the clear-blue stage, let it cool, re-polish the surface until all trace of the unsuccessful blueing has gone, and start again. Keep the rod turning, moving it along as it colours, and try to get a uniform blue over as large an area as possible. The knack will come with practice. There are various chemical formulae and processes for browning, blacking and blueing. If the worker would like to experiment with some of these methods he will find them described in many technical books on metal work or engineering.

Guns and pistols with highly polished brass barrels and fittings are attractive items in a collection. Fortunately, badly neglected brass may nearly always be made like new. If the parts are coated with verdigris it can be removed by boiling in a solution of household washing soda, using about a tea-cup to each quart of water. Boil them for about an hour, then lift them out and immediately, while still hot, scrub them with a stiff bristle brush under running hot water. The softened deposit will brush away leaving an absolutely clean surface of a dark bronze colour, a finish which can be attractive in some circumstances. The bright polished finish is generally preferred, however, for which any suitable metal polish can be used.

I boil my brass gun fittings in an old saucepan, but the brass barrel of a blunderbuss posed a problem which was overcome by using a metal watering can and boiling and cleaning first one half and then the other. The smell of boiling brass is not generally liked but it soon goes.

The wood stocks of guns and pistols and the grips of revolvers were usually made of walnut, sometimes of maple or other fancy hardwoods, and over the years many of them have become dented or cracked. Cracks which have sprung open may have become filled with dust and dirt and cannot be closed by pressure until this accumulation has been scraped out. For this purpose a table knife, worn thin and with a few notches like saw teeth ground into the edge, is quite an effective tool. Sometimes the crack can be sprung open further to facilitate cleaning out, but on occasion it saves time and trouble to complete the fracture and so allow the separate pieces to be thoroughly cleaned and then replaced, so that the repair is almost invisible.

Plate 48 (*A*) shows how splints and binding are applied in the repair of a cracked stock, in this case that of the blunderbuss whose barrel was boiled in the watering can. When this gun came into my possession, the stock was split for about 6" from the muzzle end, starting along the ramrod groove for about 3" and then running out along the grain toward one side. I managed to spring this crack open a trifle more and to clean the inside so that it could be completely closed.

Tube glue was worked into the crack with a thin-bladed knife. The barrel and also a length of tube of the same diameter as the wooden ramrod were placed in position to ensure that their respective grooves, and incidentally the sides of the stock, would be accurately lined up.

Short laths of wood were placed on either side of the stock and the whole was wrapped tightly with string. The metal tube was substituted for the ramrod to avoid surplus glue adhering to the wood.

As a further protection, the metal tube and the barrel were previously given a wipe of oil and, when the glue had been given a couple of days to set, they both came away quite easily. The string which had become firmly attached was loosened by the application of warm water, which also removed the extruded glue.

The stock was otherwise in excellent condition and had retained its original high polish; when the job was finished, the repair was unnoticeable.

Plate 48 (*B*) shows another typical repair where a small piece was broken from the butt of a gun-stock and was missing so that a new piece had to be made.

First the brass butt plate was removed and the surface of the break, which was along the grain, was flattened with coarse sandpaper wrapped round a wood block.

I had some walnut with a similar grain which I chiselled to approximately the required shape to complete the stock, being careful to match up the grain.

The surfaces to be joined were left with a rough sandpaper finish as a key for the glue with which they were liberally coated, and the new piece was placed in position.

The butt plate was put back and the lower screw put in just tight enough to prevent the tip of the new wood, which was a little oversize, from sliding backward. (The photograph shows how it was held in place.) The upper screw was left partly projecting to stop the binding string from slipping along the smooth tapering stock.

A 6″ length of 1″ by $\frac{1}{4}$″ wood lath was put underneath the stock, with soft rubber pencil-erasers inserted at either end, and all was then bound with string as shown. The function of the rubber buffers was to transmit the pressure evenly over the whole length of the new piece, firmly but not so tightly as to squeeze out all the glue.

The job was left for a week to ensure that the glue should have set hard and would hold the joint while the new tip was finished with chisel and sandpaper to the exact shape. The sandpapering having of necessity been carried on to the adjoining surface of the stock, the repair was then stained and polished to match up to the old finish, and the butt plate replaced.

Before applying stain to newly sandpapered wood, it must be "whiskered". When the job is finally smoothed down with the finest grade of sandpaper, rub the surface over with a wet cloth and leave to dry. It will be found that the grain has risen and that the surface is almost as rough as before it was sandpapered. After several repeated sandpaperings and wettings, with the wood drying progressively smoother, it will finally dry as smooth as it was before it was wetted.

The arrangement shown on *Plate 48* (*B*) was set up again for the photograph after the job was finished, so that the new piece is not apparent, but a chalk mark indicates the line of the joint. A carefully-made glued joint should be amply strong and I prefer not to reinforce a stock repair with panel pins or screws.

Most shoulder guns and many pistol stocks carry a pattern of checkering which provides a non-slip grip. This normally consists of two series of parallel grooves of triangular section crossing each other at an angle of about sixty degrees, producing an attractive regular pattern of small diamond-shaped pyramids.

As the sides of the grooves also form an angle of about sixty degrees, a file of triangular section will fit into them and a fine Swiss file, used with care, will effectively clean and trim small areas of checkering damaged by knocks or scrapes. This treatment should be given sparingly so as not to destroy the old darkened and polished surface, and leave a light-coloured patch more noticeable than the original blemish it was intended to remove.

I have a small pin-fire pepper-box revolver, commonly referred to as an Apache gun because of its popularity with the one-time Apaches or toughs of Paris. Somebody at some time had clamped this pistol in the vice by the handle, leaving a flat patch on the cheek of each grip with the tips of the diamond checkering crushed and broken. One can readily accept scars on an old gun legitimately received during its long life, but defacement caused by carelessness I find intolerable, so I set about repairing the damage to the Apache gun.

The grips were taken off and the oval nut and counter-bored washer removed. One grip was then screwed to a flat piece of wood about 1½″ by ½″ by 8″ long to serve as a comfortable handle with which to hold the grip firmly. A countersunk screw was used which allowed the head to lie in the recess well below the surface, leaving the whole of the checkered side accessible for filing.

Starting at the edge of the flattened portion, the surface was worked over with a medium-cut flat file until it showed a continuous curve and the flat had disappeared.

This, of course, considerably spread the area over which the checkering was affected, but now the diamonds where the flat had been were more than half gone and the tops of the surrounding diamonds were filed away by a progressively diminishing amount until they merged into the undamaged pattern.

The next stage called for patient and accurate work. It consisted of filing into the grooves until they reached the original depth, again creating the diamond pattern. No great skill was required as the bottoms of the grooves were there to act as guides. The second grip was similarly treated and afterwards both were lightly rubbed down with the finest grade of sandpaper to soften the sharp edges of the newly cut checkering, and then stained and polished. When the grips were replaced, no sign of the damage was apparent. *Plate 49* shows one of the grips fixed to the temporary wood handle and the grooves being filed.

Provided the fibres of the wood have not been broken, dents in a stock may sometimes be partially or wholly removed by the use of wet newspaper and a hot iron. The paper, soaked and made into a pad of about a dozen layers, is laid over the dent and the iron applied to generate steam. Frequently inspect the mark to see how the treatment is taking effect, and move the pad about to bring new wet areas into contact.

This method is quickly effective on softwood and will raise a dent in a minute or two, but hard old walnut will not respond so quickly and the dent may not be entirely eliminated. Also the wood would need to be repolished where the steaming process had been applied.

Experimenting on scrap material will help the worker to decide whether this treatment is worth while. He may, like myself, not be unduly worried by a few minor scars on a veteran firearm. It is only in very special circumstances that a complete stock should be cleaned down to the wood and refinished. If the stock has, say, been badly varnished, or even painted, I agree that it is reasonable to scrape, sandpaper, and stain and polish it again, not forgetting to "whisker".

Repeated applications of raw linseed oil on unpolished wood, persistently rubbed in over long periods, give a fine finish, but this process necessitates a good deal of time and energy. Gunsmiths sell special preparations which give a good finish much more easily, and there are the home-applied french polishes which I have found satisfactory when used according to the manufacturers' instructions. A good wax polish repeatedly applied also looks well.

I have referred to a stock which had actually been painted—green, of all colours and, believe it or not, I was once offered an old Colt which had been entirely *chromium plated*!

CHAPTER TEN

BARREL OBSTRUCTIONS

WHENEVER I acquire a new firearm, one of the first things I do is to measure the distance the ramrod will go down the barrel to see whether it is clear down to the vent. Occasionally it will be found that there is something there, usually occupying the last inch or two at the breech. It may, however, be stopped at any point, even near the muzzle, and one cannot be sure whether the barrel is full to that point or whether the obstruction is local. Most collectors will agree with me that if there is an obstruction, whatever it is, it ought to come out. *Plate 50* shows a number of tools for dealing with obstructed barrels.

No. 1 is a double-thread worm used to grip wads, paper, cloth or any other soft packing. These are sold in several sizes with a threaded boss to attach to a rod of suitable length for the job in hand.

No. 2 is a home-made version of No. 1 made from a piece of $\frac{1}{2}''$ outside diameter by $\frac{3}{8}''$ bore steel tube. Two spiral cuts were made starting from opposite sides of the tube, the angle of the cuts being such that the width of the resultant prongs was about $\frac{1}{8}''$, each cut making about one complete turn round the tube. The prongs were drawn out with the round-nose pliers until they assumed the shape shown in the photograph. A little file work on the points and raw edges put the finishing touches to a perfectly efficient tool. The completed worm was cut off leaving about 1" of plain tube which was pressed on to the reduced end of a 3 ft. length of $\frac{1}{2}''$ wood dowel and secured by two 3/32" copper rivets. The points of the prongs should be led in by turning in a clockwise direction and the movement maintained while withdrawing the obstruction. The tool would be equally efficient if the prongs had a counter-clockwise lead-in.

No. 3 is an old bullet extractor from a cased gun. This also has a double thread and there is a brass cap which fits over the screw when not in use.

No. 4 is my own version of No. 3. It is an ordinary No. 10 steel wood screw, 1¼″ long with the head cut off and welded on to the end of a 5/16″ iron rod. Before welding, the screw was centred in a ¼″ deep hole in the rod end, and it is used in conjunction with drill No. 5.

No. 5 is a ⅛″ twist drill welded to a piece of 5/16″ iron rod. It is used to make a preparatory hold to facilitate the entry of the screw into a lead bullet. Again a hole was drilled in the end of the rod ¼″ deep and of the same diameter as the shank of the drill to locate it before welding.

While, for this particular purpose, it does not really matter if the drill loses some of its hardness, bronze welding or brazing, which works at a lower temperature, is recommended.

The handles necessary for these tools may be short lengths of smaller diameter rod driven through holes, as in the case of nipple keys (see *Plate 11*). Alternatively, a cut may be sawn down the end of the rod and a piece of mild steel strip inserted crosswise and secured by a rivet. I used ½″ by 1/16″ mild steel strip about 2½″ long. To make the 1/16″ wide slots to receive these, two blades were used side by side in the hack-saw.

To keep the leading point of the drill central in the bore of the gun, a hole was made, using the drill itself, down a piece of hardwood dowel about ¾″ long and 1/16″ less in diameter than the bore. This was pushed over the drill until stopped by the rod, and is shown in position in the photograph. It can be tipped out should it be left behind when the drill is withdrawn, which is the reason for making it a slack fit in the bore.

Patience is needed to put a ⅛″ drill through a lead bullet, making half a turn at a time while pressing down on the tool. Occasionally it will bind in the lead and have to be freed by reversing and withdrawing.

Before starting the drill into the bullet, make a mark on the rod about ½″ clear of the muzzle, so that progress can be judged; when the mark is level with the muzzle, the drill should be withdrawn and the screw inserted.

In general, lead balls can be extracted fairly easily, but there are occasions when nothing seems to go right. As soon as the drill has nicely entered the ball, it begins to twist round with the drill. You withdraw the drill, and if the ball comes with it, well and good. If it stays behind, you try to grip the thing with the screw. It comes half-way up the barrel and then falls off and settles in the breech with the partly drilled hole across the bore. You start again, with the same exasperating result.

No. 6 on *Plate 50* is a tool I made to deal with a situation of this kind. A fellow collector brought a percussion pistol along which had a ball down in the breech. Measurement showed the front of the ball to be about 1″ in front of the nipple, so we quite logically imagined that the gun might be loaded; actually, there were two balls, one behind the other. He had tried to use an extractor, but the ball turned round in the breech before any grip could be obtained with the screw. It was, in fact, riding on the ball underneath like a spherical bearing and, though it would turn fairly easily, it could not be coaxed along the barrel. Could I suggest any way of getting the bullet out except by removing the breech? I could, and we soon had the ball out.

The method devised was quite simple. The bore of the pistol was just over ½″. A piece of tube ½″ outside diameter and 2″ longer than the barrel was held upright in the vice and, using a triangular file, a series of deep notches were filed around one end, producing a ring of pointed teeth. The inside diameter of the tube was immaterial so long as it would accommodate the 5/16″ rod carrying the drill. There was ample clearance, so a wooden bobbin ½″ long was made to sit on the drill to centre it in the toothed tube. The tube was put down the barrel and given several smart blows with the mallet to bed the points of the teeth in the lead ball.

With the pistol suitably protected and fixed at a convenient angle in the vice, the drill with its centring bobbin was inserted down the tube. Holding the projecting tube end in pliers with one hand and keeping it tight against the ball to prevent it rotating, the drill was pressed in and turned, and in a few minutes it was drilled through.

Still keeping the ball gripped with the tube, the screw was then turned into the hole and the ball pulled out without any difficulty, bringing the tube with it. The second ball, which occupied the space where we thought there might have been powder, was extracted in the same way. *Plate 51* shows the simple arrangement adopted, using a pistol of similar proportions set up for illustration purposes.

Here is an amusing story of the behaviour of a lead ball in a barrel. I have a pistol with a screw-off, smooth-bore cannon barrel, in the breech of which I keep a ball to show the method of breech loading. The bore is slightly chambered at the breech to accommodate the bullet which should be a driving fit for the rest of the bore.

On one occasion, when I had screwed off the barrel to demonstrate this arrangement, the ball, which was on the small side, had slightly entered the bore proper. I held the barrel, breech down, and struck the muzzle with a mallet, but the ball did not drop out. After several more blows without result, I looked at the breech end and was surprised to see that the bullet was now half way up the barrel. I turned it round again and continued to strike the muzzle and the ball went on climbing until it appeared at the muzzle. I reversed the barrel and used the mallet on the breech and immediately the ball began to travel upwards and finally came to rest in the breech chamber and dropped out when the barrel was up-ended.

The explanation would seem to be that each time the barrel moved under the blow of the mallet the inertia of the heavy lead ball was sufficient to overcome momentarily the friction between itself and the bore and consequently to move the ball a less distance than the barrel. The degree of tightness in the barrel had to be just right to produce this effect.

The job of clearing the barrel of a pocket pistol is usually fairly easy. Generally, with a short, large-bore barrel the obstruction can be seen even if its nature is not apparent. Probing with a piece of pointed rod (a domestic steel skewer is ideal for the purpose) will indicate whether the surface of the blockage is soft, like paper or rag, semi-hard, like lead, or very hard, like iron or brass.

I had to deal with a "fixed"-barrel pocket pistol of ½" calibre where the breech was blocked for the last inch. The top material was paper, as scraps could be detached with the point of the skewer, so the worm was called for. As the only worm I had at the time was too large to enter the barrel, I used an ordinary corkscrew. This brought out the paper wad and uncovered another object which the probe indicated was very hard and smoothly

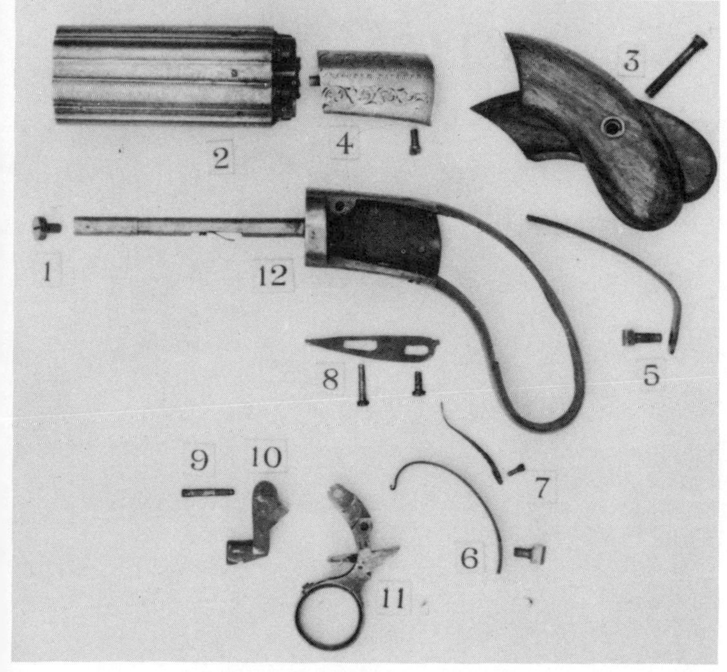

Plate 39. Underhammer pepperbox by Cooper of Birmingham.

Plate 40. Exploded view of the Cooper pepperbox above. The parts are numbered in the order in which they are removed.
1. Barrel block retaining screw. 2. Barrel block with nipples. 3. Wood grips with fixing screw. 4. Side plate with fixing screw. 5. Mainspring with screw. 6. Trigger spring with screw. 7. Spring controlling sliding member with screw. 8. Sliding member which rotates barrels with screws. 9. Pivot screw for hammer and trigger. 10. Hammer. 11. Trigger with catch and spring. 12. Frame with spindle.

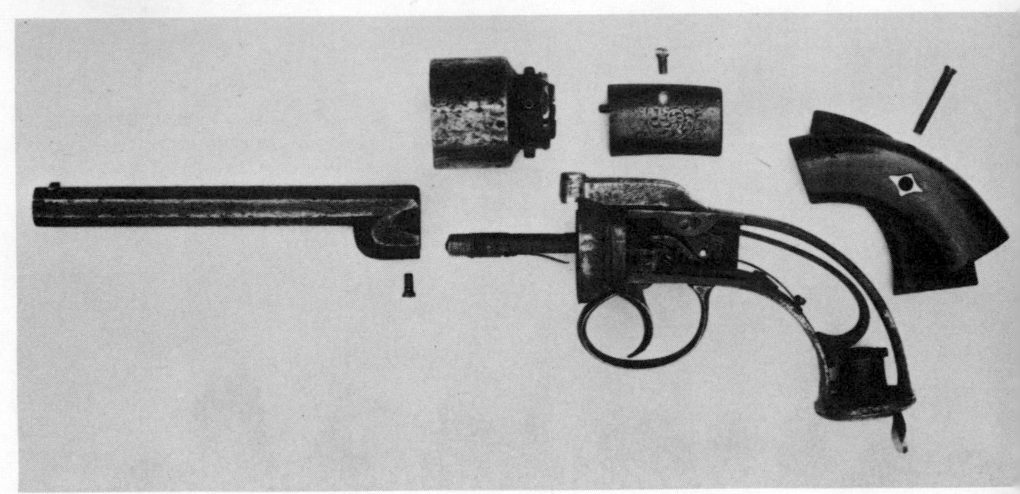

Plate 41. Top: Transition revolver with bar hammer. *Bottom:* The same revolver partly dismantled. The mechanism is very similar in principle to that of the pepperbox (*Plate 40*). The object behind the butt plate is a cap box with hinged spring cover.

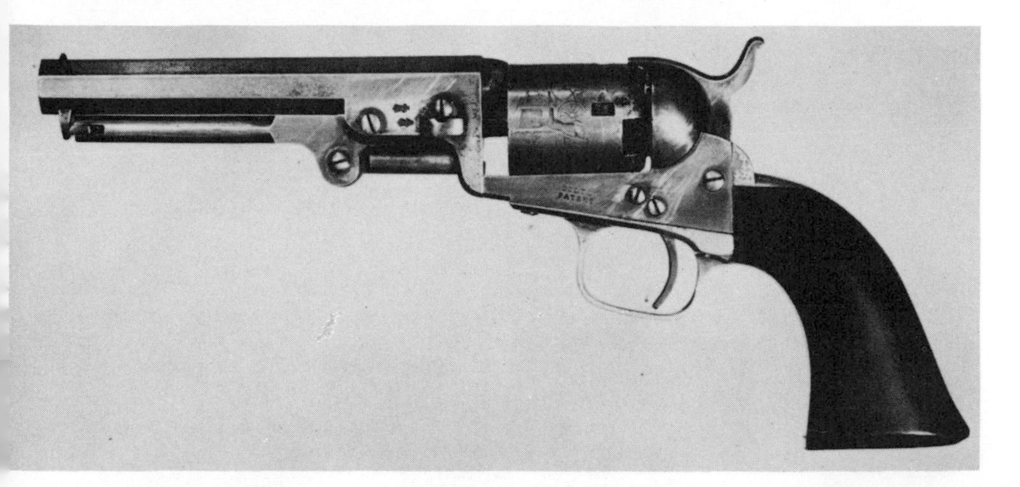

Plate 42. Colt revolver. 5-shot—.31 cal.

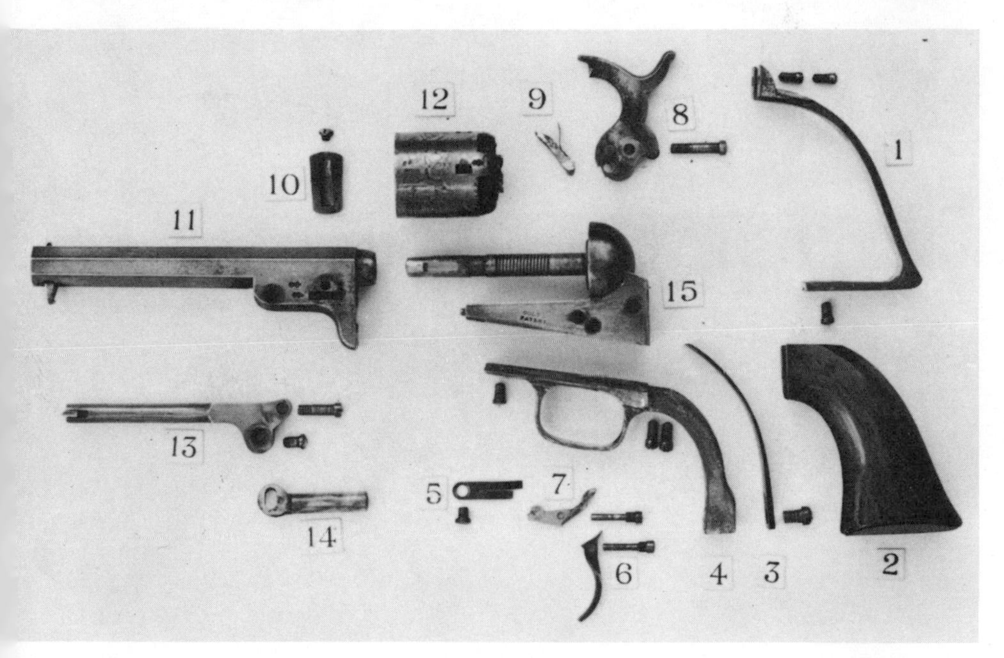

Plate 43. Exploded view of Colt revolver above. The parts are numbered in the order in which they are removed.

1. Butt strap with fixing screws. 2. Stock. 3. Mainspring with fixing screw. 4. Trigger guard with fixing screw. 5. Double sear spring with fixing screw. 6. Trigger with pivot screw. 7. Bolt with pivot screw. 8. Hammer with pivot screw. 9. Hand with spring (which rotates cylinder). 10. Wedge with retaining screw (which fixes barrel). 11. Barrel. 12. Cylinder with nipples. 13. Loading lever with spring catch and pivot screws. 14. Rammer. 15. Frame with spindle.

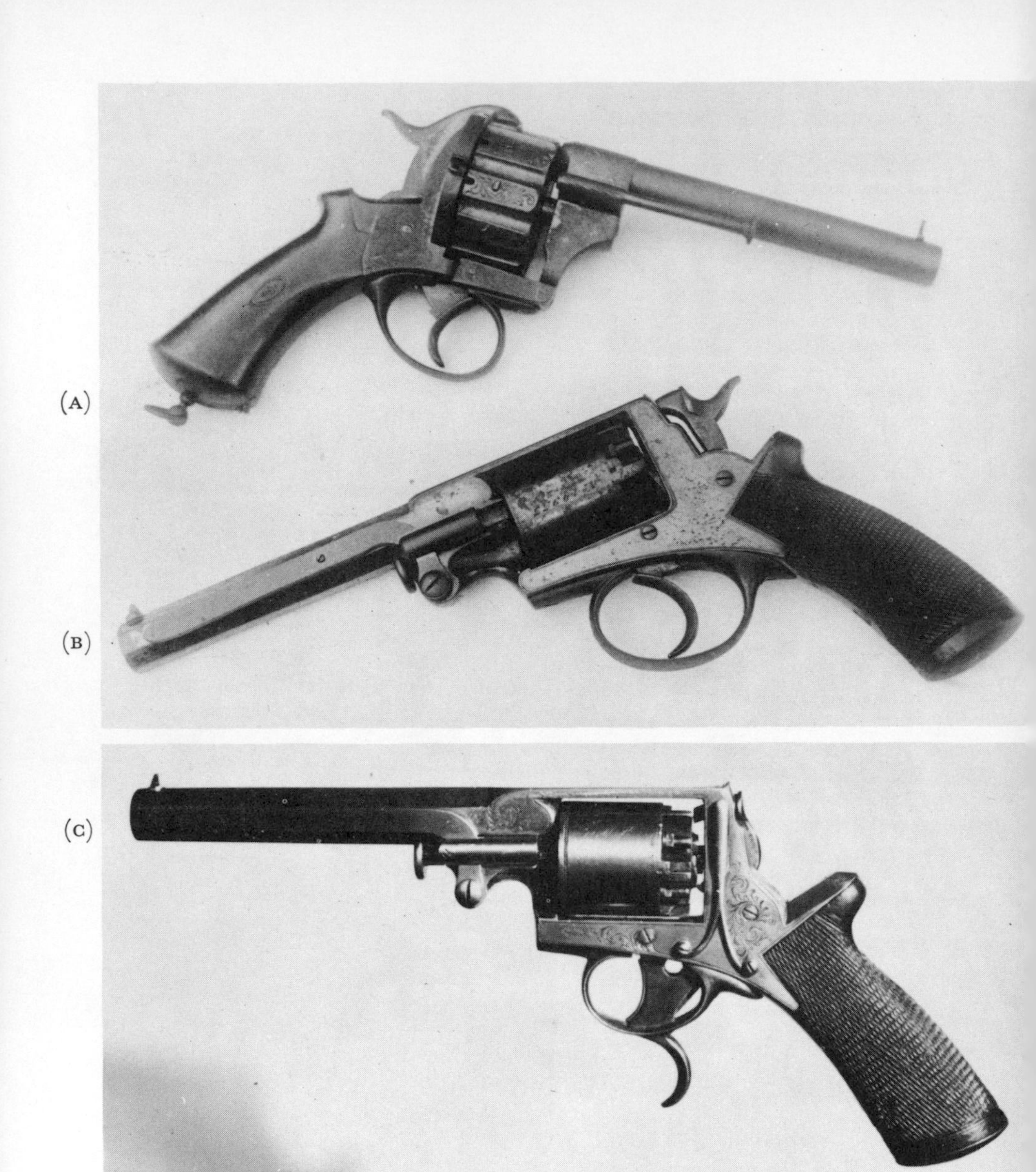

Plate 44

Top: Le Faucheux revolver. 10 shot. 12 m/m cal.
Centre: Adams revolver. 5 shot. .44 cal.
Bottom: Tranter double trigger revolver. 5 shot. .44 cal.

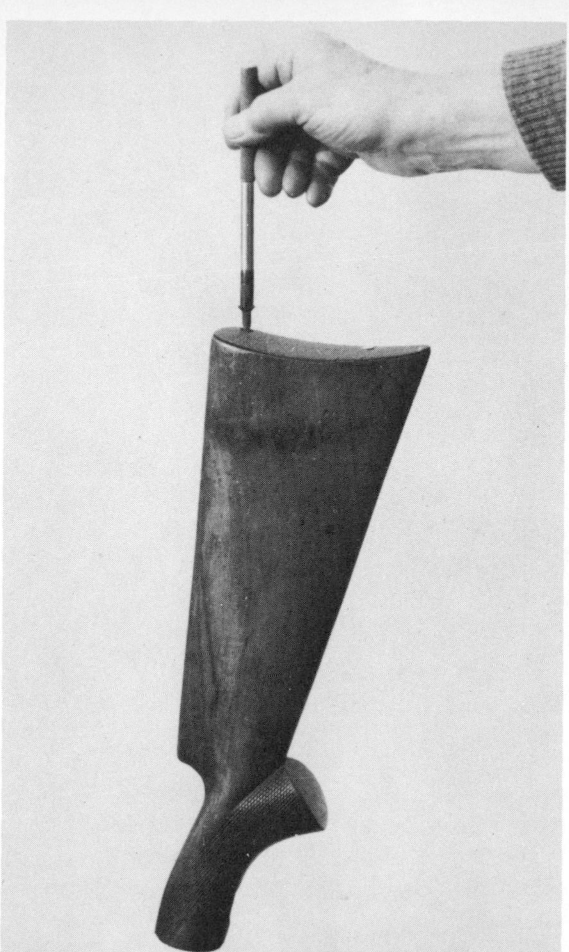

Plate 45.

Screw-holder used for removing wood-screws from stripped holes. The tool firmly grips the sides of the slot in the screw head without marking it. The walnut gun-stock is suspended by the grip of the tool in the slot.

Plate 46.

Pegs fixed in vice to hold revolver cylinder when removing stiff nipples.

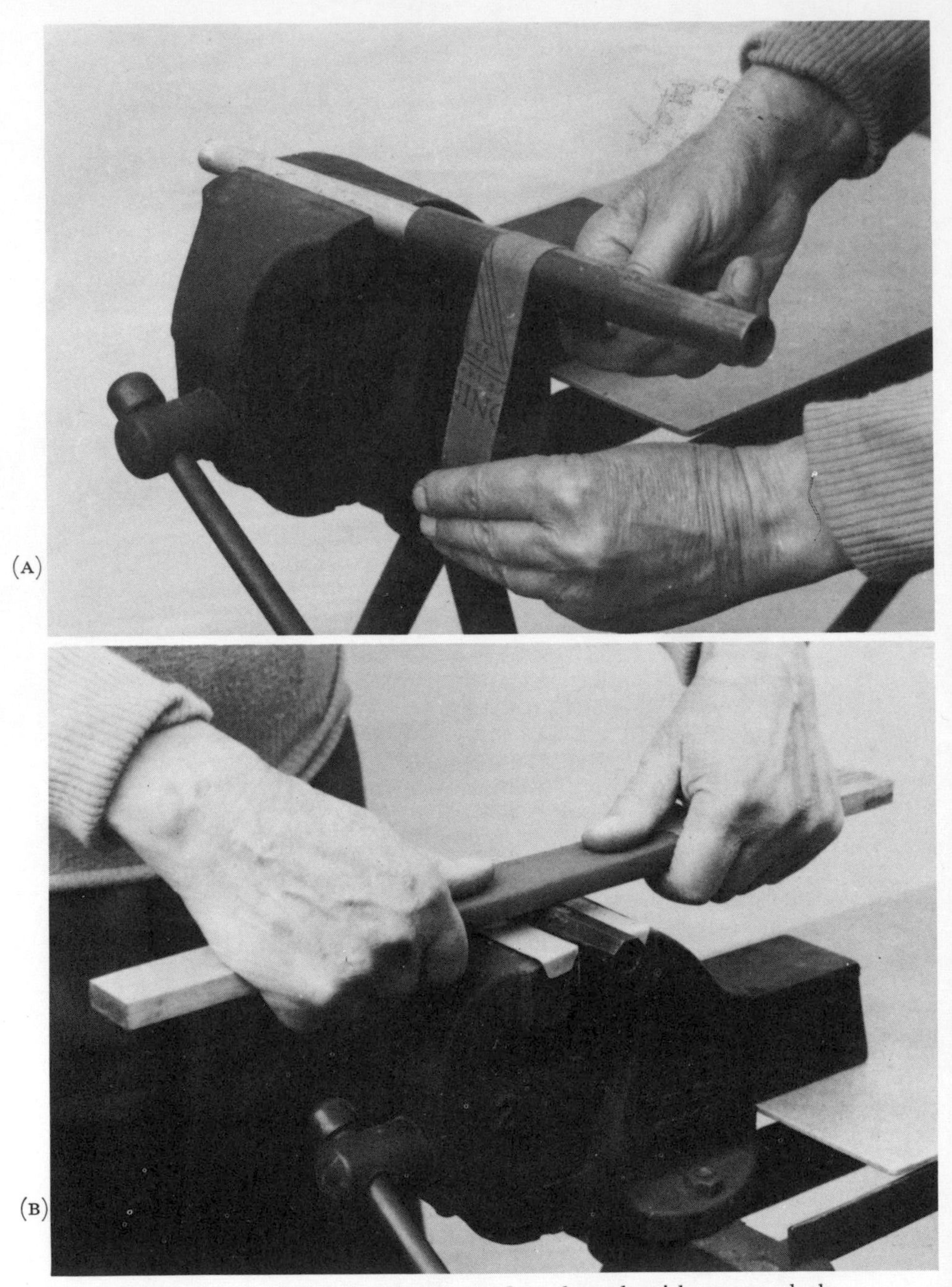

(A)

(B)

Plate 47. Removing deep rust from barrels with emery cloth.
Top: Round barrel on wood rod clamped in vice. *Bottom:* Octagonal barrel in vice with smooth jaw covers.

rounded. Pointing the muzzle downward and tapping it with a mallet, which will occasionally dislodge an obstruction, had no effect, so I decided to unscrew the barrel.

First two centrepunch dots were made close together on the underside, one on the breech and one on the barrel, to locate the final position of the barrel when replaced. The flat-sided box or breech, suitably protected, was clamped in the vice with the barrel projecting vertically. The round barrel was wiped over with petrol to remove any oil, and then tightly wrapped midway with enough turns of insulation tape to form a covering about 3/16″ thick for a length of about an inch.

A long pair of adjustable grips with curved serrated jaws was then applied and used like a spanner with the serrations squeezed down into the tape. The arrangement is shown on *Plate 52*. After a short initial movement while the grips were bedding down and tightening the tape, the barrel began to turn and was then easily screwed off.

With the barrel detached, the obstruction was knocked through the breech by using a piece of brass rod. It was a small stone with some sand behind it; apparently some youngster had amused himself by pretending to load the pistol.

In a case of this kind the tape should be wound round the barrel in a counter-clockwise direction when looking down on the muzzle, so that, when the outer layers are gripped and unscrewing pressure applied, the binding will tend to tighten. If the barrel is very tight, two wrappings can be made and two pairs of grips applied from opposite sides, and both hands used.

In another short-barrel pistol a lead bullet had been hammered down and tightly jammed in the bore. This was drilled out with a ½″ twist drill clamped in a joiner's brace. It may reasonably be stated that it is not good workshop practice to use a round parallel drill in a chuck designed to take a taper square shank, but I can only reply that it works and, if one is careful, the chuck will not be damaged.

With a long-barrel pistol or shoulder arm the tools have to be mounted on rods of adequate length. First remove the barrel from the stock for convenience of handling. Using the worm, get out any soft packing. If the solid obstruction is a bullet, a few scraped splinters of lead may come out after the worm has been used. Hold the barrel upright, breech upwards, and strike the muzzle twenty or thirty times with the rubber mallet. Check the position of the obstruction with the ramrod and, if it has started to move, continue, and it may come to the muzzle and fall out. If not, use the extracting screw on its rod and you will probably bring it out without much difficulty.

If it is definitely known that there is no powder behind a bullet, and the original finish of the barrel has gone, it is possible, by applying heat to the breech, to melt a bullet and let it run out, but never do this with a gun which might have been left charged. I have removed powder from a gun which was known to have been lying away for many years, and it was still active, so no chances should ever be taken.

I have heard it suggested that, if a gun appears to have been left charged and loaded, one might shoot the obstruction out, but it is a method I do not like. The only time I did it was in a basement with the gun in a vice and myself outside the door with a string to the trigger. It was quite successful, but I felt that anyone who was careless enough to leave a firearm permanently loaded might well be capable of charging it with a dangerous overload.

If ordinary methods fail, the collector must decide whether he will leave the obstruction where it is, or get at it by removing the breech plug. As a rule I prefer not to disturb a breech plug which afterwards must be screwed back to its precise former position. However, should it be necessary, it is as well to know how to do it.

The plug has a coarse thread which is screwed into the thickened breech of the barrel for a depth roughly comparable with the diameter of the bore. To afford the necessary grip, it normally has across the back a heavy vertical rib, which at the top extends into a tang with a screw hole for attachment to the stock. The thread is a tight fit and the plug is screwed in extremely firmly to ensure a gas-tight joint under the pressure of the explosion.

The final position of the plug in relation to the barrel as originally determined by the gunsmith is sometimes marked with a punched line across the joint, and the positions of sights, vent or nipple and any barrel-eyes for fixing-pins or keys are all accurately located relative to the position of the tang. The plug, therefore, should not be removed unless it is really necessary.

If you do decide to take it out, make suitable tackle to hold the barrel and to grip the plug very firmly. If not already indicated, mark the position of the plug by punch marks exactly opposite to one another on the plug and on the barrel.

Plate 53 shows a long gun barrel clamped between wood blocks and a long home-made spanner in position on the breech plug. In the case of a round parallel barrel the wood clamping-pieces are prepared by boring a hole the same diameter as the barrel through a block of hardwood which is then sawn in two to leave a semi-circular channel in each piece. The channels are coated with powdered resin and the barrel, free from any trace of grease, is tightly clamped up. If the part of the barrel to be clamped is of octagon section, the hole should be drilled undersize and chiselled to an octagon shape to fit the barrel.

The barrel shown in the photograph was tapered at the breech, the hole in the wood block being bored to clear the greater diameter. Insulation tape was wrapped round the barrel until a parallel surface was obtained to spread the grip of the wood clamps over their full area. The proportion of the wood grips can be judged from the photograph. The maximum diameter of the barrel was 1 1/16" and the wood block, before being cut in two, was 2" by 2" by $4\frac{1}{2}$". The block will be seen to be longer than necessary, but the piece of wood of that length was there. There was no point in reducing its size, though a shorter block would have served the purpose.

For some reason the gripping projections on breech plugs are seldom made with parallel sides and therefore will not take an ordinary adjustable spanner, so a wrench with a slot to fit has to be made for the particular plug which is to be dealt with. This can be made from a piece of iron or steel strip $1\frac{1}{4}$" by 3/16" bv about 18" to 20" long. With the slot in the middle, both hands can be used to apply the pressure. The shape of the slot should be set out with a steel scriber and a row of holes drilled almost touching and progressively diminishing in size, to take out as much metal as possible. (Here is where the electric hand-drill will save time and hard work.) With a round file clear the webs between the holes until a thin flat file can be introduced and the slot finished to the scribed outline.

The wrench shown in the photograph was made up from a fitting which I had in my scrap box. While it gives the necessary leverage, I would recommend the double-ended tool described as being more convenient.

The breech plug illustrated was very stubborn but, after repeated applications of penetrating oil and several heatings with the blow-lamp, it finally came out. The obstructions were driven out at the breech by a long rod from the muzzle end.

This barrel was no less than 55″ long and I had found an obstruction, which I could not move, lodged, as I thought, about a foot from the breech. When the plug was out, the barrel was found to be packed solid for the last foot with a collection of odds and ends of which some pieces of pencil, a small key and a glass marble offered the most stubborn resistance. It took quite a time to get the barrel clear.

Given a sufficiently tight grip on the barrel, and with a long enough leverage on the wrench to apply adequate turning pressure, the most stubborn breech plug should come out but, if it cannot be moved by the method described, I would suggest that it be left where it is. I once tried to extract a breech plug without success and finally found that, in addition to being screwed in, a substantial rivet had been put sideways through plug and barrel.

When replacing a breech plug the most important point is to ensure that it is screwed back to the precise position which it occupied before removal. A close approximation will not do. The locating line or centre punch marks must match up exactly.

One sometimes finds bullets in percussion-revolver cylinders, particularly in cased specimens where the bullet mould or stock of bullets were ready to hand and someone felt that he must test the action of the lever rammer. These can usually be knocked out with a piece of rod through the nipple hole but, in some old revolvers like the transition type and pepper-boxes with radial nipples, one must drill and extract with a screw.

CHAPTER ELEVEN

BROKEN SPRINGS; MISSING HAMMERS AND SIGHTS

WE have considered in some detail the cleaning and adjustment of antique firearms, the methods of dealing with rust, stubborn screws and some minor repairs, and the collector who has successfully carried out renovations on these lines should be feeling confident to handle the more intricate work of actually making some replacement parts.

It would not be practicable, in a single book, to cover every kind of problem which might confront the restorer, but I shall describe some typical examples which I have dealt with on firearms that have come my way.

Collectors usually consider it a matter of importance that the lock of an old firearm should function properly, but the lock is very vulnerable. One may acquire a gun where wear on the sear or tumbler notches has put the half-cock or full-cock setting out of action; where the mainspring or, less frequently, one of the other springs is broken, or where the top jaw and cock screw, or even the whole hammer, of a flint gun is missing. Take the case of the worn sear and tumbler first.

The experienced collector can usually detect the amount of wear on these parts by feel and sound, without removing the lock for visual inspection. Draw the hammer slowly back, and if the notches and sear nose are unworn, the sear nose, when it reaches the lip of the half-cock notch, will drop with a sudden sharp snap.

When the pressure is taken off the spur it will move back by, perhaps, $\frac{1}{8}$" and the trigger will be rendered inoperative. If the cocking of the hammer is slowly continued until the full-cock position is reached, the sear nose will again fall into position with a clean snap and the hammer will remain without any return motion when relieved of the cocking pressure. A firm, smooth pull on the trigger of about 4 lb should release the hammer. If this test is satisfactory, the action may be taken as being in sound condition.

If, however, the half-cock position is indicated by a dull click and there is little or no movement when the thumb pressure is taken off; if, also, a sharp pull on the trigger releases the hammer from half cock or the hammer will hardly hold at full cock and falls at the lightest touch of the trigger; then the action is badly worn and requires attention.

Before dismantling the lock remove the mainspring so that the action can be manipulated without danger of trapping the fingers. If the hammer will not stay safely at full cock to hold the main-spring closed while putting on the hand-vice, tie or wedge it back until the spring is taken out.

With the mainspring out, the movements of the hammer, sear and tumbler may be studied unhindered. *Fig. 16* shows a typical sear and tumbler as they should be, and also as they are frequently found when badly worn.

At (A) in the drawing the tumbler (1) is represented in the position it occupies when the hammer has fallen with the nose of

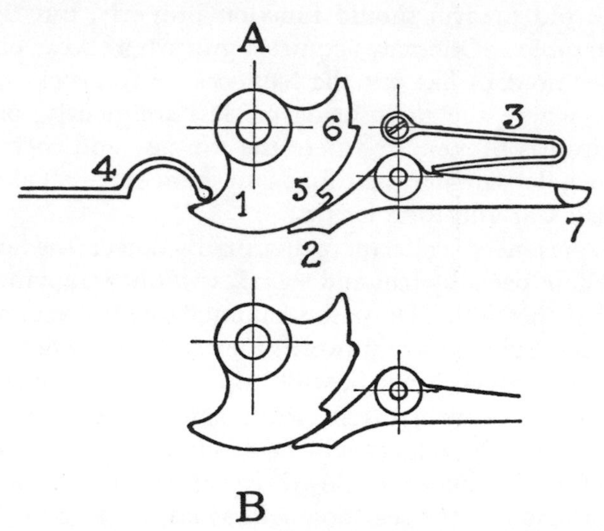

Figure 16. Wear on tumbler and sear.

A. Correct shape of nose of sear and notches in tumbler.
B. Shows effect of excessive wear at these points.

sear (2) idle and resting on the smooth part of the face of the tumbler with which it is held in contact by the pressure of the sear spring (3).

The end of the mainspring (4) is shown exerting a downward force in front of the tumbler and trying to turn it in a counter-clockwise direction; but the movement is checked by the hammer which has been stopped at the end of its fall.

Cocking the hammer turns the tumbler clockwise against the power of the mainspring until the sear nose rides over the lip of the half-cock notch (5) and enters the slot as thumb-pressure on the hammer spur is released. As this slot is undercut, the sear nose cannot be disengaged by pressing on the trigger.

Further cocking of the hammer brings the step (6) round until it reaches the end of the sear nose which springs behind it and holds the hammer at full cock, until released by the lifting action of the trigger on the tail of the sear (7).

Fig. 16 (B) shows the rounded sear nose and notches much as they would be found in a defective action due to excessive wear and which would need to be reshaped in line with those at (A).

The sear and tumbler in some common locks will be found to be of relatively soft metal, which is one reason for their worn condition, and in these cases careful work with the fine Swiss files will put them back into efficient working order. In most good-class locks, however, these fittings will be sufficiently hard to resist the file.

Bringing the parts to a dull red heat in the flame of the blow-lamp for a minute will soften them sufficiently for the file to bite. The corners and faces can then be trimmed to the angles shown at (A). The miniature hack-saw or a small knife file is useful for shaping the half-cock recess.

Try to reduce the hardness of the metal by the minimum amount to render it workable. Personally, I do not re-harden, as future wear will be negligible, although, when I made a new tumbler from mild steel, I had it professionally case-hardened.

Re-shaping the sear nose and tumbler notches will slightly advance the position of the hammer at half and full cock by perhaps $\frac{1}{8}''$ but, unless this has been done several times before, it is of no consequence.

Broken Springs. I have, once or twice, adapted a flat spring to a revolver by grinding, but I do not make springs. The firms who supply antique gun parts can provide most types of springs of the exact pattern for many of the common makes of firearms, or near enough to be adaptable to less standardised weapons. It might be necessary to drill a new hole in the lock plate to receive the locating peg, but this is a simple matter.

Keep any broken lock springs as, apart from being useful as patterns for replacement purposes, the parts can sometimes be adapted for use elsewhere. For instance, I had a carbine with a patch box in the stock. The spring which held the cover in the open-and-shut position was broken but, on removing the hinge plate, I found the parts still lying in the recess underneath. It was a straight flat spring with a hooked end just like the bottom half of a flint-lock mainspring, and my box of old spares produced the half of a broken flint-lock spring. After a little trimming on the grinder it fitted exactly.

MISSING OR INCOMPLETE HAMMERS

The cock screw and top jaw are sometimes missing from flint-lock guns. Apart from the ramrod, these are the two most easily detachable parts of a flint gun which may have been removed for some reason in the past, or broken, and never replaced.

Making a cock screw is a fairly simple turning job, but the man without a lathe can order both screw and jaw from the antique-parts suppliers. If, however, the worker can make the cock screw or have it made locally, he may as well make the top jaw himself. In fact, he may have no alternative if it is of unusual pattern.

Fig. 17 shows the sequence of operations in making a top jaw for a flint hammer. If a duplicate of the gun concerned is available, an accurate dimensioned sketch could be made but, failing this, the style and proportion will largely be governed by the design of the body of the hammer.

The example given in the drawing was made for a holster pistol of the type shown on *Plate 30*. The width of the lower jaw was 11/16″ and the maximum thickness of a similar size top jaw on a comparable pistol was 7/32″. Taking a 6″ length of $\frac{3}{4}$″ by $\frac{1}{4}$″ mild steel strip, I coated one end on both sides with colour wash to take a pencil lay-out of the jaw. (*Fig. 17 (A)*.) The diameter of the cock screw hole and the distances from its centre to the front tip of the jaw and the rear flat were measured from the bottom jaw.

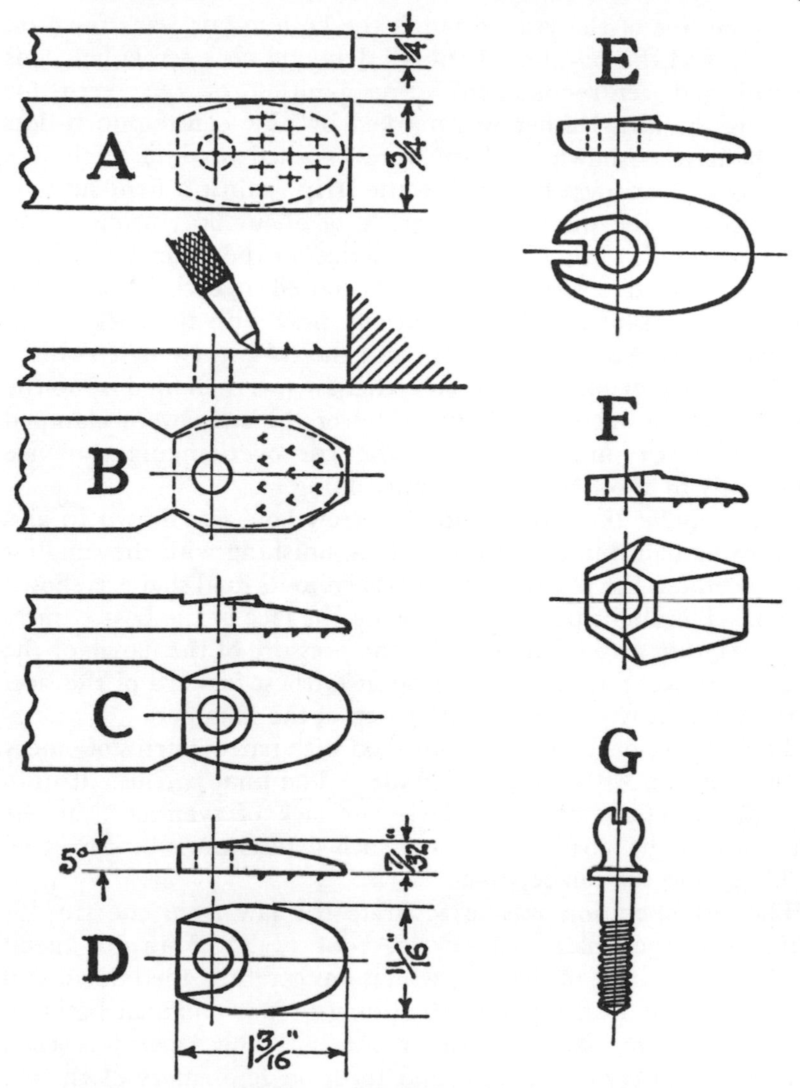

Figure 17. Making a flint top jaw for a flint-lock hammer.

A. Outline of jaw, position of hole for cock screw and centres of teeth set out on underside of steel strip.
B. Cock screw hole drilled, teeth punched up (note angle of centre punch) and surplus metal cut away by hacksaw.
C. Top side of jaw after filing to shape and polishing with emery cloth.
D. Finished jaw cut off the strip.
E, F. Other patterns of top jaws.
G. Typical cock screw.

The outline of the jaw to match the bottom jaw was drawn on the strip and the position of the $\frac{1}{4}''$ diameter cock screw hole was marked and centre-punched. The position of the teeth for gripping the flint leather was marked by nine centre-punch dots in a pattern as shown. These were knocked up into teeth like those on a wood rasp by placing the strip against a firm support and applying the punch at an angle of about 60°, using a 1-lb hammer. (*Fig. 17* (*B*).) A little practice on the other end of the strip will enable a sharp tooth to be raised at each blow of the hammer. Surplus metal was next cut away with the hack-saw to the rough shape as shown at (B), and the cock screw hole drilled. With the strip gripped in the vice, the jaw was then filed up to the correct outline, after which the sides of the strip were clamped with the teeth underneath and the jaw overhanging the vice sufficiently to allow free action when filing.

The shape of the boss round the screw hole was drawn in and then, using half-round and round files, finishing with the smallest and smoothest, the jaw was worked down to its final shape as shown at (C). The slight backward slope on the face of the boss ensures the maximum grip of the flint by the pressure of the flange of the cock screw being applied at the point farthest forward of the heel of the top jaw, which rests on the step of the hammer.

The top face of the jaw was polished with narrow strips of emery cloth, finishing with the finest grade. The final polish will indicate by reflection any irregularity or lack of symmetry in the curvature of the surfaces, and any such defects must be corrected by filing, and the job repolished.

The last operation was to separate the jaw from the surplus strip, using the small hack-saw. About 1/32″ of surplus metal was left at the back of the jaw, which was carefully filed down and repeatedly tested until a smooth sliding fit was obtained between the flats on the jaw and the hammer. The back was then smoothed by drawing it back and forth on fine emery cloth laid on a flat board, and the jaw was complete as at (D).

If the first attempt to make a top jaw results in failure, possibly through trying to work too quickly, leave it for a day or two and start again. Go more slowly, with patience, until you can produce a job comparable with the best professional work.

Referring again to *Fig. 17*, another type of top jaw is shown at (E) which, instead of a locating flat at the back, has a slot which engages with a narrow comb on the hammer.

The one shown at (F) is from a pistol where both jaws, the underside of the pan and the frizzen were formed with flat faces. The possibility of getting a commercial replacement of this pattern is extremely remote but, after a little practice, this and other variations will not present any great difficulty.

A typical cock screw is shown at (G). The pattern of the heads of these can vary slightly. Sometimes, particularly in the case of military weapons, there is a hole to take the ramrod as a tightening lever in addition to the slot for a screw-driver. The length of plain shank on a cock screw should be equal to the thickness of the top jaw plus not more than $\frac{1}{8}''$.

If the entire flint-lock hammer is missing, it must be considered to be beyond the capacity of the great majority of amateur mechanics to make a new one. The nearest available pattern will have to be ordered from one of the dealers in these gun parts and the necessary adjustments made.

The "throw" or distance from the centre of the hammer boss to the tip of the lower jaw is the key dimension, and the style must be chosen to suit the particular gun. Obviously it would be absurd to put a massive military hammer on a duelling pistol or a delicate swan-neck on a heavy rifle, so send a sketch of what you want (see *Fig. 8*, Chapter 3) and give the fullest particulars of the weapon.

In the case of a percussion hammer the "throw" is measured from the centre of the boss to the centre of the nose which strikes the cap and this dimension should be exact; in the case of flint-ignition a tolerance of 1/16" either way would be of no consequence.

A percussion hammer which is a fraction short or long may possibly be corrected by setting the hole for the tumbler square slightly out of centre in the boss and filing the edge of the boss to make it concentric with the hole. I do not like the trick, but it is worth knowing if it proves impossible to get a hammer of exact size.

I have stated that, unless the gun we are dealing with is a standard, named weapon and hammers are listed specifically for it, the hammer should be ordered without a hole for the tumbler projection. The square hole must be made to suit the particular gun and be a tight fit on the tumbler with the internal sides of the square quite true and at precisely the correct angle.

Assume we are dealing with a flint hammer. Provide a short piece of metal rod—a headless nail will do—which will just fit down the tapped hole for the tumbler screw. Centre-punch the position for the hole in the middle of the outside face of the cock boss, and drill a preliminary hole just large enough to take this piece of rod.

Glue a disc of thick paper to the inside face of the cock boss and pierce it to coincide with the newly drilled hole. Next, carefully select a flint of the right width and of average thickness and length and clamp it in the cock with the flat side uppermost. (Most collectors will recognise the correct proportions of a flint for a particular lock.)

Using a nipple key or a small adjustable spanner, set the tumbler to the half-cock position. Put the piece of rod through the hole in the cock boss and into the tumbler screw hole to act as a temporary pivot for the hammer. Swing the hammer back out of the way and bring the frizzen to the closed position. Bring the hammer forward until the striking edge of the flint is approximately $\frac{1}{8}''$ clear of the frizzen, which is its correct position at half cock.

Take a piece of tube a little longer than the rod and a slack fit over it, and drop it over the rod so that it rests on the hammer boss. A smart but not heavy hammer blow on the end of the tube will impress in the paper the exact position for the square hole. Make a centre-punch mark through the paper very accurately at each corner and, after soaking off the paper, scribe the square in the metal.

The hole must now be drilled out to a size which only just touches the sides of the square. The square hole is then produced by filing. To achieve a tight and true fit will again demand the utmost care and patience. As the hole approaches its final shape and size use a finer file, testing it on the tumbler square after every half-dozen strokes, with the squares in their correct relative position, to allow for any slight wear or irregularity on the tumbler square.

The hammer should be a fairly tight fit on the tumbler and, when tapped home and locked by the tumbler screw, should stand true and parallel to the lock plate without any play, with the centres of the jaws and frizzen in line.

If this desirable state of affairs is achieved at the first attempt, the job is highly satisfactory. However, what is more likely to be found on critical examination is that the hammer has a slight amount of sideways and radial play and perhaps is a trifle askew on the tumbler.

If the defects are really bad I suggest that the square be weld-filled and a new start made; but usually small errors can be rectified fairly easily. Where the plane of the hammer boss is satisfactory but there is play due to imperfect filing, remove the hammer and place it on the anvil with the jaw and spur overhanging the edge so that the boss lies flat.

Using a punch with a flat nose about 3/32" diameter, and a ½-lb hammer, work around the square corners of the hole on both inside and outside faces. Don't strike the punch hard; half a dozen light blows around each corner will probably be all that is necessary. As the metal is compressed it is displaced and reduces the size of the hole until the hammer is a tight fit on the tumbler with all play eliminated.

If it sits slightly askew on the tumbler, careful filing away of surplus metal on one side, combined with tightening up with the punch on the opposite side, will correct or improve this. The punching process can, of course, be used to tighten up an old hammer which, through wear or other causes, has become loose on the tumbler. *Plate 54* shows a hammer being "tightened up".

The procedure is the same for fitting a new percussion hammer except for the method of setting up the tumbler and hammer when determining the position of the square.

In this case the position of the hammer at half cock is not important. The governing condition is that the hammer nose should strike the nipple before it comes to the end of its travel and that, when the nipple is taken out, the hammer should reach the end of its travel before the nose would strike the nipple seating.

To find the appropriate angle of the square, put the tumbler at half cock and remove the nipple. Holding the tumbler square in the spanner or nipple key, operate the trigger and allow the mainspring to turn the tumbler until it is checked by the internal stop.

Assemble the hammer on the locating rod as described before, with the loose tube in place, and set the hammer so that the nose clears the nipple seating by $\frac{1}{8}$″. In this position strike the impression of the square on the paper glued to the inside face of the hammer boss.

The suggested $\frac{1}{8}$″ clearance is for a hammer with a hooded nose recessed to about $\frac{1}{8}$″ deep and a nipple about $\frac{3}{8}$″ high. For a deeply recessed hammer nose or a squat nipple, the clearance might well be reduced to 1/16″.

When the hammer is firmly fitted to the tumbler, it may need to be adjusted to strike true and central. With a flint hammer the flint itself can usually be set to correct any slight error of alignment, but a percussion hammer must be exact and may call for a final setting to make the hammer strike the nipple centrally. To do this, detach the hammer and clamp the boss in the vice with the jaw-covers on. The hammer neck is brought to a dull red heat with the blow-lamp and the necessary adjustment can be made with a pair of pliers.

MISSING SIGHTS

One of my percussion pistols had the front sight missing, but otherwise was in excellent condition. The seating for it was an undercut or dovetail, taper slot across the top flat of the octagon barrel, the back sight being in a similar but parallel slot, allowing lateral adjustment.

A straight-edge laid over the sights of a number of percussion pistols showed a noticeable variation in the relative heights of the front and back sights but, taking the average, the practice appeared to be to set the top of the back sight higher than the tip of the front sight by approximately 1/16″ in 6″.

The back sight of my gun being 3/16″ above the top of the barrel suggested a height for the new front sight of $\frac{1}{8}$″ plus the depth of the slot, which was less than 1/16″. The greatest width of the slot was just under $\frac{1}{4}$″, so a piece of $\frac{1}{4}$″-square mild steel rod about 3″ long was used to make the sight.

Fig. 18 shows the sequence of operations. The square rod was gripped in the vice for about half its length, leaving half overhanging. Two opposite sides of the overhanging piece were filed to an angle to fit the dovetailing of the slot, and also to taper towards the outer end to fit the taper of the slot, as shown at (A).

This is less difficult than it sounds and, if the first attempt is not satisfactory, one can work back along the rod until a perfect fit without any play is obtained when the rod is pushed in by hand.

When this was achieved, the rod was tapped in further until it was really firm. As this was to be its final permanent position,

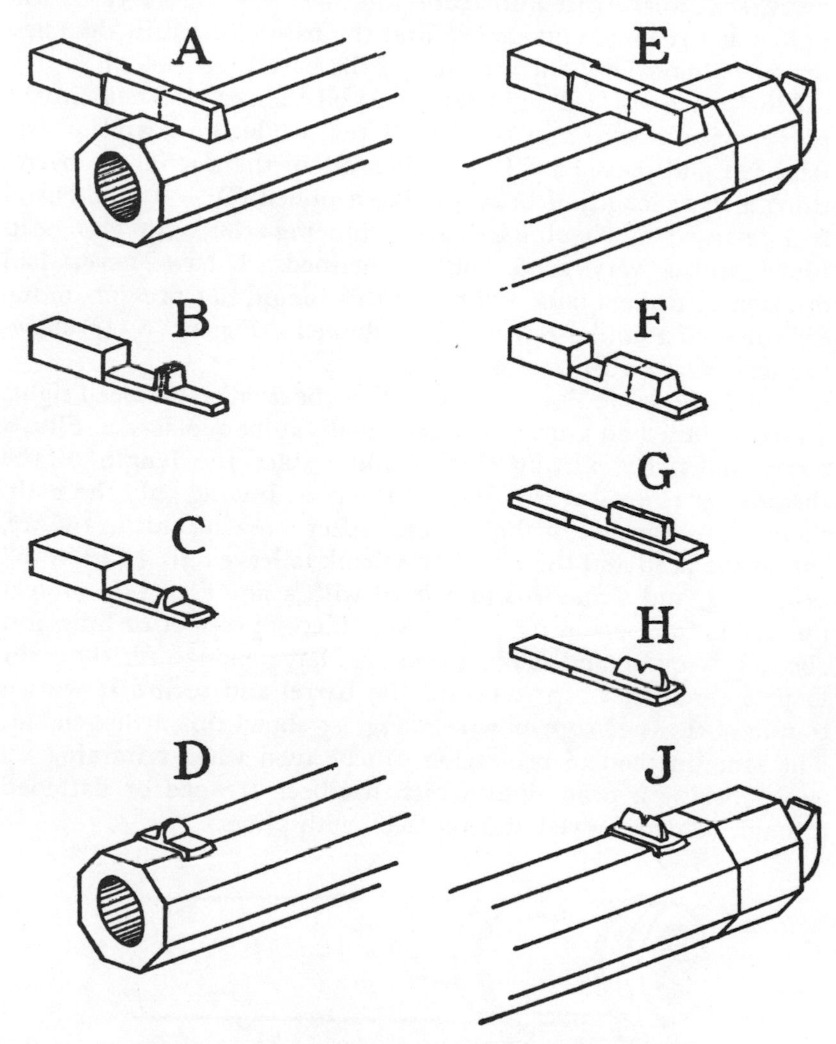

Figure 18. Making sights: sequence of filing operations.
A, B, C, D for front sight. E, F, G, H, J for back sight.

the centre line for the vertical sight itself and the outline of the top and sides of the slot were scribed on both back and front faces of the rod, which was knocked back out of the slot and the sight roughed to shape with file and hack-saw as shown at (B).

The surplus at the narrow end was then sawn off, as at (C) and, by careful work with miniature files and fine emery cloth, the sight was narrowed and shaped and the base reduced in thickness to come almost level with the top of the barrel.

Finally the finished sight was sawn off the rod and held in the hinged vice mounted in the bench vice while the sawn end was trimmed and polished. It was then set in the slot in the barrel using a short length of brass strip as a punch (D). As the barrel had retained much of its original blueing, the sight was heat-blued and a very good match obtained. I have never had occasion to make a back sight, but this should not present undue difficulties if a similar technique is adopted. *Fig. 18* (*E*)–(*J*) shows the suggested sequence of operations.

While discussing sights, we note that the small front bead sights sometimes used on guns have occasionally to be replaced. Find a screw to fit the existing thread and reduce the length of the threaded part until it will just fill the hole, leaving only the plain shank above the face of the barrel. After screwing this in tightly, cut off the head and the top of the shank to leave only $\frac{1}{8}''$ or $3/16''$ projecting, and shape this to a bead with a fine file. To protect the barrel from being marked, take a piece of copper or brass foil about $1\frac{1}{2}''$ square and make a hole just large enough for the sight to pass through; wrap it round the barrel and secure it with a couple of turns of copper wire. *Fig. 19* shows this arrangement. The same method of protection can be used when trimming up and polishing a bead sight which has been scraped or flattened through being removed and replaced with pliers.

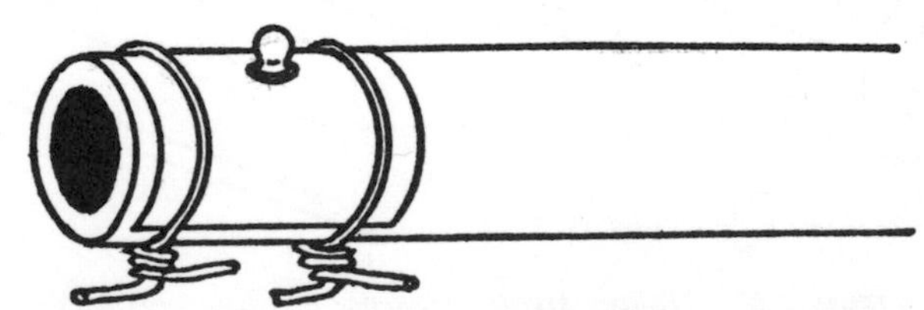

Figure 19. Foil to protect barrel when filing front bead sight.

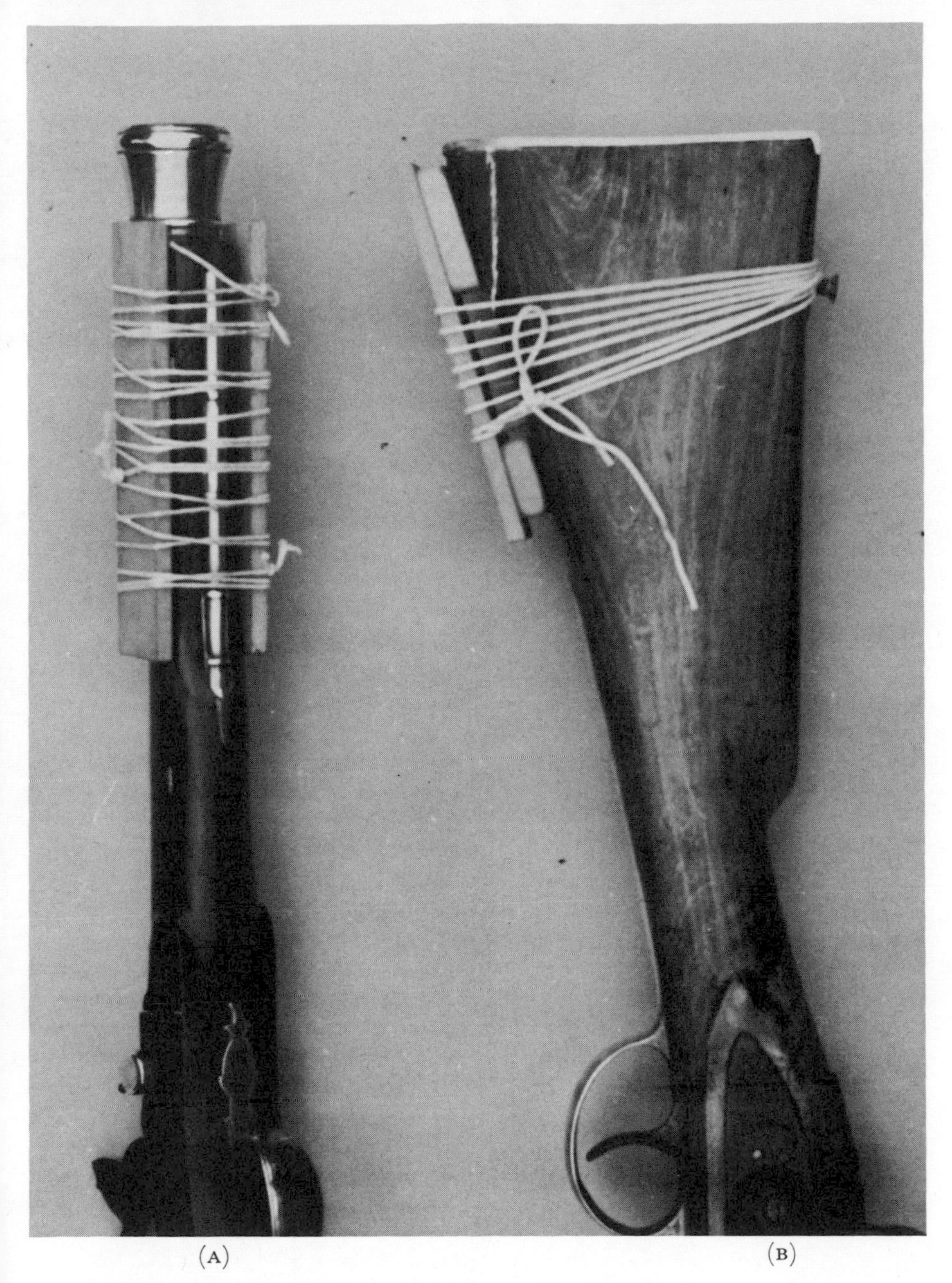

(A) (B)

Plate 48. Repairs to wood stocks.
Left: Blunderbuss stock, split down the ramrod groove. *Right:* Gunstock with piece split off underside of butt (indicated by chalk mark).

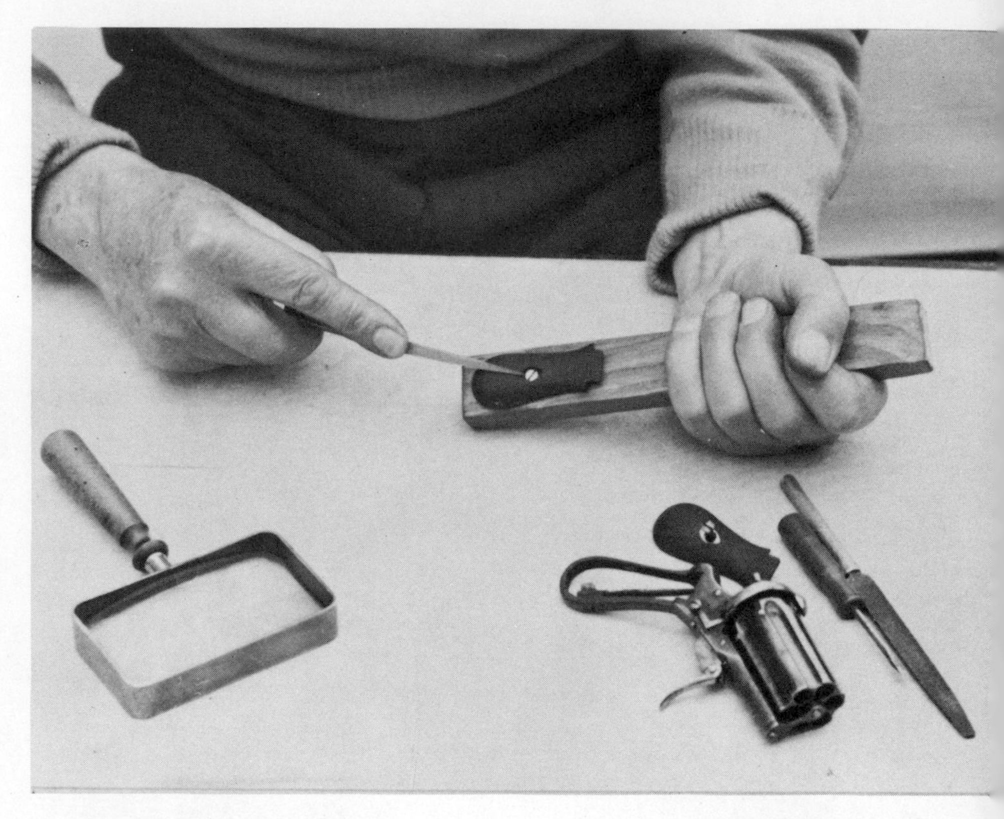

Plate 49. Restoring checkering on the wood grips of a pepperbox revolver.

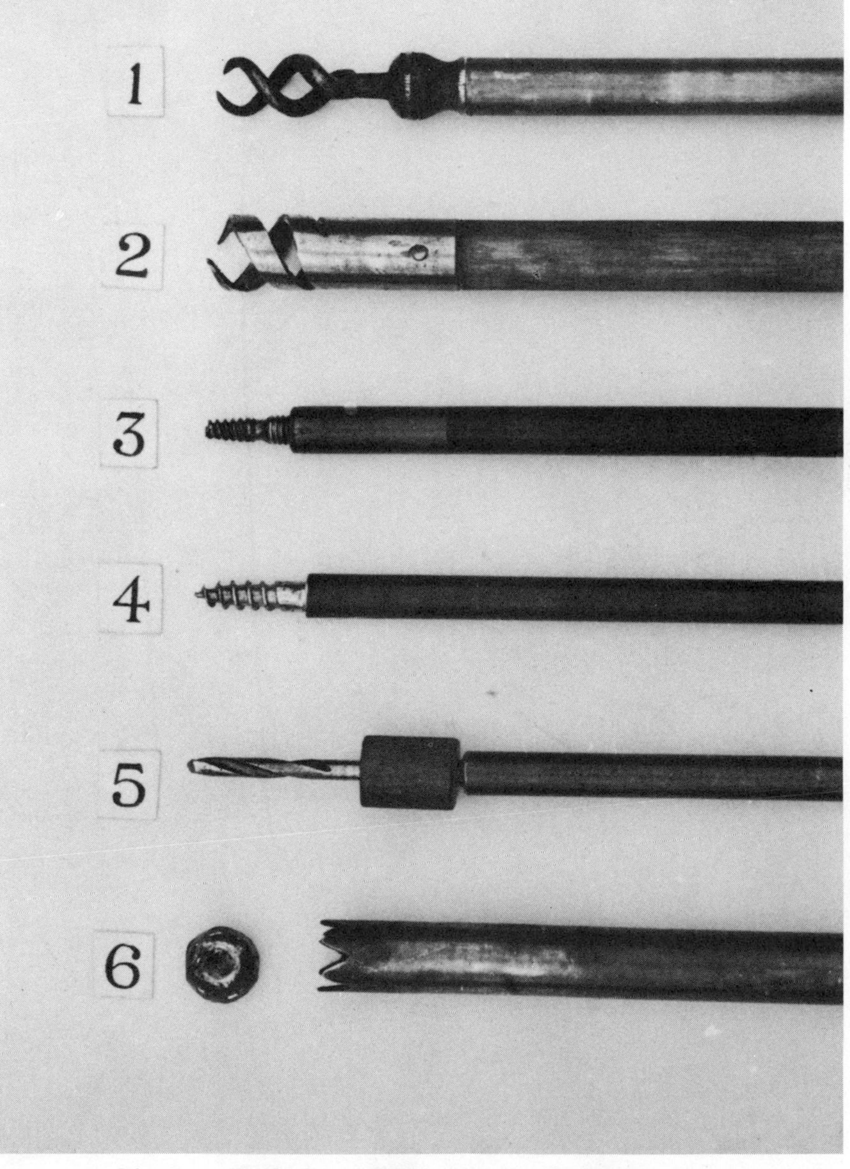

Plate 50. Tools for removing barrel obstructions.
1. Worm for removing wads, paper, etc. 2. Home-made version of No. 1. 3. Bullet extractor. 4. Home-made version of No. 3. 5. Drill with centreing bobbin in position. 6. Tube with tooth end to prevent bullet from turning when Nos. 5 and 4 are being used. *Note.*—Lead ball after extraction.

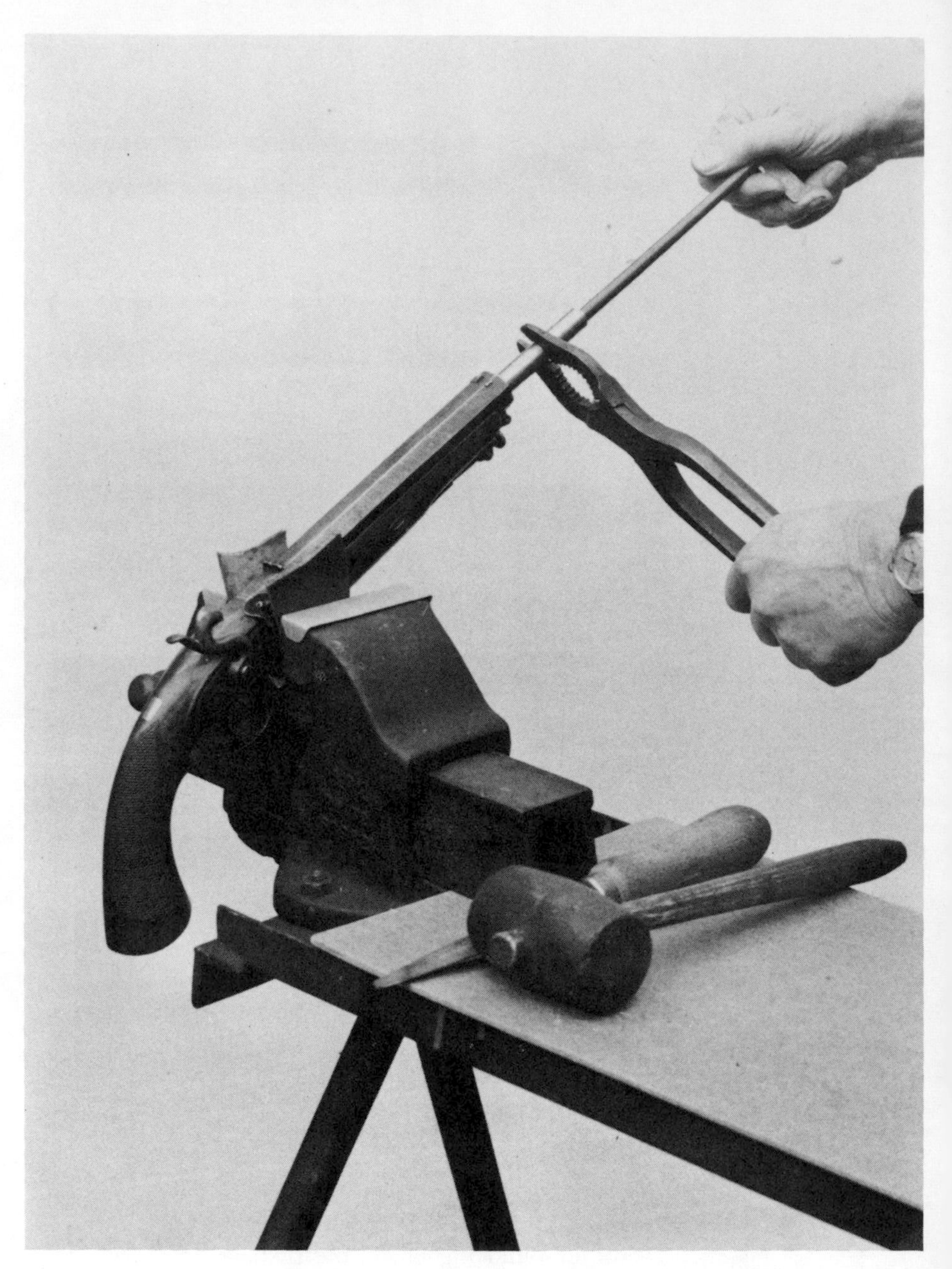

Plate 51. Extracting a lead bullet from a pistol barrel.

Plate 52. Removing a 'fixed' screwed-on barrel of a box-lock pistol to clear an obstruction from the barrel. Note the leather packing between pistol and vice jaws and wrapping of insulation tape around barrel.

Plate 53. Taking the breech plug out of a barrel.

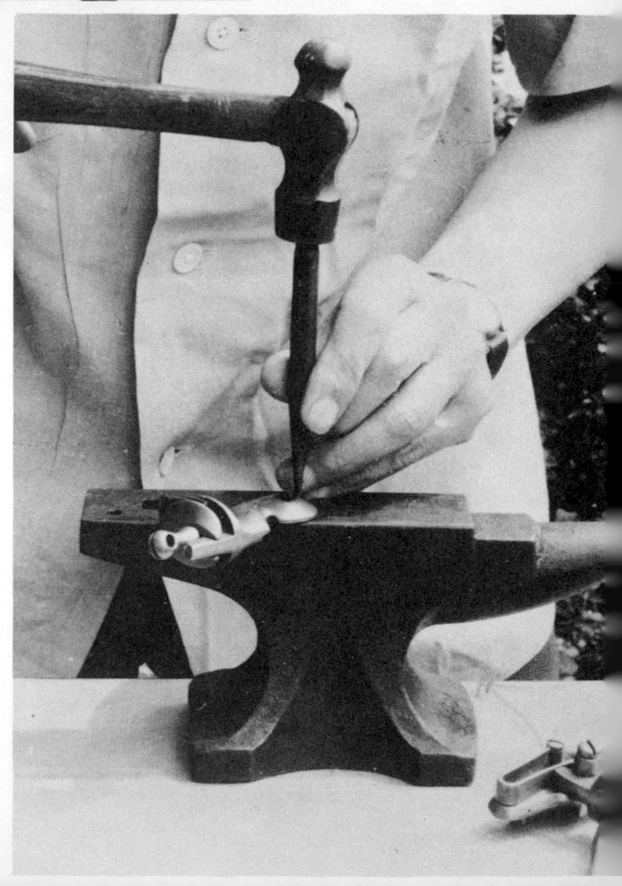

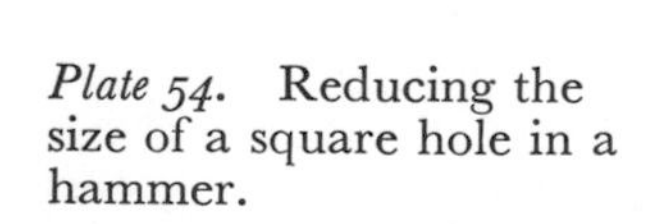

Plate 54. Reducing the size of a square hole in a hammer.

CHAPTER TWELVE

RAMRODS

EXCLUDING the built-in rammers on revolvers and the linked or stirrup ramrods mechanically attached to some pistols, the ordinary straight wooden or iron ramrod carried by muzzle loaders is probably the item most likely to be missing. Even if a gun has one, it may quite likely be a replacement. The ramrod was used for every loading and, during a century or more, could easily be lost or broken. Usually, however, it is not difficult to make a new one.

Plate 55 shows a number of different patterns in wood and metal. *No. 1* shows part of a heavy iron ramrod for a big swivel boat gun tapering from 9/32″ to 7/16″ with a button tip 11/16″ diameter, and it is forged all in one piece.

Nos. 2 and 3 are iron ramrods without taper and with cupped tips to fit the ball. Both are from military type percussion pistols.

No. 4 is an iron captive ramrod from a heavy percussion holster pistol.

No. 5. A brass rod from a flint-lock pistol. This also has a cupped tip.

No. 6 is a long wooden rod from a flint-lock blunderbuss. It has a black horn tip with a slight shoulder where the horn joins the wood.

No. 7. Again a wooden rod from a Customs Officer's brass-barrel flint-lock pistol, also with a black horn tip which merges into the wood in a continuous curve.

No. 8 is another wooden ramrod from a flint duelling pistol, with a flat-faced tip of ivory. I am inclined to think that either the tip or the whole ramrod is a replacement, as ivory seems out of keeping with the otherwise severely plain finish of the weapon.

No. 9 is an ebony ramrod with a cupped ivory tip. This accords quite well with the highly ornamented pistol to which it belongs.

It will be apparent from the diversity of the few patterns illustrated that, when fitting a gun with a new ramrod, some discrimination must be used in selecting material and pattern to suit the weapon.

The size of the hole in the ramrod pipes, whether the front pipe is parallel or tapered, and the groove under the stock will indicate the approximate diameter of the original rod at different points along its length and whether it was of wood or metal.

A tapering iron ramrod like *No. 1* is a blacksmith's job, rather beyond the skill of most amateurs. If such a rod is required, I suggest that a dimensioned sketch be made and, if the dealers in antique gun parts cannot supply anything suitable, the rough forged rod might be obtained from a blacksmith ready for file finishing.

An iron or brass rod of uniform section throughout its length is simple to make. A length of rod is selected of a diameter large enough to be a fairly easy push fit through the ramrod pipes and down the hole in the stock.

Make sure that this hole is clear for its full length. One can usually tell by sound and feel whether the rod end is stopping smartly at the end of its travel. If there appears to be an accumulation of dust and dirt at the end of the hole, file a couple of grooves at right angles to each other across the end of the rod, using a triangular file. When the grooves are about ⅛" deep they will form four sharp teeth which, when rotated in the hole, should clean it out.

File the teeth off and cut the rod to length, so that, when pushed right home in the stock, it projects an inch or so beyond the gun muzzle.

The metal tip is a simple turning job, with a hole slightly smaller in diameter than that of the rod, drilled to within ⅛" of the face of the tip. Reduce the rod end by turning or filing for a distance 1/16" less than the depth of the hole, until it is a driving fit, and push it well home into the tip.

A 3/32" rivet will finally secure the tip. The hole for the rivet must be slightly countersunk at each side and the ends of the rivet well spread so that, after filing and finishing with a strip of fine emery, it will be invisible. The arrangement is shown in *Fig. 20* at (A). Naturally, the proportions of rod and tip must be governed by the size and type of gun for which it is intended.

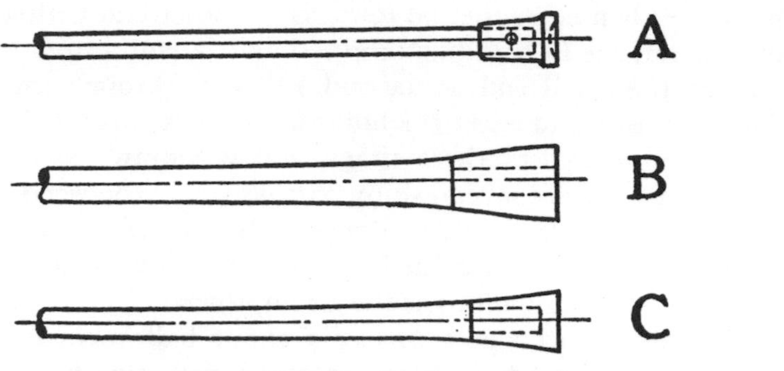

Figure 20. Methods of fixing ramrod tips.

A. Metal tip on metal rod.
B. Horn tip glued on to wood rod.
C. Ivory tip glued on to wood rod.

The idea of cutting the rod 1″ over its finished length is to provide a margin for a second fitting if the filed end should be reduced too much and prove a loose fit in the tip. Assuming, however, that a firm, tight assembly has been made, adjust the length of the ramrod to bring the face of the tip to its correct position, which is usually level with, or slightly behind, the muzzle; then finish the completed rod with fine emery.

Wooden ramrods were frequently made of hickory, and lengths of from one foot to four feet of hickory rod can be bought in several diameters from $\frac{1}{4}$″ to $\frac{1}{2}$″, or the tough hardwood dowel used by cabinet makers and sold in similar sizes will serve. Tips or buttons of horn or brass are catalogued in a great variety of sizes. *Fig. 20 (B)* shows the usual method of fitting a horn tip. The wood is reduced in diameter for a length slightly greater than the length of the tip, and the horn drilled right through to fit. The inside of the hole is roughened by wrapping a piece of coarse sandpaper round a thin taper file pushed tightly into the hole and twisted round.

The end of the rod which fits into it is also roughened, and both the hole and the rod end are coated with glue. The tip must be kept well pressed against the shoulder on the rod for at least twenty-four hours. Shape tip and rod together into a continuous curve and level the projecting ends of the rod flush with the face of the tip. Then taper the rod towards the other end with a joiner's spoke-shave, the fit being determined by trial and error.

When the small end of the rod will pass through the ramrod pipes and begins to enter the hole in the stock, press it lightly in, turn it round two or three times, and withdraw it. It will be found that there are several shiny patches where the wood has been rubbing. Shave these off and repeat the process; each time the rod will slide in a little further and the shiny surfaces become larger and more numerous as the fit improves.

When the ramrod goes in easily about half way, discard the spoke-shave and work with coarse sandpaper and then medium, until it will go down to within an inch or so of its length. Leave it for about a week to allow for any shrinkage and then, for the final stage, use the finest sandpaper, wetting and "whiskering" to a smooth finish until it is a reasonably tight fit when it bottoms. Again leave it for another week, not fully pushed down, for any further shrinkage, and, if it is still tight, ease it with fine sandpaper and finally stain and polish it to match the stock.

Fig. 20 (*C*) shows how an ivory tip is fixed on the ramrod of one of my specimens where the wood is glued into the tip but does not come right through.

A too slack metal ramrod, particularly a long one, can be "adjusted" by giving it an almost imperceptible bend.

One might expect that a linked or stirrup ramrod attached to a pistol barrel would be reasonably secure against loss, but the links, swivel and ramrod complete can be detached by the removal of one small screw on which the links are pivoted to the boss under the barrel. I had a holster pistol from which the linked ramrod had been taken off and never put back, for which I had to make a replacement. If the collector is ever faced with this job, he will find that it is not so formidable as it might appear.

Fig. 21 shows the various parts dimensioned to suit the particular pistol for which they were made. If a pistol with a similar ramrod to the one missing is not available to use as a pattern, the drawing will serve as a guide.

The material to use is mild steel. The dimensions which might have to be modified are:

(*a*) The width across the swivel, which must be the same as the width of the boss under the barrel. Make the swivel 1/16″

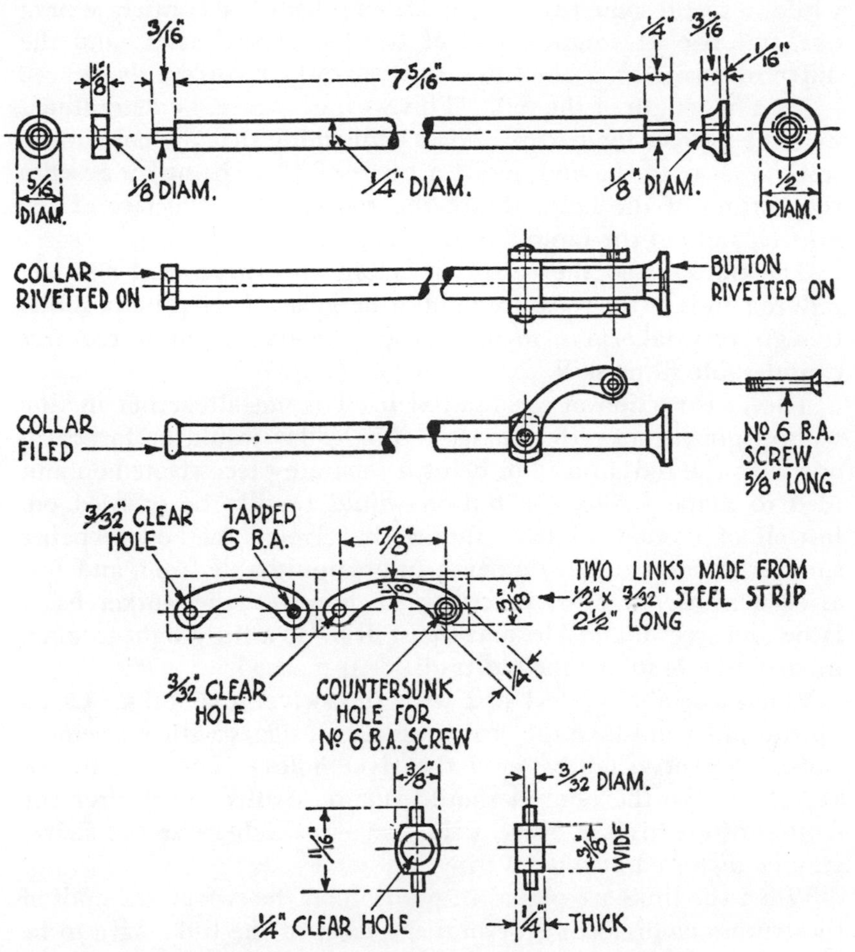

Figure 21. Parts to make a stirrup or linked ramrod.

thicker than the final required dimension, and the length of each little trunnion 1/16″ more than the thickness of the links.

(*b*) The distance between centres of the links. This must be such that, when swung up, the rod comes opposite the centre of the barrel and, when swung down, opposite the hole in the stock.

The curve of the links has to fit the curved underside of the front of the stock when the rod is pushed into its socket. Before making the links, I would suggest that it would be well worth while to spend some time at the drawing board, accurately setting out, full size, the muzzle end of the barrel and stock, and the different positions of the links, to ensure their correct shape.

(*c*) The length of the rod. This will, of course, be determined by the length of the barrel. After confirming that the hole in the stock is clear to the end, insert a piece of $\frac{1}{8}''$ rod until it reaches the bottom of the hole. Mark the rod opposite the face of the muzzle, and cut the ramrod to this length.

The button and the retaining collar, the swivel and also the reduced ends of the rods, are light lathe jobs. It is quite possible, though very laborious, to make them by hand, but it requires considerable filing skill.

The construction of the ramrod itself is not altogether in line with original gunsmith practice. The collar would be forged in one with the rod, instead of being a separate piece riveted on and filed to shape. Also, the button would usually be screwed on, instead of riveted. I have shown the riveted method as being simpler to construct while being indistinguishable from, and just as efficient as, the older practice. If, however, the worker has a lathe and screwing tackle, and the skill to do a little light forging, he may like to follow the old traditional method.

When assembling, deal first with the swivel and links. Clean up the links and take the sharpness off all edges with fine emery cloth, and very slightly bevel the rivet holes. The hole in the swivel to take the ramrod should not be drilled until after the trunnions are riveted over in the link-ends, otherwise the swivel may be distorted during riveting.

When the links are placed in position on the swivel, the ends of the trunnions projecting beyond the faces of the links have to be formed into circular, domed rivet heads, like enlarged pin heads, which must allow the links to swing freely without appreciable side play.

Before attempting this job for the first time I suggest that a little experimenting on the following lines will be well worth while and possibly avoid spoiling the work and having to make new parts.

Take a short length of $3/32''$ mild steel rod and clamp it very firmly in the vice with one end projecting vertically about $\frac{1}{4}''$ above the jaws. Strike the rod end with the flat face of a $\frac{1}{2}$-lb hammer until the diameter is enlarged by about fifty per cent.

Examine the rod and it will be found that the expanded end tapers to the normal diameter in a length of about $\frac{1}{8}$″. If the rod end had been through a hole in one of the links, it would have expanded and gripped the link immovably. Normally this is just what is required when riveting parts together but, where the shank of the rivet has to act as a free bearing, it must retain its original diameter right up to a flat underface at the rivet head.

Cut the hammered end off the rod and firmly clamp it up as before. Now, with the ball peen of the 4-oz hammer, tap the rod end, working round the edge and striking always at a slight outward angle as though one were trying to roll the edge over, which is exactly what we want to do. This will gradually expand the edge outward and downward and the enlarged dome will begin to form with a flat underside. Constantly correct any tendency for the head to work to one side or to form on the slant. Patient, continuous light tapping is the secret of success. After a little practice one should be able quickly to produce a circular, smooth, domed head every time.

When the actual job is to be done, clamp the swivel in the vice with only a trunnion projecting vertically. Clamp up very tightly without using the jaw covers, as the swivel must not move when the hammer is applied. Put one of the links in position which will leave 1/16″ of trunnion projecting which, for a diameter of 3/32″, is exactly the amount necessary to form the head. When this is nearing the correct proportion, keep moving the link and watch for the first sign of friction. Stop when the link will just swing easily without side play.

Turn the swivel over and repeat with the second link, working at the end of the vice jaws to accommodate the first link. When the work is released, the sides of the swivel will bear imprints of the jaw pattern which must be filed off, using the jaw covers this time. It was to allow for filing on both sides that the width of the swivel was left 1/16″ oversize.

Now the $\frac{1}{4}$″ clear hole in the swivel can be drilled, the ramrod inserted, the collar and button riveted on, and the collar filed into a bulb small enough to enter the stock but not so small as to pass through the hole in the swivel. This will slightly shorten the overall length of the rod. The screw which attaches the links to the gun should be adjusted so that the links swing freely without side play, and the projecting end of the screw filed down until almost level and lightly hammered to lock the screw in position. When the ramrod is pushed home into the stock, the face of the button will lie about $\frac{1}{8}$″ short of the muzzle.

When the restorer can make and fit a stirrup ramrod indistinguishable from an original fitting, he should not find any insurmountable difficulty in producing a replacement for a revolver lever rammer. Parts for Colt rammers are still catalogued for most models.

RAMROD PIPES

It is not often that ramrod pipes are missing and, when it happens, it is usually the front one that has gone. However, I had one brass-furnished flint pistol without either pipe. Brass pipes could be castings or formed out of sheet. Usually they were provided with lugs through which they were pinned to the stock, though sometimes those made of sheet were secured by the two projections which formed the lug being taken through a slot in the stock and bent apart into shallow recesses inside the stock below the barrel.

I used sheet brass No. 16s B. & S. gauge, approximately 1/20″ thick. The recesses in the ramrod channel under the stock determined the length, diameter and taper of the pipes, and the position and size of the lug slots and pinholes indicated the dimensions of the lugs, so that an accurate sketch of the pipes could be made before starting work.

Plate 56 shows the different stages in making a pair of ramrod pipes. (1) is the piece of sheet brass for the front pipe. This should be cut about $\frac{1}{4}$″ longer and $\frac{1}{8}$″ wider than will finally be required. The middle portion has to be bent into a tapering pipe, leaving the ends projecting in a rib along its length.

A piece of tapering rod is required round which to bend the brass. Amongst my tools I keep an old butcher's steel (7) which has just about the average ramrod taper for the last 4″, reducing from slightly over $\frac{1}{2}$″ to 3/16″. The worker may have to file the end of some stock round-iron rod to the required dimensions if he cannot put his hand on a piece already suitably tapered. In the case illustrated, the pipe was $\frac{7}{8}$″ long tapering from $\frac{3}{8}$″ to 5/16″

internal diameter, so it would not have been a big job to taper the last inch of a $\frac{3}{8}''$ rod by 1/16″.

Brass varies considerably in both its composition and hardness and it will probably make for easier manipulation if the piece to be used is softened. Heat it slowly and uniformly in the flame of the blow-lamp to dull red heat only and then allow it to cool in the air. Never attempt to work brass in the hot state or it may break into pieces. It will harden again as it is being worked.

Bend the brass round the rod into a "U" shape and, leaving the taper rod in position, close the sheet round it by squeezing the free ends between the jaws of the vice. Do not use smooth jaw covers, but help the rough jaws to grip the brass and keep it tight over the taper rod by pressing the work down, or tapping it down with a light hammer as the vice is slowly screwed up. The vice marks can be seen in the illustration.

With care and perhaps a certain amount of luck, a nice tapered pipe may be produced at the first squeeze, but it may be necessary to bring it to shape with a little light hammer work around the rod.

The ends of the pipe will be thrown a little askew by the tapering hole and must be filed to bring them to a right angle with the axis of the pipe and also to reduce the length of the pipe to fit exactly into the cavity in the stock. A pipe at this stage is shown at (2).

Next cut away the surplus metal, using the miniature hack-saw, leaving only a projecting lug of the correct width to fit the slot in the stock. This lug will meet the underside of the barrel before the pipe is bedded in its recess, so it must be progressively reduced until it just clears the barrel when the pipe is properly seated. At this point the vice marks can be filed off the faces of the lug. Now file grooves round the ends of the pipe to give the conventional beaded effect. These are usually only carried round the exposed portion. The pipe should then be worked smooth with emery cloth, the finest grade being used to impart the finishing polish. A finished front pipe is shown at (3).

A rear pipe is a little more intricate to make. It need not be tapered, which simplifies matters, but it is quite a tricky business to shape up the conventional slender-pointed neb which fits into the stock and covers the end of the tunnel in the wood.

At (4) is shown the shape of the flat piece of sheet brass which is to be bent into a pipe as previously described. Trim away the surplus metal until the neb is approaching the size of the recess in the stock and then make the offset, or "lift" to the point as shown at (5).

This is the critical part of the job. The brass has to be stretched where the shouldered offset is formed so, to avoid the risk of cracking, the roughly shaped pipe should be softened before starting. Even if it was softened before being bent, it will have started to harden again while being worked, so bring it to a dull red heat again and let it cool.

Fig. 22 shows one method of forming the offset.

(A) is the ramrod pipe.

(B) is a wood block drilled to fit the outside of the pipe and sawn in two to enable the pipe to be firmly gripped in the vice. The saw cut on one side must be extra wide to accommodate the double thickness of metal of the lug for the pin.

(C) is a piece of steel rod about 3" long of a suitable diameter to fit inside the pipe.

(D) is a piece of steel tube about 2"–3" long of a diameter to slide over the rod (C). One end of this tube must be chamfered to the shape indicated.

The rod (C) is put through the ramrod pipe, the pipe inserted between the halves of the wood block, and the whole clamped firmly in the vice (E). The tip of the neb must be bent slightly away from the rod to allow the chamfered end of tube (D) to be inserted and hammered down to form the off-set.

When this is partly formed it may be necessary to soften the brass again to allow it to stretch more easily without splitting. As the tube is driven down, the point of the neb will curl away from the rod unless it is restrained by pliers or a piece of larger diameter tube. In any case, when the off-set shoulder is formed, the neb can be hammered back against the tube.

The ramrod pipe may now be removed from the clamp and the neb filed to fit the recess in the stock, the lug formed and bored for the pin and the pipe ornamented and polished.

Referring again to *Plate 56*, a finished back pipe is shown at (6). This and the corresponding front pipe are shown on the actual wooden ramrod which they accommodate.

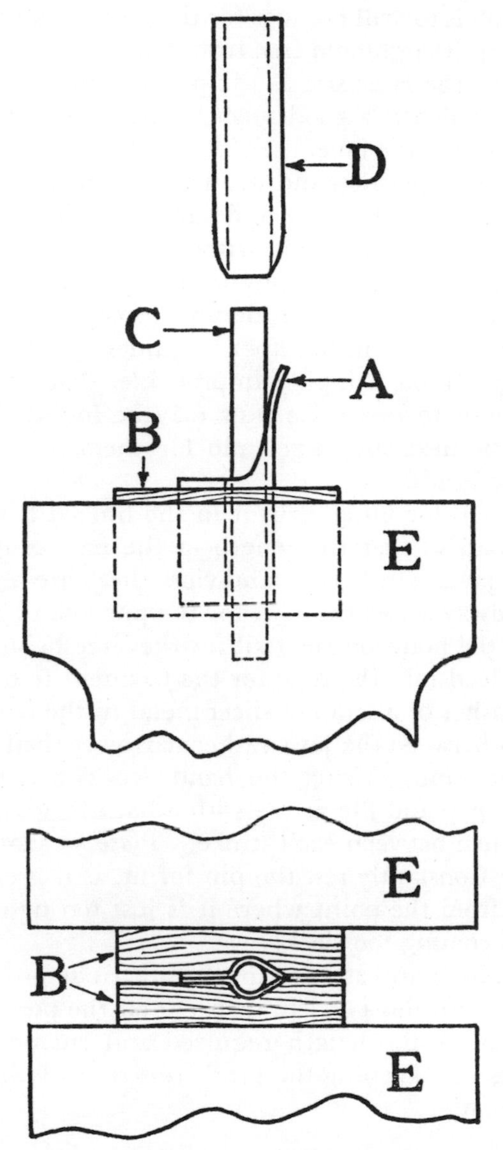

Figure 22. Shaping the neb for a back ramrod pipe.

A. Ramrod pipe.
B. Wood clamp to grip pipe.
C. Steel rod gripped in pipe.
D. Steel tube with leading end shaped to expand neb of pipe.
E. Vice jaws.

The final job is to drill the lugs for the pins so that the assembled pipes will be quite tight and free from play.

Select a drill the same size as the pin-hole in the stock. If you have not one which is a good push fit, use a drill a shade larger and pass it through the hole.

Put the pipes in position and wind a dozen turns of strong string round each pipe, and the stock and barrel, pulling the string tight at each turn and tying it firmly without letting the tension relax. Keep the string clear of the pin-holes. The pipes will now be pressed into the stock with considerable force and the lugs may be drilled, using the holes in the stock as guides.

It is possible, though highly improbable, that perfectly fitting round wire nails to make the pins may be found in your stock. If not, take the next size larger and file them down to suit, first cutting off the heads.

To hold a nail for filing, grip it in the hinged hand-vice by $\frac{1}{4}$" at the head end so that the length of the nail projects at right angles to the jaws. In many hand-vices there are a pair of small V-notches midway across the jaws for the purpose of gripping thin pins. Leave the point on the nail for the time being, as it makes a convenient lead into the hole for the frequent tests for size.

Clamp a washer or a scrap of sheet metal in the bench vice so as to leave a gap between the jaws rather narrower than the required diameter of the pin. Using the hand-vice as a handle, lay the nail along the gap and file across with a flat file, giving the nail a fraction of a turn between each stroke. *Plate 57* shows such a pin being made. Constantly test the pin for fit, as it is easy to reduce the diameter from the point where it is just too tight to where it is suddenly becoming too slack.

When the pin is an easy driving fit so that it progresses about $\frac{1}{8}$" at each tap with the 4-oz hammer, cut off the point, set the pin in the stock, mark the length required and cut off the surplus. Trim the ends and, keeping the pipe pressed firmly into the stock, pin it in position.

CHAPTER THIRTEEN

MISCELLANEOUS REPAIRS

WELDING REPAIRS

OCCASIONALLY the repair of broken gun parts may be simply effected by welding, but it would not pay the amateur to acquire the necessary equipment for the occasional use he might make of it and, apart from this consideration, welding is a skilled job demanding much practice and experience before one could safely use it in gun restoration.

In general, it is satisfactory to entrust simple welding work to a garage, provided exact instructions are given, and that no finishing is attempted by the welder.

A good weld should be virtually as strong as the original metal and, when filed up and polished, ought not to leave any visible traces. Ask for the weld to be well built up and, before beginning to file off the surplus, break away the brittle, hard scale by tapping it all over with a cross-peen hammer, otherwise it will damage the file.

I have had various such jobs done, and a selection of these is shown on *Plate 58*. The black arrows indicate the positions of the welds.

(1) is a flint hammer which broke at the neck. It is usually the thin swan-neck hammers which fail in this way but, strangely enough in this instance, it was a ring hammer with a double neck which snapped.

(2) is a percussion hammer which had a broken spur. It was being used to replace a missing hammer on a pistol and, as the square hole was at the wrong angle, this was weld-filled at the same time that the spur was attached, and redrilled and correctly squared by the method previously described.

(3) This slender trigger guard belongs to a long Arab flint-lock gun. There is an ornamental pierced hole opposite the arrow and at some time the guard had broken in two at this point.

(4) is the trigger of the same gun. The pivot hole was worn almost through the side, and was weld-filled and redrilled.

(5) The lower tang of a box-lock pistol which was broken at the screw hole. After welding, the outside only was filed up and smoothed. When the butt was replaced, the thickened metal inside was not visible, so it was left to reinforce this weak spot. It is just discernible in the photograph.

(6) shows the handle and percussion lock of an under-hammer walking-stick gun. The hammer end with its spur was broken off and missing and a new one had to be made by hack-saw and file, and welded on to the remaining stump of the neck. As no similar example or illustration could be found, the new hammer end had to be designed to be proportional to, and in keeping with, the trigger.

(7) A flint-lock frizzen which was broken at the pivot boss when the gun was dropped.

I have not been able to include some other examples as they are no longer in my possession; but one instance might usefully be mentioned. There was, for a period, a considerable vogue for flint and percussion box-lock pistols with folding triggers. Normally the trigger lies in a recess under the lock and frequently the fit is so meticulously accurate that the outline of the trigger is hardly visible, particularly if it has been decorated with engraving. On cocking the hammer, the trigger springs out to the usual position and, after firing or lowering the hammer, can be snapped back into the recess.

The connection between hammer and trigger is very simple. It consists of a small projecting ridge across the hammer boss which, as the hammer is being cocked, meets two small projections on the boss of the trigger and swings it out of its recess. The weakness of this arrangement is that the projections are necessarily so small and delicate that, after much use, wear takes place and the action ceases to function.

An appreciable proportion of folding-trigger pistols will be found to be defective. The trigger may not swing out when the hammer is cocked, or may come only part-way out, or the hammer and trigger may become jammed.

The only practical cure is to build up the worn projections by welding. Because of their minute size this is a job only for an expert welder who must deposit no more than a sufficient surplus of metal to allow the projections to be re-formed to their original size by filing. Great care must be taken to stop filing as soon as the trigger operates correctly. A few unnecessary strokes may well put the action out of order again and necessitate a fresh start.

REPLACING REVOLVER GRIPS

I have had several revolvers with wooden grips so badly damaged that new ones had to be made. Revolver handles may consist of a separate wooden grip on each side of a butt strap held by a connecting screw as in the case of the Cooper pepper-box (*Plates 39 and 40*), or a single wooden butt held by a continuous butt strap sunk in a groove in the wood in the manner of the Colt (*Plates 42 and 43*) or by a tang and screws, as used on the Adams and Tranter revolvers (*Plate 44*).

Many revolver grips were checkered, whilst others were plain. Checkering is highly skilled work and I have never had occasion to attempt a complete job, so I cannot offer any guidance about it. If there is an existing foundation pattern, it is fairly simple to renovate checkering, but to start from the smooth wood is a very different proposition. Plain polished grips have the advantage of showing up the full beauty of choice grained wood.

Plate 59 shows (top) a pair of badly broken revolver grips, (bottom) the finished new grips which were made to replace them and (middle) a pair of rough-sawn blanks before shaping; a description of the procedure in this particular case will suggest the method of approach in a similar instance.

The screw was taken out, the broken grips were removed and the diamond-shaped nut and counter-bored washer knocked out. These were of German silver in good order and were used again.

The thickest part of the discarded grips was $\frac{3}{8}$" so, to allow for shaping and sandpapering, the blanks were made from $\frac{1}{2}$" thick walnut. A piece I had in stock was just large enough to provide four blanks with the grain of the wood running down the length of the grips, which is why there is a spare pair in the rough to complete the illustration.

The blanks were cut to allow about $\frac{1}{4}$" margin all round, and the top ends were planed true to lie against the frame of the revolver. The mainspring was taken out to leave an unobstructed space inside the butt strap, against which the blanks were held in turn while an outline of the outer and inner edge of the butt strap was scribed on each blank, one on either side of the strap to give the right- and left-hand grip (see *Plate 59*). It would be easy to forget this and to find oneself with two grips of the same hand.

The blanks were then chiselled down almost to the outer line, leaving only about 1/16″ of margin. The scribed inner line was taken a little deeper with a sharp ¼″ chisel and the wood at the edges removed up to this line to a depth of about 1/32″. This located the grips in the butt strap and prevented any movement when they were screwed into place.

It requires a steady hand to pare away the wood to a uniform depth exactly to the line, and it helps if the central screw holes are drilled and the blank fixed to a length of wood to act as a handle, similar to the arrangement shown in *Plate 49*. The screw holes in the new grips must be in the same position as in the old ones to obviate any risk of the fixing screw fouling the mainspring or other working parts.

The recesses were made for the diamond-shaped nut and washer, which were sunk until, when tightened up with the grips in position on the revolver, the end of the screw just came flush with the outside face of the nut. This took nut and washer below the face of the wood.

With the grips still in position on the revolver, the surplus wood was then cut away with a ½″ chisel, care being taken to keep the two contours symmetrical, until they were nearly down to the final shape and size. They were then taken off the revolver and finished, first with a rasp and then with progressively finer grades of sandpaper, "whiskering" as the final stage was reached. The grips were slipped into position at frequent intervals and, when they were a perfect fit, exactly following the curve of the butt strap, and with the outside faces of the nut and washer coinciding with the surfaces, they were given a final smoothing with the finest sandpaper and then stained and polished. Keep any scraps of attractively figured hardwood such as walnut, rosewood or old mahogany which could be used for grips, and, of course, ivory or horn are excellent for the purpose.

Plate 55. Various patterns of ramrods.

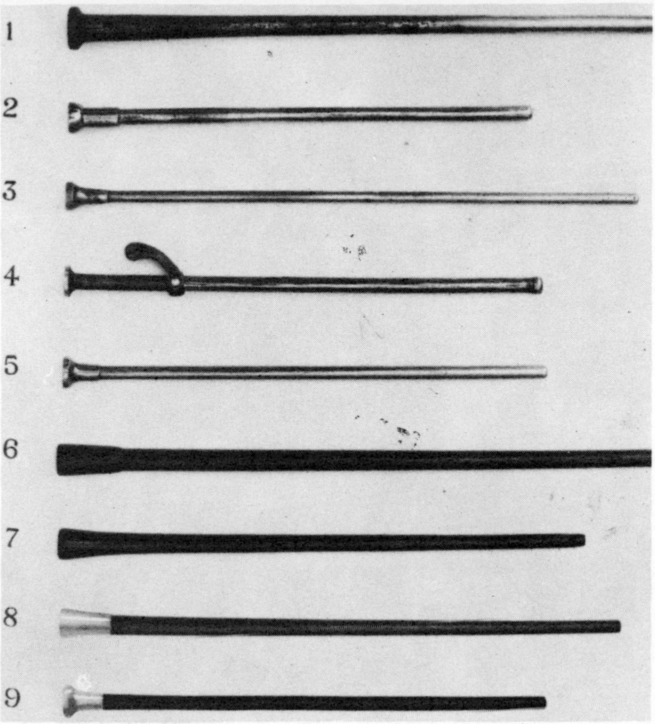

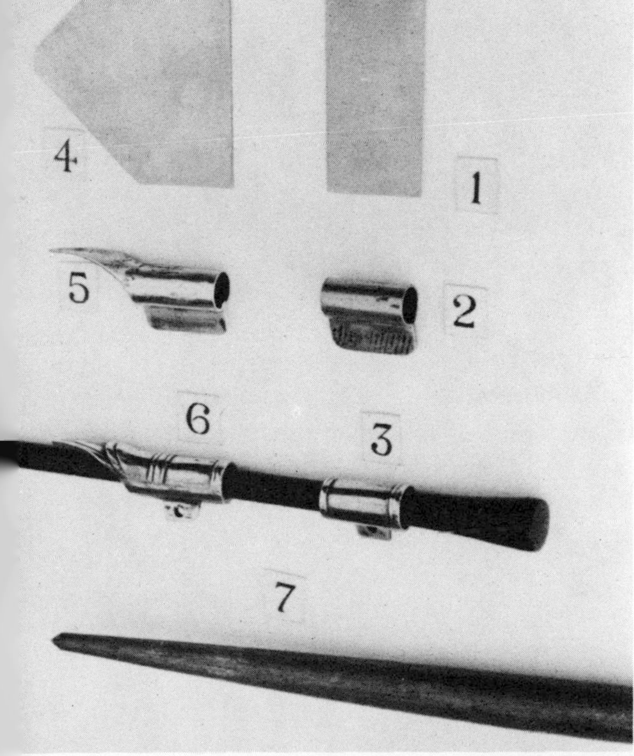

Plate 56. Making a pair of ramrod pipes for a flint pistol.

Plate 57. Making a pin out of a round wire nail.

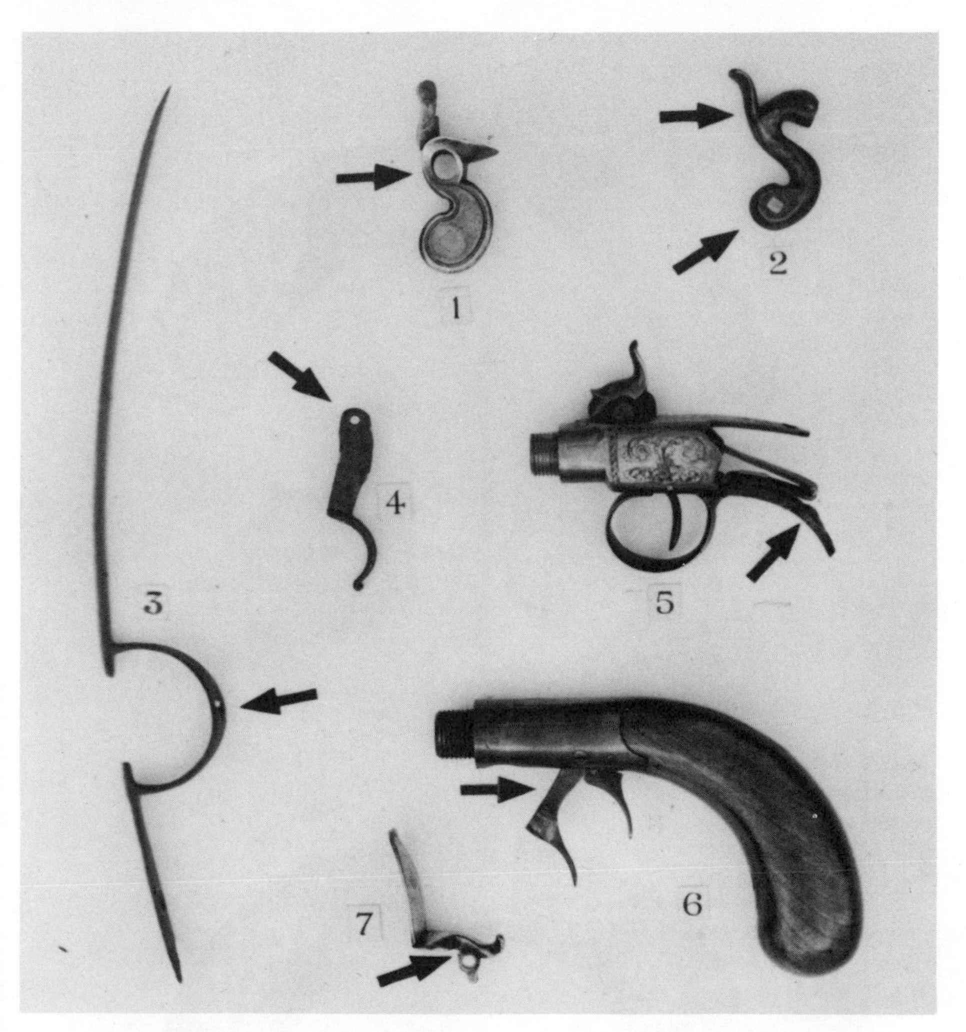

Plate 58. Various parts which have been repaired by welding. 1. Flint hammer broken at neck. 2. Percussion hammer. Spur broken off. Hammer used as a replacement which necessitated weld filling the hole in the boss and re-drilling and squaring at a different angle. 3. Long trigger guard broken into two pieces. 4. Trigger. Worn hole filled and re-drilled. 5. End of tang broken at screw hole: note built-up weld left inside for extra strength. 6. Under-hammer broken off and missing. A new piece was made and welded on. 7. Frizzen – broken at pivot boss.

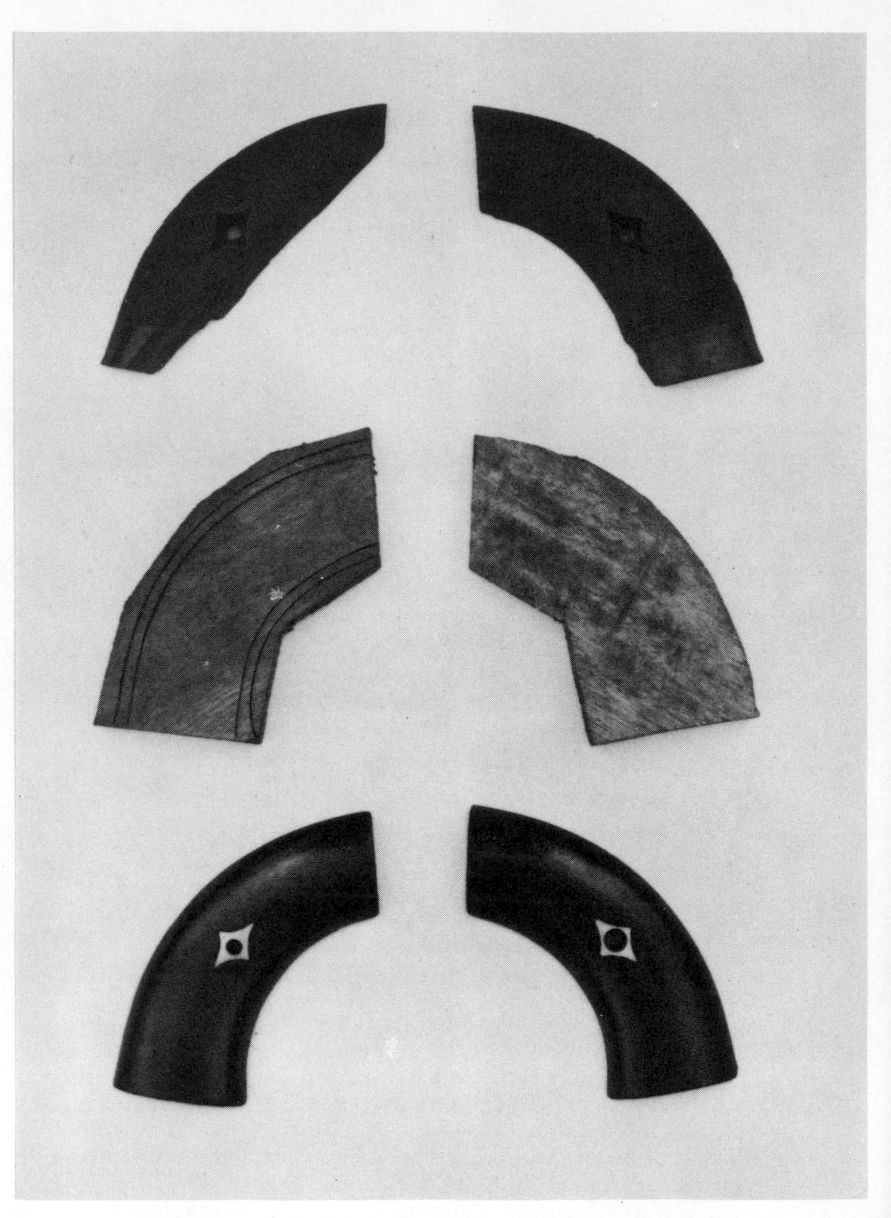

Plate 59. Replacing a broken pair of revolver grips.
Top: The discarded broken grips. *Middle:* Rough blanks for new grips.
Bottom: The finished grips stained and polished.

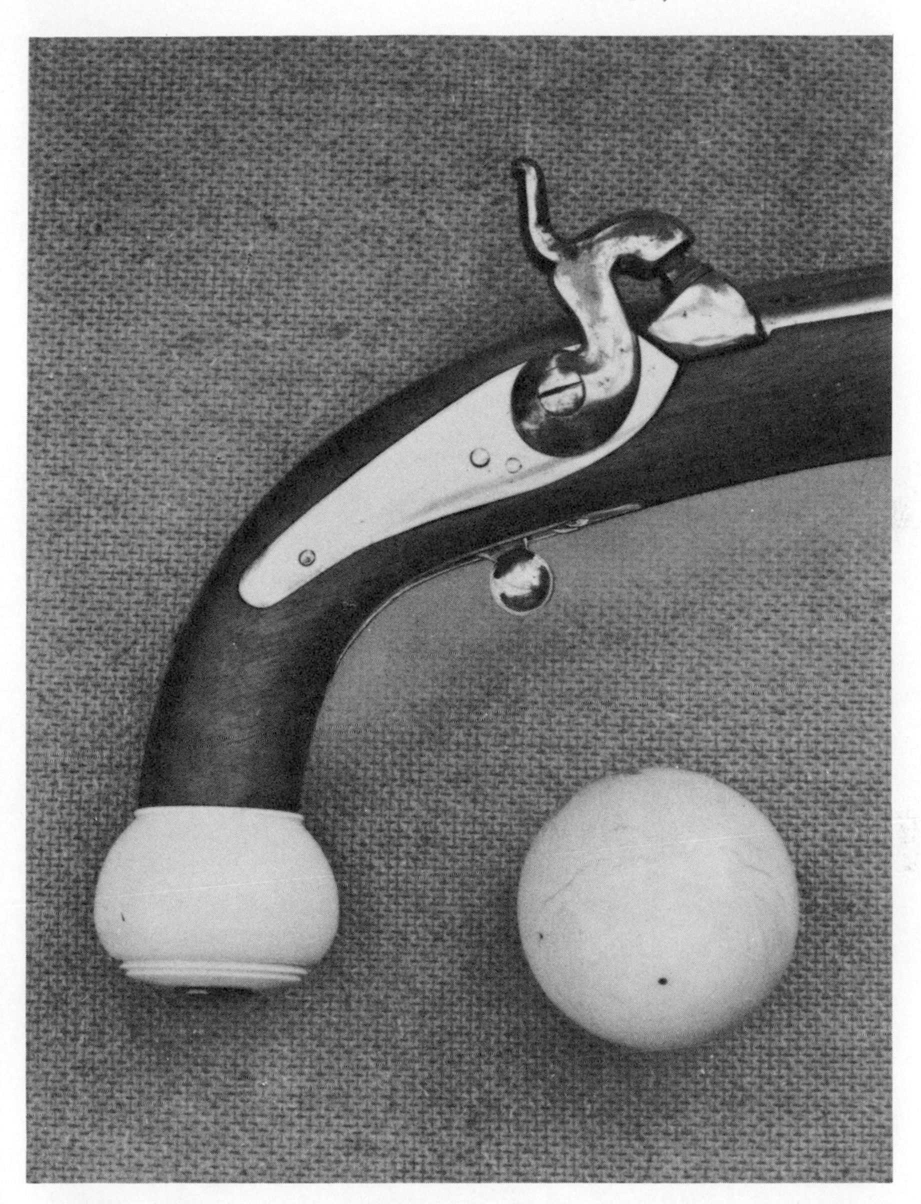

Plate 60. The ivory ball on the butt of this Cossack pistol was missing. The replacement illustrated was made from a discarded billiards ball. The corresponding 'spot' ball is included in the photograph.

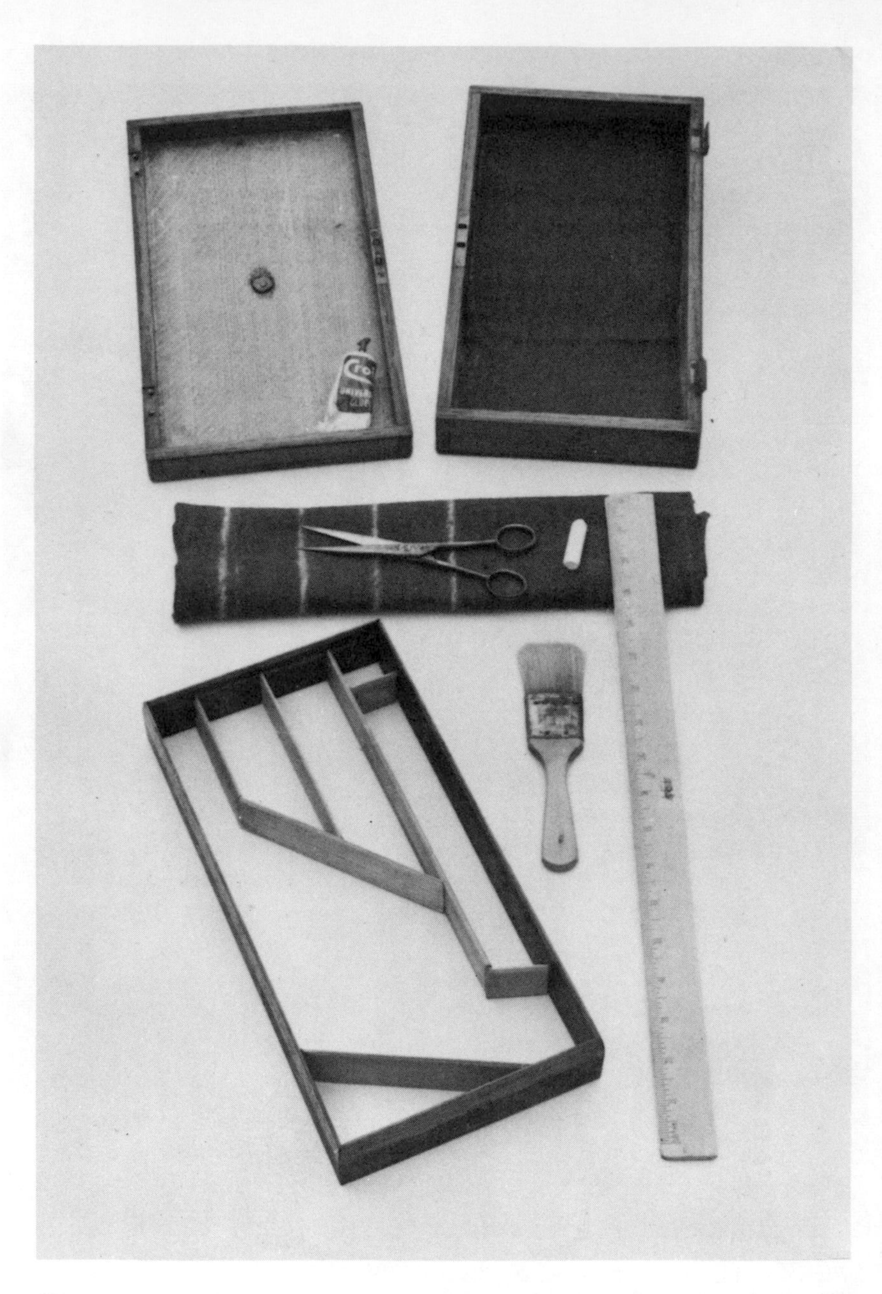

Plate 61. Oak case for Adams revolver and accessories being fitted with new partitions and re-lined.

AN IVORY BALL BUTT

For some years a couple of old ivory billiard balls lay in my "miscellaneous" box. It seemed unlikely that they would be required for gun repair until one day I acquired a long Cossack or Circassian percussion rifled pistol with the usual three-ring barrel fixing, back-action lock and ball trigger, all in excellent condition, except that the ivory ball butt was missing.

Plate 60 shows the replacement which was turned on my lathe from one of these balls with the other (spot) alongside. An actual pistol, of similar type, was not available to use as a pattern. Illustrations showed, however, that the ball butts varied both in size and design, and I based the proportions of my replacement on one which appeared to me to be the most pleasing. After turning and smoothing with the finest sandpaper, the final rich, deep polish which so enhances the beauty of ivory was given by the application of plate powder and olive oil mixed to a smooth creamy paste, the ultimate gleam being achieved with a piece of old silk.

CASES—REPAIRS AND RE-LINING

Many pistols and guns were originally sold in polished mahogany or oak cases lined with baize or velvet and partitioned to accommodate tools and accessories; naturally these are especially prized by the collector.

Apart from missing accessories, broken or loose partitions and worn or torn linings constitute the most common defect in cased sets. External damage to the case is usually a matter of refinishing and polishing and, if necessary, replacing hinges and lock.

The more intricate job of re-lining the inside and fitting new partitions needs only patience and care to ensure success. If the interior of the case is really dilapidated, it must be taken out and have all the lining removed, new partitions made where necessary, and the whole re-lined.

Plate 61 shows the oak case of an Adams revolver in course of being refitted. When I got it some well-intentioned person had started the job but, after prising out the partitions and splitting most of them, and tearing away most of the baize from the box and lid (incidentally destroying a perfectly good and genuine gunsmith's lid-label), he had presumably lost interest and packed the lot—revolver, accessories and débris—back into the case and got rid of it.

To deal with a complete refit such as this, first detach the lid to facilitate working inside the body of the box. Soften the glue, using a sponge with warm water, and remove the partitions and the strips which line the sides and ends. These lining strips which project above the box and fit into the lid, when closed, can be used again provided they are not damaged. They are made of the same kind of wood as the box and are stained and polished to match on the outside face and top edge.

Soak the baize off all the parts with warm water, first noting exactly how it has been folded and wrapped, particularly where one partition joins another or meets the lining strips. If there is a maker's label in the lid, carefully steam if off before removing the baize. Dry the label and clean it with stale bread and, in due course, replace it in the newly-lined lid.

The partitions are made of wood strip $\frac{1}{8}''$ or 3/16″ thick, made to taper slightly towards the top which is radiused. Wood of the required thickness can be bought in sheets from hobby shops.

The old pieces will give the dimensions of thickness, height and length of each strip and indicate the angle of the ends of those which do not meet at right angles. These partition strips need not be smoothed or "whiskered"; the material will adhere all the more firmly if they are left rough.

When the partitions are made, put them all in position and tack them to each other and to the lining strips with spots of glue, to check that each part fits.

The new baize should be of good quality, as near a match in colour to the original as possible, and no thicker, or the partitions will look clumsy. A piece about 24″ square will suffice for an average-size case accommodating a single pistol with the usual flask, bullet-mould and other simple accessories.

Use a good, fairly thin tube glue and coat the wood only. Press the dry baize into contact with it and smooth it out firmly to avoid ridges. The baize will stretch a little in the process and may need a slight trim before the last edges are stuck down. Glue the underside of the partitions as well as the vertical joints where their ends meet each other and also where they meet the lining strips.

A few $\frac{3}{8}''$ fine panel pins may be inserted at suitable points to give rigidity at the partition joints but, if each joint is properly glued, pins are not really necessary. Sometimes a compartment may be closed with a shaped, baize-covered lid and this replacement should present no difficulty.

Where the original outside polish of the case is sound, clean off any dirt with mild soap and warm water and, when thoroughly dry, finish with a good wax polish.

As before-mentioned, velvet was sometimes used for lining and I have a Colt revolver in a red-velvet-lined case which looks very attractive.

The photograph shows the Adams revolver case after it was completely stripped with the lid detached. The new partitions are seen temporarily stuck together within the lining strips, to check all lengths and angles. They have been lifted out of the box and are ready to be separated and to have the baize stuck on. The roll of baize is marked out in chalk for cutting, with a piece already cut and in place in the bottom of the box, but not yet stuck down.

The round object in the middle of the lid is a nut sunk into the wood which secures an inset brass escutcheon on the outside; while the nut was accessible, I took the opportunity to take the plate off and clean it, together with the brass hinges and lock.

POWDER FLASKS

Most of the accessories accompanying a cased gun are unlikely to have been damaged. Bullet-moulds, screw-drivers, nipple keys, cleaning rod, etc., are all strong and solid enough to withstand rough usage and need only to be cleaned and oiled.

The one item in the case which is susceptible to damage is the copper powder-flask. Occasionally the shutter return spring will be either broken or missing. In general the amateur cannot expect to equal the quality and finish of commercially made springs and, as flask springs are catalogued in various sizes, I suggest that they should be ordered when required.

This leaves us with the problem of removing dents and flats from the body of a flask. I would be inclined to leave a flat on the seam where the two sides meet, as any attempt to hammer it out might result in opening the seam. The defects, however, will almost always be on the faces of the pressed copper sides and, with patience and care, can be removed.

Dented metal is actually stretched and it must be compressed to eliminate the dent and restore the original form. The method is to use a piece of hardwood which will enter the body of the flask when the cap is screwed off. One end must be shaped to fit the contour of the flask where the dent is situated.

With the wood fixed in the vice, the flask is placed over it so that the dent bears on this curved end, the position being ascertained by measurement, alignment and feel. The dent is then beaten out by repeated light tapping all round it so that, in effect, it is the curve of the hard wooden block which raises the depression.

Large intricately embossed flasks are the easiest to deal with. For these a light cross-peen hammer is suitable, with the peen wrapped with surgical tape to reduce the risk of marking the copper. The cross-peen will pass between the raised parts of the embossing and, provided the job is done carefully and neatly, the pattern will minimise the effect of any slight hammer marks.

It is, however, the small perfectly plain flask usually found with cased sets which demands the greatest care and patience, and a strong warning must be given here that careless or hurried work is likely not only to leave the dent itself unaffected, but to surround it with a ring of dimples and scratches. Good antique flasks are too rare to be damaged in this way; the work, therefore must be done slowly and accurately.

Plate 62 shows a small flask in position on the wooden block. This flask had several dents all on one side, one of them a sharpish groove. These were each in turn located over the curved hard wooden block and worked round with the taped face of the 4-oz hammer. Bringing up the indented surfaces was a slow job, and there could be no question of softening the copper by heating, as this would almost certainly have opened up the soldered seam.

This flask was brought back to almost its original condition by the method which I have described and now, without close examination by reflected light, no trace of the former damage is apparent.

Before working on an actual flask, I would suggest that a few dents be knocked in a piece of 20s gauge sheet copper and a little practice put in until one feels confident to deal with a flask.

CALIBRE AND RIFLING GAUGES

Two simple accessories which constantly will be useful to the collector are a taper gauge for quickly measuring calibre in either decimals of an inch or millimetres, and a sliding gauge to pass down a rifled barrel to determine the rate of twist.

Fig. 23 shows the calibre gauge which can be made from a 1" by 1/16" by 10" long strip of alloy or brass. The lay-out is self-explanatory and the advantage of making the gauge just 10" long is that the divisions on the "inches" side can be transferred directly from an ordinary rule graduated in inches and tenths, and these measurements along the length of the gauge correspond to tenths and hundredths of an inch across the width. Similarly on the millimetre side, the divisions can be taken from a metric rule, the measurements along the length being in centimetres, corresponding to millimetres across the width. For example, at 5" and 6" from the point the width of the gauge indicates calibres of ·5" and ·6" respectively. The intermediate divisions indicate the second figure after the decimal point, i.e. if the gauge will enter the barrel to the depth of, say, 5·6", the calibre is ·56". On the metric side, each increase of 1 mm in calibre allows the gauge to go 1 cm further down the barrel. On the gauge shown each cm is subdivided so that the gauge reads to a half mm. Accurately made and graduated, a gauge of this kind should measure calibres to the nearest hundredth of an inch or a quarter of a millimetre.

After the gauge has been set out in pencil, the graduations and numbers can be permanently marked with a sharp steel scriber. The first inch at the point, shown dotted on the drawing, may be cut off as it is inconveniently fragile and unlikely ever to be used. The gauge will not accurately measure the calibre of a large-bore pistol with a short barrel, as it will come against the breech before it reaches the appropriate depth. The difficulty does not arise with a screw-off barrel but, with a fixed barrel, one can cut a tapering slip of cardboard, mark it where it stops at the muzzle, and read the corresponding dimension from the gauge.

A gauge to ascertain the amount of twist in the rifling of a gun barrel can be made from a rod about 3' long which will freely pass

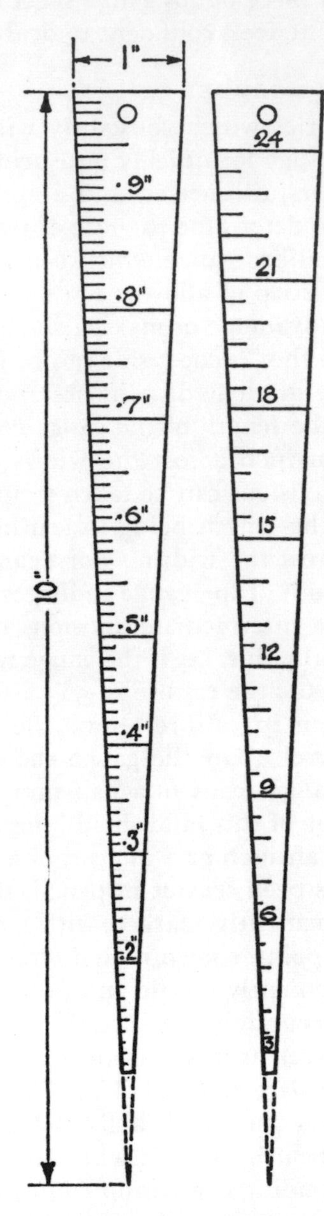

Figure 23. Home-made gauge for measuring calibre in fractions of inches or millimetres.

down the barrel, with a piece of thin, say 16s gauge, brass sheet fixed by a counter-sunk screw into a saw-cut at one end, as shown in *Fig. 24*.

Make the piece of brass 1/16" wider than the diameter of the calibre and file it down until it will enter the barrel with the sides just fitting in two opposite rifling grooves and will pass fairly easily

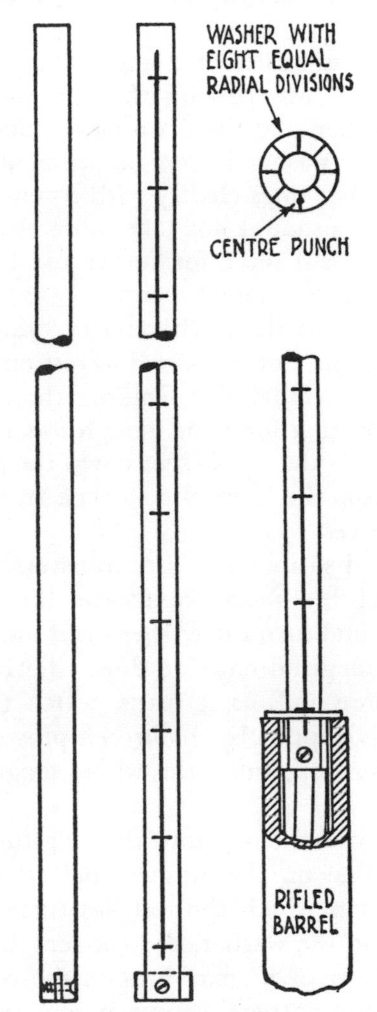

Figure 24. Home-made gauge for determining twist of barrel rifling.

down the full length of the barrel without appreciable play. As this brass blade slides up and down the barrel and follows the twist of the rifling, the rod will slowly turn.

We want accurately to measure the distance in which the rifling would make a complete turn. Rule a straight line along the full length of the rod; then, starting near the brass slide at the leading end, put a transverse mark across this line at 1″ intervals, as shown in the drawing.

Next take a washer of sufficient diameter to pass over the rod and scribe two lines across, passing through the centre and at right-angles to each other, and then two more lines between them, accurately dividing the washer into eight segments (see drawing). Mark one of these radial lines clearly with a centre punch.

Preparing these parts should not take more than half an hour, after which the gauge will serve for future use by substituting a new brass slide for each different firearm.

To determine the twist, insert the end carrying the slide into the barrel, drop the washer over the rod to rest on the muzzle and hold it there with the left hand. Holding the rod in the right hand, apply a light turning force (as though to screw it in), which should be maintained as the rod is sent down the bore, the object, of course, being to keep the brass slide always in contact with the same sides of the grooves.

Now, adjust the rod so that the first transverse mark near the leading end is just visible above the face of the washer, as indicated in the drawing, and turn the washer until the centre-punched mark is against the longitudinal line down the rod. Then pass the rod down the bore and, as it turns, watch the line moving round until the rod is stopped by the breech plug of a pistol or, in the case of a shoulder gun, until the whole length of the rod is inserted.

Then slowly draw back the rod until the longitudinal line comes opposite the radial line on the washer that it had just passed. Note the angle through which the rod has turned by reckoning 45° to each division on the washer, and the length it has travelled by counting the number of 1″ markings on the rod between first and last positions. From these figures it is a matter of simple arithmetic to calculate the rate of twist.

For example, if the rod has turned through one division (that is, one eighth of a revolution) in, say, $6\frac{1}{4}''$, the rifling will make a complete turn in:

8 multiplied by $6\frac{1}{4}''$ equals 50″

or, if it has turned through six divisions, that is, three-quarters of a revolution in, say, $31\frac{1}{2}''$, it will make a complete turn in:

$31\frac{1}{2}''$ divided by $\frac{3}{4}$ equals 42″

If it is preferred to express the rate of twist in calibres, simply measure the calibre and divide into the length of a complete turn. For example, supposing a calibre of ·6″ and one turn in 42″, the twist could be expressed as one turn in 42″ divided by ·6 equals 70 calibres.

The specification of the rifling, including the number and width of grooves, and whether right or left-hand, as well as the rate of twist, will add interest to the description of individual specimens.

CHAPTER FOURTEEN

A MAJOR RESTORATION

THE foregoing chapters cover no more than the stripping, cleaning, adjustment and restoration of a limited selection of guns of the kind and period which most collectors of antique firearms will possess.

Rarities such as highly decorated match- and wheel-locks are in relatively few private collections and, as a general rule, the amateur who is fortunate enough to acquire rare specimens should consider very carefully before embarking on any extensive work on weapons of value. One would need exceptional mechanical aptitude and experience on work of this kind to handle the older and more valuable guns, and the advice given earlier, never to start on a job which one cannot feel quite sure can be carried out successfully, is worth repeating.

The question might well be asked, to what degree of dilapidation a firearm might deteriorate before it reached a condition beyond hope of restoration. Naturally, the answer must be qualified according to the nature of the defects and the value of the specimen, and perhaps a description of an actual major renovation which I carried out on a flint-lock pistol may be of interest here.

Plate 63 shows a view of this pistol after the work had been completed. It is 13½″ overall, barrel 7½″ long ·57 calibre, octagonal at the breech merging to round and tapering in thickness to about 1/16″ at the muzzle. Its weight is 1 lb 12 oz.

The barrel, butt cap, trigger guard and an ornate escutcheon are of steel, deeply chiselled in an intricate pattern and inlaid with gold. The steel side plate is elaborately fretted and inset flush with the stock. There is also some engraving on barrel and lock, and the walnut stock is attractively carved round the various fittings. The outer faces of the hammer jaws, the underside of the flash-pan, the back of the frizzen and the ramrod pipes are formed with flat facets, and the ramrod is of ebony with an ivory tip.

Altogether, it is a very handsome specimen and one of which I am rather proud, as I literally saved it from destruction. To my regret, there is no photograph of it showing the condition it was in when I got it, as any idea of restoration appeared then to be out of the question. My reason for buying it was to salvage the lock and to keep the barrel and some of the fittings as examples of decoration.

Really, I had never seen what had once been a fine pistol in such a shocking state. Someone had tried to take it to pieces without removing the pins and screws. The fretted side plate had been prised up and bent out at each end, breaking away some of the wood.

The side tangs of the butt cap had been levered out of the stock and an attempt made to take out the ornamental boss which secures the butt cap but, as this was attached by a screw through its tang concealed under the trigger-guard strap, the result was a bent and distorted butt cap and boss and two sizeable pieces split off the stock.

The trigger-guard strap was also bent out at each end in an attempt to wrench it off without removing the pins. The barrel pins had been taken out, splitting off the fore end of the stock as far as the back ramrod pipe. The ramrod was missing but, surprisingly, the cock screw and top jaw were in place, though the tip of the top jaw had been bent down by constant impact with the frizzen without a flint. The fittings had been roughly hammered back into the stock, doing more damage, and the barrel and broken stock bound round with copper wire.

Also, the pistol appeared to have been used at some time as a fire poker, as the fore-end of the broken stock was completely charred away for about 2" and the front ramrod pipe had gone. The muzzle end of the barrel was flattened underneath and dented all round, as if it had been used to crack coal. Finally the pistol had been laid away to rust.

I took off the lock, dismantled and cleaned it and straightened and trimmed the jaw tips. With its engraving, it seemed a good spare for stock. The barrel looked as if it might be shortened, cleaned up and kept as an example of decoration. I managed to get the flat out of the muzzle by local heating and hammering over the horn or beak of the anvil, but could only get rid of the dents and burrs round it by taking about $\frac{1}{8}''$ of metal off.

The film of rust was largely on the surface and, as the chiselling was deep and the inlay slightly sunk, slow and careful work with fine files and emery cloth on a wooden block got the barrel into good shape without affecting the inlay. It looked as good as new after a final polishing with flour-grade emery, and this encouraged me to tackle the other metal parts.

The fretted side plate was removed, hammered flat and then smoothed with a fine file; after polishing, it showed no trace of its ill-usage. The ends of the trigger guard and tangs of the butt cap were straightened out and the butt cap and its boss restored to shape by carefully beating out the dents and distortions, again without any harm to the inlay.

By this time the metal parts were looking so fine that I thought they might justify a new stock, although the carving in relief and the sinking of the fretted side plate would make this a formidable job. It had not occurred to me that anything could be done with the original walnut stock and, at this stage, I wondered whether it could possibly be made good. I finally decided to attempt the job, as nothing except my time would be lost should the result be unsuccessful.

The fore end of the stock was glued back into position, leaving the charred portion as it was, for the time being. After giving the glue a week to set thoroughly, the charred end was cut away at an angle following the run of the grain, and the broken surfaces at the butt end were cut back to flat faces.

I had some old walnut of a colour and grain almost indistinguishable from that of the stock. Pieces of this were cut to roughly the required sizes and shapes, taking care to match up the angle of the grain in all cases. These were glued in position and again left for the glue to set. At this stage the stock was a remarkable sight, with lumps of walnut bound with string sprouting from its extremities.

When the glue had set, work was commenced with chisel, files (which I know perfectly well are not supposed to be used on wood) and sandpaper. The walnut sawdust was collected and sieved through a tea strainer, the finest part of it being mixed with tube glue to make plastic wood of a matching colour to fill the numerous cuts and dents.

Shaping the fore end of the stock to give a smooth continuation to the hollow for the barrel and to the groove for the ramrod, and also restoring the contours of the butt, took time but, when all was finished, the joints were scarcely perceptible to the touch. Some of the wood which filled the open frets of the side plate had been broken away, and this was built up again with plastic wood.

The old finish was scraped off down to the natural wood by working carefully over the carving with the fine pointed blade of a pocket-knife. A little of the carving on one side was badly chipped, so this was chiselled away without interfering with the general motif and the opposite side was modified to match. After the stock was finally smoothed and had been stained and wax-polished, it required close examination to detect that it was not one single piece of wood.

A new front ramrod pipe was made by the method described earlier. To match the rear pipe this had to have a fine double beading and slightly curved facets lengthwise. The work was done with fine files and finished with the finest emery paper wrapped round slips of wood. It took a long time, but looked very pretty when it was finished, and perfectly matched the pattern of the rear pipe.

The stock had to be slotted to accommodate the pin lug on the barrel through which the pin passes to anchor it to the stock. This now came in the new part and careful calculation was necessary, when the holes were drilled through the stock to take the pin, to make these coincide with the hole in the lug. The fixing of the front ramrod pipe, for which a slot also had to be made, was simpler since, once the location was decided upon, the drill could be sent right through stock and lug. The ivory-tipped ebony ramrod was made to be in keeping with the ornate design of the pistol. This is not shown in the photograph, which was taken with a temporary ramrod in position (which was afterwards discarded).

This restoration, as may be imagined, entailed a tremendous amount of work, but the result was a very satisfying reward, and ordinary inspection would not reveal that the pistol had ever been damaged.

Ideally, as I have tried to convey, the standard of work on gun restoration should be such as would not be apparent to the expert, except under close scrutiny. It is true that a fair degree of natural mechanical aptitude and skill is essential to success measured by this standard. There are many people, however, who believe that they have little or no mechanical ability simply because they seem to lack that natural facility in the use of tools which is innate in others. There are, however, comparatively few who, given a little guidance and plenty of practice, will not develop a useful standard of skill with simple tools.

This, of course, is not all that is necessary for the work of successful restoration. Equally essential are patience, and more patience, that takes no account of time while on a job; the ingenuity to devise original methods of approach to a mechanical problem; the ability to work slowly, very slowly, continually testing and fitting, and to continue steadily until the job is perfect; to finish meticulously work which, when it is assembled, will be out of sight.

These, I believe, are some of the qualities which distinguish the craftsman. I believe, also, that all of them can be cultivated, always making allowances for personal limitations.

Even this is not all. Without some outside stimulus, such work may in time become a task rather than a pleasant recreation; but fortunately the gun collector has the continual gratification of seeing the specimens in his collection improved and enhanced by his own hands, and this will constantly maintain his enthusiasm. Also, the capable and experienced restorer will develop a far greater knowledge of firearms and a wider interest in collecting.

CHAPTER FIFTEEN

HOUSING THE COLLECTION AND PHOTOGRAPHIC RECORDS

THE ideal provision for the accommodation and display of an extensive firearm collection is in airtight glazed cases in a dry, warm room or rooms, solely used as a private museum. Few amateur collectors can aspire to such an arrangement and, as I know from early experience, circumstances may compel a collection to be restricted to a few specimens kept in a drawer or a suitcase.

For most of us the possibilities lie somewhere between these extremes but, whatever the conditions, some thought and planning should be applied to make the most of individual resources. It is not really feasible for weapons to be kept on permanent display unless there is a room which can be used exclusively for that purpose.

Even if the collector has a room or "den" of his own, I feel that it is a mistake to cover the walls with firearms. To maintain full interest in any collection, I am of the opinion that it should be out of sight, except perhaps for one or two outstanding pieces: a handsome blunderbuss, say, in a strategic position in the entrance hall; or a fine pair of pistols displayed in an appropriate setting.

Specimens which are continually in view are seldom examined and soon pass unnoticed, whereas the occasional display of the collection or part of it for inspection, either alone or with interested friends, is a recurring source of enjoyment of which one never tires.

Still, if the collector feels a compelling urge to exhibit some of his pieces, I suggest that it is worth while making, or having made, a shallow case with accurately fitting glazed doors, something on the lines of the one shown on *Plate 65*.

The case is 3 ft. by 3 ft. by 5½″ deep inside and will accommodate about twenty pieces. The back is of softwood, ½″ thick, to take long thin panel pins to support the specimens, which permits them to be changed from time to time. A superimposed back of peg board will allow this to be done more readily if one does not mind the pattern of holes in the background. Personally, I find it somewhat distracting.

A stack of shallow drawers about 3″ deep, of the type used in drawing offices to keep plans, affords excellent storage, particularly for pistols, flasks, etc. It has the advantage that no fixing is needed. The guns are merely laid in position and the drawers can be taken out without disturbing the arrangement. Unless the individual weapons are kept in bags, the drawers should be lined with felt or baize or thin cork sheet.

Almost certainly the bottoms of these plan drawers would need to be reinforced to prevent them sagging under the unusual weight of a load of firearms. These commercial plan drawers can be obtained with drawer areas of 2 ft. by 3 ft. up to 3 ft. by 4 ft. and a stack of ten would house a sizeable collection.

Plate 65 shows a small stack which takes some forty pistols and powder flasks. It measures only 22″ wide by 25″ high by 15″ from front to back, with five baize-lined drawers.

I have seen the deeper drawers of an ordinary domestic chest adapted to take removable trays. It was economical of space in proportion to its capacity, but care had to be taken not to overload a piece of furniture which had never been intended to be used as an arms chest.

Quite a number of my own guns are accommodated in a tall cupboard similar to that in the workshop, described in Chapter 2. It is 6 ft. high by 3 ft. wide by 18″ deep and so is very economical of floor space.

The cupboard has been fitted with three shelves carried the full width at the top and a series of smaller ones down each side. Each of these small shelves will take four large pistols or revolvers longways, or almost double that number of pocket pistols lying across the shelves. The top shelves carry cased sets, longer pistols and powder flasks, and the space underneath takes shoulder guns.

This cupboard will comfortably hold one hundred to one hundred and twenty or more specimens, including up to a dozen shoulder guns. It can stand, locked, in a corner of the workshop, on a landing or in a spare guest room and completely solve the storage problem of a man with a small collection.

Plate 62. Removing a dent from a copper powder-flank, using a shaped wood block. Note the tape wrapping on the hammer head.

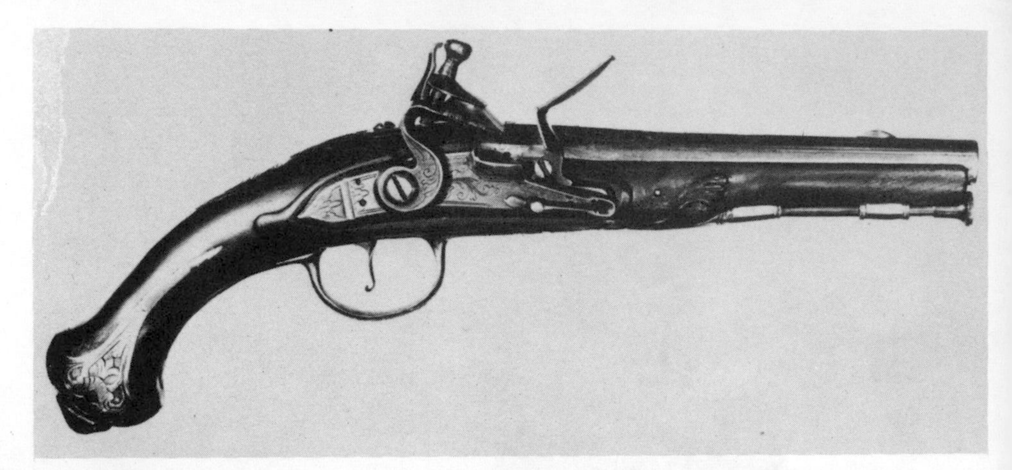

Plate 63. This handsome flint-lock pistol was extensively damaged by fire, rust and abuse. The photograph show the pistol after restoration.

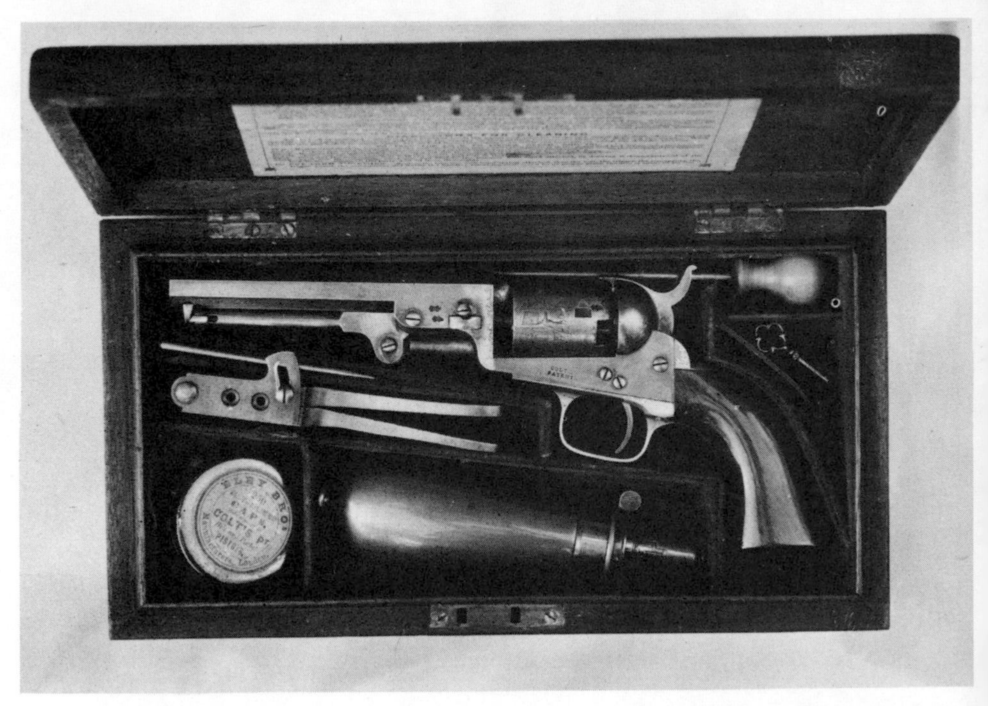

Plate 64. A Colt percussion revolver in perfect shooting condition, in velvet-lined mahogany case, complete with accessories including spare mainspring, key for case, and maker's label and instructions for loading cleaning and dismantling.

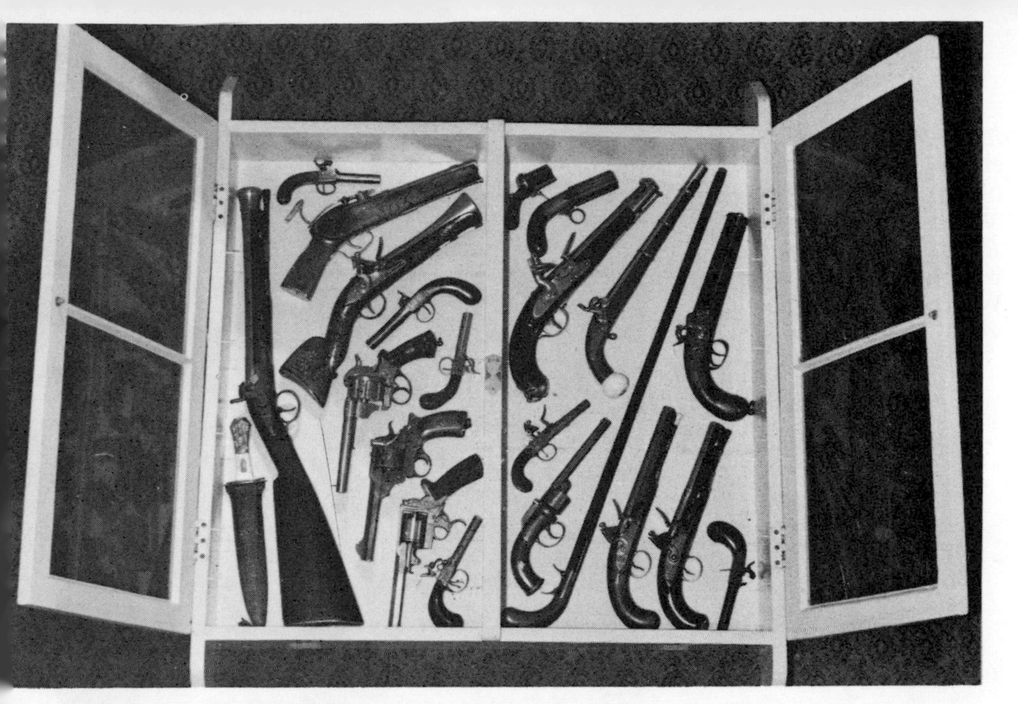

Plate 65.

Above:
Wall-mounted case 3 ft. 0 in. by 3 ft. 0 in. by $5\frac{1}{2}$ in. deep with glazed doors. Suitable for a display of about twenty selected specimens.

Left:
Small stack of drawers suitable to accommodate about forty pocket pistols, powder flasks, etc.

Plate 66. Arrangement to eliminate shadows when photographing a gun out of doors in daylight.

Right: Gun supported on rod pushed into ground. White cloth background about 18 in. behind gun.

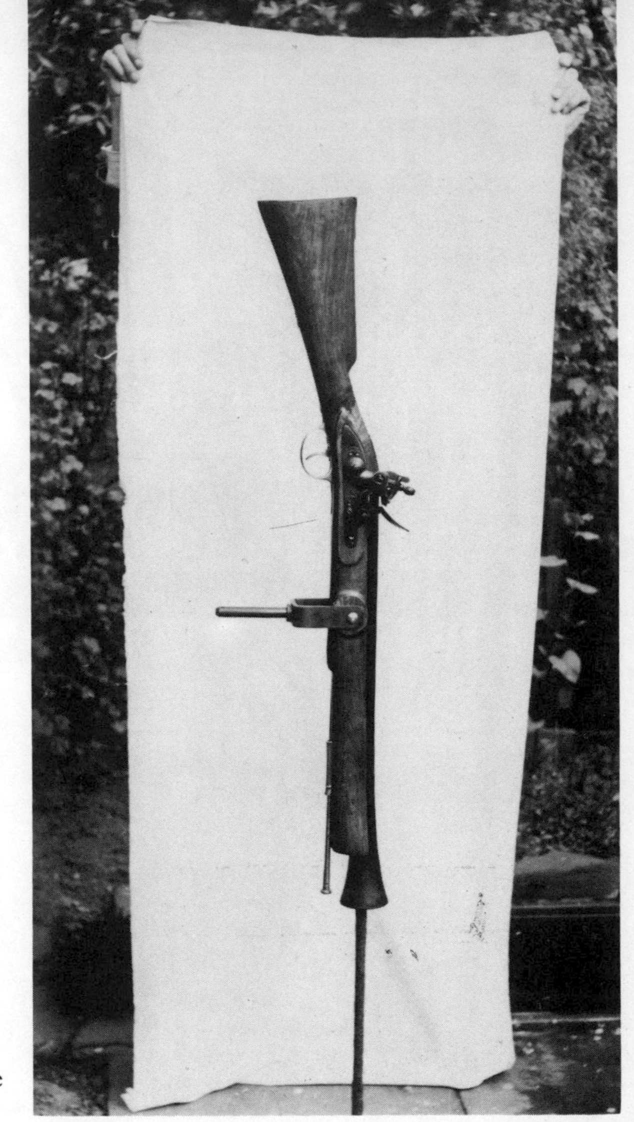

Below: Finished photograph with supporting rod touched out.

Note: The swivel was wedged at right angles to the gun so as to appear to be hanging vertically in the finished photograph.

The best protection for individual guns is a special wooden case fitted with compartments for the weapon and all its accessories. Only a small minority of guns were originally so provided and, of these, many have become separated from their cases and equipment, so that cased pistols in fine condition with all their original accessories are now exceedingly difficult to come by.

Plate 64 shows a cased Colt revolver in perfect shooting order with part-numbers all matching and every original accessory, including even a spare mainspring and the key for the case lock, and with the maker's label and printed instructions. This is an ideal collector's item, but unfortunately most of our guns will not be cased and for these some form of individual protection is desirable.

All except my cased pistols are kept in bags, home-made from thick woollen cloth. They are about 5″ wide at the open end, tapering to about half that width at the bottom. Each is a few inches longer than the pistol for which it was made and has a draw-tape to close the open end. These bags effectively protect their contents from knocks and scratches. Attached to each one is a small label bearing detailed particulars of the gun inside; for example:

> F.L. duelling pistol by Tow—London, 1770–1793—½″Cal.—9″ oct. barrel—Length 14½″—Weight 1 lb 13 oz—London Proof Marks—Note frizzen spring roller.

The labels are loosely looped to the bag tapes and can be slipped off and attached to thc trigger guards when the weapons are laid out for display. Not only do they give the visitor full information and save a lot of questions, but they keep the details of every piece fresh in the owner's memory and serve to identify any specimen without opening the bags.

My pistols, however, are arranged in roughly chronological order and I can quickly locate practically any gun by feel through the bag.

Finally, whatever the storage plan adopted, the iron or steel parts should regularly be wiped over with an oily cloth. Perspiration will almost immediately start rust patches on steel. Even the commercial vaporising rust-inhibitors, which may be useful in drawers and cupboards to prevent rusting of clean surfaces, will not be effective through greasy perspiration patches. The only safe protection is to clean and re-oil after every handling.

PHOTOGRAPHY OF FIREARMS

While this may be somewhat outside the scope of this book, some collectors have, as I have myself, made a photographic catalogue of all the firearms they possess or have owned in the past.

Filed and indexed in loose-leaf binders, a photographic record is valuable since it will contain in handy reference form, not only a picture and description of each item in the collection, but can include photographs of rare or attractive specimens from other collections, as well as close-up views of engraving and similar interesting details.

I generally take with me a selection of such pictures when I am away from home, in the hope of meeting a fellow enthusiast; even non-collectors have shown a keen interest in pictures of antique firearms.

Basically, gun photography is like any other kind, but it has its own techniques and, as I am not aware that there has been any published information about the photography of firearms, the following notes may be useful.

Apart from the camera, tripod, universal head, which will allow the camera to be directed vertically downward, and other apparatus which the photographer is likely to possess already, he will need a piece of hardboard about 2′ 0″ by 2′ 6″ and another about 2′ 0″ by 5′ 0″ to which can be pinned white or tinted paper or cloth to serve as backgrounds for pistols and long guns. He will also need a sheet of plate glass about 2′ 6″ by 1′ 6″ for indoor work by artificial light, and a small circular spirit level is useful.

Almost any type of camera can be used successfully, but naturally some types are more convenient than others. The older pattern of camera with long bellows-extension, or its modern counterpart, the technical camera, using plates or cut films in individual dark slides and with a ground glass focusing screen, is the ideal instrument for the work.

With a lens of focal length equal to the diagonal of the negative, which is the usual proportion, a large pistol will fill the negative, leaving the usual working margin, when about 3 ft. away from the camera, and with a negative size of $2\frac{1}{2}''$ by $3\frac{1}{2}''$ or larger, the image on the screen can be satisfactorily arranged and critically focused. Furthermore, the photographs can be taken and developed one at a time, enabling a test negative to be made to determine correct exposure for subsequent shots.

In firearm photography, external shadows should be either eliminated or rendered unobtrusive, at the same time retaining the shadows on and between the various parts of the weapon to emphasise contours and to give the appearance of solidity. The easiest set-up to achieve this effect is to take the photograph out of doors on a clear, bright day, away from the shadows of houses or trees.

When a pistol is to be photographed, the smaller board will serve and, if the gun has no bright parts, use a white background; but, if there are parts which will photograph white, use the tinted paper—preferably buff or grey. Lay the board flat on the ground and pack under it, where necessary, until the circular spirit-level shows it to be horizontal in each direction; place the pistol in the middle. Erect the tripod to straddle the board with the camera pointing down vertically and as nearly as can be judged over the centre of the board. Roughly focus and adjust the tripod height until the image nicely fills the available space and level the camera by applying the spirit-level to the ground-glass screen. If the image is out of centre, move the pistol on the board until it is right. Now focus accurately at full aperture and then stop down to, say, f/11 to ensure the necessary depth of field, which is very restricted in close-up work of this kind.

If there is a wooden butt with a nice grain of a reddish tone, a red or orange filter will lighten it and bring out the figure. Shade the pistol from any direct sunlight and the hard shadows will disappear and what are left will hardly be noticeable. The exposure should be made with a cable release to avoid vibration.

The photographs for *Plates 37 and 39* were made in the open by this method and, in the latter case, an orange filter was used to bring out the beautiful figure of the wood grips. Faint external shadows can be detected, but they are not intrusive.

With photographs taken by artificial light external shadows can be entirely eliminated, with the further advantage that, once the set-up has been standardised and the correct exposure and developing routine have been determined, negatives of uniform quality can be produced on subsequent occasions.

For this, the sheet of $\frac{1}{4}''$ plate glass previously referred to will be required. This must be supported at each narrow end about 12″ above the floor with only an inch or so of the edges resting on the supports, leaving a clear space below. A sheet of white paper (or whatever else is selected for the background) of the same size as the glass is placed underneath it on the floor. The glass should be carefully cleaned as any specks or marks will show clearly against the highly illuminated background. The pistol is placed on the glass, the camera and tripod are erected and the image focused, exactly as was done for the outside photograph.

The light is provided by two lamps of equal power of, say, 100 watts each (there is no need for any higher power). They should be arranged at opposite diagonal corners at such a height that they illuminate the pistol and background at a downward angle of about 45°. The lamps must be shaded above so that the camera and tripod are not illuminated, or these are likely to be reflected from the glass and show on the negative. They must also be adjusted so that the tripod legs, the supports for the glass and the edges of the glass do not cast any shadows across the background.

Care must be taken that the lights are not reflected direct into the lens by some bright surface on the pistol. The flat side of an octagon barrel or the curved surface of a cylinder can do this very effectively and spoil the picture. One great advantage of the ground-glass focusing-screen is that any effect of this kind is at once apparent and the angle of the lights can be suitably adjusted.

All this may sound rather complicated and, the first time it is set up, some experimental arrangement and re-arrangement may be necessary but, once it has been successfully done, it will be standard for future lay-outs.

The correct exposure must be found by experiment. With cut film or a plate in a dark slide it is easy to make a test negative by closing the slide in steps, giving a series of graduated strips of different exposure times in doubling sequence in the way that a bromide paper test-print is made; and it is well worth doing as, at the expenditure of one or two pieces of film, the correct exposure with the particular lighting, film and stop in use, can be determined for all future occasions.

The photographs for *Plates 15 and 42* were taken by this method and it can be seen that not only are there no external shadows, but that the white background is visible through every space between the components, however small. For example, in *Plate 15* between the sides of the mainspring and the legs of the hinged vice, and in *Plate 42* through the narrow slit between barrel and rammer lever and at the lower ends of the cylinder.

If the pistols had been lying direct on the white background instead of being supported well above it on the glass, these spaces would have been obscured by internal shadows.

I have found that the use of the glass support is not equally successful out of doors, as the reflections of the camera and tripod legs are liable to produce an out-of-focus ghost image on the negative. Probably this difficulty could be overcome by the use of a polarising filter and the photographer may like to experiment with this.

A shoulder gun is best photographed out of doors. The longer background board is needed for this and the photograph taken at an angle as high as the fully extended tripod will permit. The gun should be at right angles to the optical axis of the camera and held in position by any suitable props out of sight behind it. Another arrangement which entirely eliminates shadows is to pass the barrel of the gun over a stout rod fixed vertically in the ground so that it is supported at a convenient height. The background board is placed behind the gun at such a distance as to be out of the range of shadows. The supporting rod would, of course, have to be touched out on the negative or print (see *Plate 66*).

Flash can be used satisfactorily if the dense shadows which usually outline the edges of the subject are eliminated either by bounced flash, or by supporting the gun well clear of the background and illuminating it at such an angle that the shadow falls outside the photographic field.

Next in convenience to the plate camera comes the single-lens reflex. Its advantage over the two-lens reflex is that, like the plate camera, the exact view that will appear on the negative is shown on its screen. At a range of 3 ft. or less, the taking lens of a two-lens reflex sees a slightly different view to that shown in the viewing lens. I do not refer particularly to the slight displacement of the entire view due to vertical separation of the lenses—this is easily allowed for by the experienced photographer—but to other small though important differences in the picture arising from the same cause. For example, a reflected flare from a bright spot may appear on the negative which was not indicated by the viewing lens, or two parts of the subject which appeared to be satisfactorily clear of each other may seem to be touching in the photograph.

I have seen very good half-plate enlargements from 35 mm negatives of guns taken with a reflex miniature, and a fellow collector uses a very simple $3\frac{1}{4}$ x $2\frac{1}{4}$ roll-film camera which can only be focused by scale, so requiring accurate measurement between subject and camera. The closest graduation is 3 ft., which is a convenient distance to adopt as standard, but it is advisable to make a preliminary test with a piece of ground glass to confirm whether the 3 ft. is from the subject to the lens or to the focal plane. This particular camera is a quite inexpensive one but, by stopping the lens well down, it gives pin-sharp negatives which produce first-class enlargements.

To make a record of a maker's name, a piece of fine engraving or proof, or other marks on a gun necessitates either a camera with double-extension bellows, or the use of a supplementary lens or extension rings to get near enough to the subject. For work of this nature a high degree of contrast is usually desirable and this may be obtained by filling the engraving or lettering with a suitable medium. The top barrel shown on *Plate 2* was bright steel and the letters and proof marks were filled with powdered charcoal; for those on the dark barrel I used powdered chalk.

For purposes of record this treatment is effective, but in my opinion it can have a rather artificial look on a pictorial photograph of a gun.

APPENDIX

The materials listed below were those which proved most useful to the author in carrying out the work described in this book. The items are page indexed to facilitate reference to their application and more detailed description.

It is not practicable to offer any standard recommendation as the requirements of the individual restorer will depend upon the scope of the work he is prepared to undertake, but by obtaining only such materials as are wanted for the job in hand, including a reasonable surplus for stock, a useful store will soon be built up.

Aluminium or alloy sheet, 26, 193
  half-round beading, 22
Brass:
  rod, 40, 58, 90, 145, 168
  sheet, 64, 174, 193, 195
  strip, 71, 160
Copper:
  sheet, 24, 193
  wire, 160
Foil, brass or copper, 81, 160
Galvanised sheet iron, 21
Glass, 210
Hardboard, 210
Horn, 28, 167, 169, 182
Ivory, 28, 167, 170, 182, 189
Lead sheet, 26, 82
Leather, 82
Nails, 40, 125, 178
Rubber sheet, 22, 79, 107, 113
Screws, 44
Steel or iron rod:
  hexagon, 129
  round, 46, 47, 116, 126, 130, 136, 168, 172, 176, 193
  square, 47, 158
Steel or iron strip, 44, 125, 136, 147, 152
Steel:
  sheet, 62
  tube, 47, 131, 135, 137, 176
Wood dowel and laths, 58, 68, 129, 131, 132, 135, 136, 169, 190

INDEX

R

S

T